CHELSEA HOUSE PUBLISHERS
Modern Critical Views

HENRY ADAMS
EDWARD ALBEE
A. R. AMMONS
MATTHEW ARNOLD
JOHN ASHBERY
W. H. AUDEN
JANE AUSTEN
JAMES BALDWIN
CHARLES BAUDELAIRE
SAMUEL BECKETT
SAUL BELLOW
THE BIBLE
ELIZABETH BISHOP
WILLIAM BLAKE
JORGE LUIS BORGES
ELIZABETH BOWEN
BERTOLT BRECHT
THE BRONTËS
ROBERT BROWNING
ANTHONY BURGESS
GEORGE GORDON, LORD BYRON
THOMAS CARLYLE
LEWIS CARROLL
WILLA CATHER
CERVANTES
GEOFFREY CHAUCER
KATE CHOPIN
SAMUEL TAYLOR COLERIDGE
JOSEPH CONRAD
CONTEMPORARY POETS
HART CRANE
STEPHEN CRANE
DANTE
CHARLES DICKENS
EMILY DICKINSON
JOHN DONNE & THE
   17th-CENTURY POETS
ELIZABETHAN DRAMATISTS
THEODORE DREISER
JOHN DRYDEN
GEORGE ELIOT
T. S. ELIOT
RALPH ELLISON
RALPH WALDO EMERSON
WILLIAM FAULKNER
HENRY FIELDING
F. SCOTT FITZGERALD
GUSTAVE FLAUBERT
E. M. FORSTER
SIGMUND FREUD
ROBERT FROST

ROBERT GRAVES
GRAHAM GREENE
THOMAS HARDY
NATHANIEL HAWTHORNE
WILLIAM HAZLITT
SEAMUS HEANEY
ERNEST HEMINGWAY
GEOFFREY HILL
FRIEDRICH HÖLDERLIN
HOMER
GERARD MANLEY HOPKINS
WILLIAM DEAN HOWELLS
ZORA NEALE HURSTON
HENRY JAMES
SAMUEL JOHNSON
BEN JONSON
JAMES JOYCE
FRANZ KAFKA
JOHN KEATS
RUDYARD KIPLING
D. H. LAWRENCE
JOHN LE CARRÉ
URSULA K. LE GUIN
DORIS LESSING
SINCLAIR LEWIS
ROBERT LOWELL
NORMAN MAILER
BERNARD MALAMUD
THOMAS MANN
CHRISTOPHER MARLOWE
CARSON MCCULLERS
HERMAN MELVILLE
JAMES MERRILL
ARTHUR MILLER
JOHN MILTON
EUGENIO MONTALE
MARIANNE MOORE
IRIS MURDOCH
VLADIMIR NABOKOV
JOYCE CAROL OATES
SEAN O'CASEY
FLANNERY O'CONNOR
EUGENE O'NEILL
GEORGE ORWELL
CYNTHIA OZICK
WALTER PATER
WALKER PERCY
HAROLD PINTER
PLATO
EDGAR ALLAN POE

POETS OF SENSIBILITY &
   THE SUBLIME
ALEXANDER POPE
KATHERINE ANNE PORTER
EZRA POUND
PRE-RAPHAELITE POETS
MARCEL PROUST
THOMAS PYNCHON
ARTHUR RIMBAUD
THEODORE ROETHKE
PHILIP ROTH
JOHN RUSKIN
J. D. SALINGER
GERSHOM SCHOLEM
WILLIAM SHAKESPEARE (3 vols.)
   HISTORIES & POEMS
   COMEDIES
   TRAGEDIES
GEORGE BERNARD SHAW
MARY WOLLSTONECRAFT SHELLEY
PERCY BYSSHE SHELLEY
EDMUND SPENSER
GERTRUDE STEIN
JOHN STEINBECK
LAURENCE STERNE
WALLACE STEVENS
TOM STOPPARD
JONATHAN SWIFT
ALFRED LORD TENNYSON
WILLIAM MAKEPEACE THACKERAY
HENRY DAVID THOREAU
LEO TOLSTOI
ANTHONY TROLLOPE
MARK TWAIN
JOHN UPDIKE
GORE VIDAL
VIRGIL
ROBERT PENN WARREN
EVELYN WAUGH
EUDORA WELTY
NATHANAEL WEST
EDITH WHARTON
WALT WHITMAN
OSCAR WILDE
TENNESSEE WILLIAMS
WILLIAM CARLOS WILLIAMS
THOMAS WOLFE
VIRGINIA WOOLF
WILLIAM WORDSWORTH
RICHARD WRIGHT
WILLIAM BUTLER YEATS

Further titles in preparation.

Modern Critical Views

NORMAN MAILER

Modern Critical Views

NORMAN MAILER

Edited with an introduction by

Harold Bloom

Sterling Professor of the Humanities
Yale University

CHELSEA HOUSE PUBLISHERS
New York
Philadelphia

PROJECT EDITORS: Emily Bestler, James Uebbing
ASSOCIATE EDITOR: Maria Behan
EDITORIAL COORDINATORS: Karyn Gullen Browne
EDITORIAL STAFF: Laura Ludwig, Linda Grossman, Perry King
DESIGN: Susan Lusk

Cover illustration by Robin Peterson

Printed and bound in the United States of America

10   9   8   7   6   5   4   3   2

Library of Congress Cataloging in Publication Data

Norman Mailer.
   (Modern critical views)
   Bibliography: p.
   Includes index.
   1. Mailer, Norman—Criticism and interpretation—Addresses,
essays, lecutures.   I. Bloom, Harold.
II. Series.
PS3525.A4152Z818   1986   813'.54   85-17518
ISBN 0-87754-656-8

Contents

Editor's Note

This volume gathers together a representative selection of the best criticism devoted to the writings of Norman Mailer during the last quarter-century, arranged in the chronological order of its publication. It begins with Gore Vidal's review-essay of 1960 on *Advertisements for Myself* and ends with my own meditation upon *Ancient Evenings* in 1983. The editor's "Introduction" addresses itself to the impossible task of making a canonical judgment upon Mailer's works, partly in response to the powerful judgments of Richard Poirier, which are reprinted elsewhere in this volume.

After Vidal's witty and generous estimate (which I acknowledge he might not be inclined to repeat today), all the rest of us become his legatees, condemned to repeat his brilliant insight: "Mailer is a Bolingbroke, a born usurper." Richard Foster's account of the early novels—*The Naked and the Dead, Barbary Shore* and *The Deer Park*—emphasizes Mailer's acute individualism, with its need to confound expectations, presumably including Mailer's own. The playwright Jack Richardson, examining Mailer's aesthetics of the will, pays tribute to the novelist's indubitable stylistic achievement in *The Armies of the Night* and *Miami and the Siege of Chicago*.

Tony Tanner, leading off the criticism of the seventies included in this volume, concentrates upon a defense of the novelistic art of *An American Dream*. A stylistic defense both of *An American Dream* and of *Why Are We In Vietnam?* is the core of the following essay by Robert Langbaum. A very different judgment is made upon Mailer and his *The Prisoner of Sex* by Germaine Greer, who dismisses him as "a typical patriarch, friend of the fetus and oppressor of the child." Much more sympathetic and even-handed is the consideration of *The Prisoner of Sex* by Joyce Carol Oates, who accurately characterizes Mailer as a puritan, "so easily and deeply shocked," very much in the tradition of the highly puritanical D. H. Lawrence.

With Richard Poirier's magisterial reflections upon *An American Dream* and *Why Are We In Vietnam?*, this volume reaches a critical center. Poirier is Mailer's canonical critic, and I dissent from him with reluctance. After Poirier, the course of Mailer criticism is essentially retrospective, which may be an indication of a relative failure on Mailer's part, despite *The Executioner's Song, Of a Fire on the Moon* and *Ancient Evenings*. A kind of elegiac intensity pervades Randall H. Waldron's return to *The*

Naked and the Dead, Robert Merrill's reconsideration of *The Armies of the Night*, and John Garvey's initial reaction to *The Executioner's Song*. This elegiac quality reaches its apotheosis in Alvin B. Kernan's essay concerning *Of a Fire on the Moon*, which sees Mailer himself as an elegist commemorating the death of Romantic art at the hands of scientific myth.

In some sense, the remaining essays center upon Mailer as theosophical or occult speculator, a mythmaker of a very Romantic kind. Jessica Gerson, trying to adjudicate the disputes between Mailer and the feminists, turns to the Kabbalah as a possible source for the archaic attitudes of Mailerian sexuality. In an essay upon *The Executioner's Song*, Judith A. Scheffler characterizes the book's "Gary Gilmore" as a demiurgic artist or occult creator, and not the "real life" culprit who was Mailer's ostensible subject. Finally, the editor's own review essay upon *Ancient Evenings*, that vast panoply of humbuggery and bumbuggery, centers itself upon the extraordinary suggestiveness of Mailer's most peculiar speculations, his wide-ranging phantasmagoria of death, copulation and rebirth.

Introduction

I

Mailer is the most visible of contemporary novelists, just as Thomas Pynchon is surely the most invisible. As the inheritor of the not exactly unfulfilled journalistic renown of Hemingway, Mailer courts danger, disaster, even scandal. Thinking of Mailer, Pynchon, and Doctorow among others, Geoffrey Hartman remarks that:

> The prose of our best novelists is as fast, embracing, and abrasive as John Donne's *Sermons*. It is polyphonic despite or within its monologue, its confessional stream of words. . . .
>
> Think of Mailer, who always puts himself on the line, sparring, taunting, as macho as Hemingway but deliberately renouncing taciturnity. Mailer places himself too near events, as science fiction or other forms of romance place themselves too far. . . .

Elizabeth Hardwick, a touch less generous than the theoretical Hartman, turns Gertrude Stein against Mailer's oral polyphony:

> We have here a "literature" of remarks, a fast-moving confounding of Gertrude Stein's confident assertion that "remarks are not literature." Sometimes remarks are called a novel, sometimes a biography, sometimes history.

Hardwick's Mailer is "a spectacular mound of images" or "anecdotal pile." He lacks only an achieved work, in her view, and therefore is a delight to biographers, who resent finished work as a "sharp intrusion," beyond their ken. Her observations have their justice, yet the phenomenon is older than Mailer, or even Hemingway. The truly spectacular mound of images and anecdotal pile was George Gordon, Lord Byron, but he wrote *Don Juan*, considered by Shelley to be the great poem of the age. Yet even *Don Juan* is curiously less than Byron was, or seemed, or still seems. Mailer hardly purports to be the Byron of our day (the Hemingway will do), but he might fall back upon Byron as an earlier instance of the literary use of celebrity, or of the mastery of polyphonic remarks.

Is Mailer a novelist? His best book almost certainly is *The Execu-*

tioner's Song, which Ms. Hardwick calls "the apotheosis of our flowering 'oral literature'—thus far," a triumph of the tape recorder. My judgment of its strength may be much too fast, as Ms. Hardwick warns, and yet I would not call *The Executioner's Song* a novel. *Ancient Evenings* rather crazily is a novel, Mailer's *Salammbô* as it were, but clearly more engrossing as visionary speculation than as narrative or as the representation of moral character. Richard Poirier, Mailer's best critic, prefers *An American Dream* and *Why Are We In Vietnam?*, neither of which I can reread with aesthetic pleasure. Clearly, Mailer is a problematical writer; he has written no indisputable book, nothing on the order of *The Sun Also Rises*, *The Great Gatsby*, *Miss Lonelyhearts*, *The Crying of Lot 49*, let alone *As I Lay Dying*, *The Sound and the Fury*, *Light in August*, *Absalom, Absalom!* His formidable literary energies have not found their inevitable mode. When I think of him, *Advertisements for Myself* comes into my memory more readily than any other work, perhaps because truly he is his own supreme fiction. He is the author of "Norman Mailer," a lengthy, discontinuous, and perhaps canonical fiction.

II

Advertisements for Myself (1960) sums up Mailer's ambitions and accomplishments through the age of thirty-six. After a quarter-century, I have just reread it, with an inevitable mixture of pleasure and a little sadness. Unquestionably, Mailer has not fulfilled its many complex promises, and yet the book is much more than a miscellany. If not exactly a "Song of Myself," nevertheless *Advertisements* remains Mailer at his most Whitmanian, as when he celebrates his novel-in-progress:

> If it is to have any effect, and I can hardly look forward to exhausting the next ten years without hope of a deep explosion of effect, the book will be fired to its fuse by the rumor that once I pointed to the farthest fence and said that within ten years I would try to hit the longest ball ever to go up into the accelerated hurricane air of our American letters. For if I have one ambition above all others, it is to write a novel which Dostoyevsky and Marx; Joyce and Freud; Stendhal, Tolstoy, Proust and Spengler; Faulkner, and even old moldering Hemingway might have come to read, for it would carry what they had to tell another part of the way.

Hemingway in 1959 reached the age of sixty, but was neither old nor moldering. He was to kill himself on July 2, 1961, but Mailer could hardly have anticipated that tragic release. In a letter to George Plimpton

(January 17, 1961) Hemingway characterized *Advertisements for Myself* as "the sort of ragtag assembly of his rewrites, second thoughts and ramblings shot through with occasional brilliance." As precursor, Hemingway would have recognized Mailer's vision of himself as Babe Ruth, hitting out farther than Stendhal, Tolstoi, *et al.*, except that the agonistic trope in the master is more agile than in the disciple, because ironized:

> Am a man without any ambition, except to be champion of the world, I wouldn't fight Dr. Tolstoi in a 20 round bout because I know he would knock my ears off. The Dr. had terrific wind and could go on forever and then some. . . .
>   But these Brooklyn jerks are so ignorant that they *start off* fighting Mr. Tolstoi. And they announce they have beaten him before the fight starts.

That is from a letter to Charles Scribner (September 6–7, 1949), and "these Brooklyn jerks" indubitably refers to the highly singular author of *The Naked and the Dead* (1948), who had proclaimed his victory over Hemingway as a tune-up for the Tolstoi match. Hemingway's irony, directed as much towards himself as against Mailer, shrewdly indicates Mailer's prime aesthetic flaw: a virtually total absence of irony. Irony may or may not be what the late Paul de Man called it, "the condition of literary language itself," but Mailer certainly could use a healthy injection of it. If Thomas Mann is at one extreme—the modern too abounding in irony—then Mailer clearly hugs the opposite pole. The point against Mailer is made best by Max Apple in his splendid boxing tale, "Inside Norman Mailer" (*The Oranging of America*, 1976), where Mailer is handled with loving irony, and Hemingway's trope touches its ultimate limits as Apple challenges Mailer in the ring:

> "Concentrate," says Mailer, "so the experience will not be wasted on you."
>   "It's hard," I say, "amid the color and distraction."
>   "I know," says my gentle master, "but think about one big thing."
>   I concentrate on the new edition of the *Encyclopedia Britannica*. It works. My mind is less a palimpsest, more a blank page.
>   "You may be too young to remember," he says, "James Jones and James T. Farrell and James Gould Cozzens and dozens like them. I took them all on, absorbed all they had and went on my way, just like Shakespeare ate up *Tottel's Miscellany*."

There are no such passages in Mailer himself. One cannot require a novelist to cultivate irony, but its absolute absence causes difficulties, particularly when the writer is a passionate and heterodox moralist. Mailer's speculations upon time, sex, death, cancer, digestion, courage, and God are all properly notorious, and probably will not earn him a place as one of the major sages. The strongest aesthetic defense of Mailer as speculator belongs to Richard Poirier, in his book of 1972:

> Mailer insists on living *at* the divide, living *on* the divide, between the world of recorded reality and a world of omens, spirits, and powers, only that his presence there may blur the distinction. He seals and obliterates the gap he finds, like a sacrificial warrior or, as he would probably prefer, like a Christ who brings not peace but a sword, not forgiveness for past sins but an example of the pains necessary to secure a future.

This has force and some persuasiveness, but Poirier is too good a critic not to add the shadow side of Mailer's "willingness not to foreclose on his material in the interests of merely formal resolutions." Can there be *any* resolutions then for his books? Poirier goes on to say that: "There is no satisfactory form for his imagination when it is most alive. There are only exercises for it." But this appears to imply that Mailer cannot shape his fictions, since without a sacrifice of possiblity upon the altar of form, narrative becomes incoherent, frequently through redundance (as in *Ancient Evenings*). Mailer's alternative has been to forsake Hemingway for Dreiser, as in the exhaustive narrative of *The Executioner's Song*. In either mode, finally, we are confronted by the paradox that Mailer's importance seems to transcend any of his individual works. The power of *The Executioner's Song* finally is that of "reality in America," to appropriate Lionel Trilling's phrase for Dreiser's appropriation of the material of *An American Tragedy*. Are we also justified in saying that *An American Dream* essentially is Mailer's comic-strip appropriation of what might be called "irreality in America"? Evidently there will never be a mature book by Mailer that is not problematical in its form. To Poirier, this is Mailer's strength. Poirier's generous overpraise of *An American Dream* and *Why Are We In Vietnam?* perhaps can be justified by Mailer's peculiarly American aesthetic, which has its Emersonian affinities. Mailer's too is an aesthetic of use, a pragmatic application of the American difference from the European past. *The Armies of the Night* (1968), rightly praised by Poirier, may seem someday Mailer's best and most permanent book. It is certainly not only a very American book, but today is one of the handful of works that vividly represent an already lost and legendary time, the era of the so-called Counterculture that surged up in the later 1960's, largely in protest against our war in Vietnam. Mailer, more than any other figure, has broken down the distinction between fiction and journalism. This sometimes is praised in itself. I judge it an aesthetic misfortune, in everyone else, but on Mailer himself I tend to reserve judgment, since the mode now seems his own.

III

Mailer's validity as a cultural critic is always qualified by his own immersion in what he censures. Well known for being well known, he is himself inevitably part of what he deplores. As a representation, he at least rivals all of his fictive creations. *Ancient Evenings*, his most inventive and exuberant work, is essentially a self-portrait of the author as ancient Egyptian magician, courtier, lover and anachronistic speculator. Despite Poirier's eloquent insistences, the book leaves Mailer as he was judged to be by Poirier in 1972, "like Melville without *Moby Dick*, George Eliot without *Middlemarch*, Mark Twain without *Huckleberry Finn*." Indeed, the book is Mailer's *Pierre*, his *Romola*, his *Connecticut Yankee in King Arthur's Court*. At sixty-two, Mailer remains the author of *Advertisements for Myself*, *The Armies of the Night* and *The Executioner's Song*.

Is he then a superb accident of personality, wholly adequate to the spirit of the age? Though a rather bad critic of novelists, he is one of the better critics of Norman Mailer. His one critical blindness, in regard to himself, involves the destructive nature of Hemingway's influence upon him. Hemingway was a superb storyteller and an uncanny prose poet; Mailer is neither. Essentially, Mailer is a phantasmagoric visionary who was found by the wrong literary father, Hemingway. Hemingway's verbal economy is not possible for Mailer. There are profound affinities between Hemingway and Wallace Stevens, but none between Mailer and the best poetry of his age. This is the curious sadness with which the "First Advertisements for Myself" reverberates after twenty-five years:

> So, mark you. Every American writer who takes himself to be both major and macho must sooner or later give a *faena* which borrows from the self-love of a Hemingway style . . .
> For you see I have come to have a great sympathy for the Master's irrepressible tantrum that he is the champion writer of this time, and of all time, and that if anyone can pin Tolstoy, it is Ernest H.

By taking on Hemingway, Mailer condemned himself to a similar agon, which harmed Hemingway, except in *The Sun Also Rises* and in *The First Forty-Nine Stories*. It has more than harmed Mailer's work. *The Deer Park* defies rereading, and *An American Dream* and *Why Are We In Vietnam?* have now lost the immediacy of their occasions, and are scarcely less unreadable. In what now is the Age of Pynchon, Mailer has been eclipsed as a writer of fictions, though hardly at all as a performing self. He may be remembered more as a prose prophet than as a novelist, more as Carlyle than as Hemingway. There are worse literary fates. Carlyle, long neglected, doubtless will return. Mailer, now celebrated, doubtless will vanish into neglect, and yet always will return, as a historian of the moral consciousness of his era, and as the representative writer of his generation.

GORE VIDAL

The Angels Are White

I first heard of Norman Mailer in the spring of 1948, just before *The Naked and the Dead* was published. He was living in Paris or had been living there and just gone home when I arrived in France, my mood curiously melancholic, no doubt because of the dubious fame I was enjoying with the publication of a third book, *The City and the Pillar*. At twenty-two I should have found a good deal more to please me than I did that spring and summer in the foreign cities. I do recall at one point Truman Capote telling me about *The Naked and the Dead* and its author, a recital which promptly aroused my competitive instincts . . . waning, let me say right off, and for reasons which are relevent to these notes. Yet at that time I remember thinking meanly: So somebody did it. Each previous war had had its big novels, yet so far there had been none for our war, though I knew that a dozen busy friends and acquaintances were grimly taking out tickets in the Grand War Novel Lottery. I had debated doing one myself and had (I still think) done something better: a small cool hard novel about men on the periphery of the action; it was called *Williwaw* and was written when I was nineteen and easily the cleverest young fox ever to know how to disguise his ignorance and make a virtue of his limitations. (What an attractive form the self-advertisement is: one could go on forever relighting one's image!) Not till I began that third book did I begin to get bored with playing safe.

I took to the field and have often wondered since, in the course of many excursions, defeats, alarums and ambushes, what it might have been like to have been a safe shrewd custodian of one's talent, playing from strength. I did not suspect then that the ambitious, rather cold-blooded

From *The Nation* (January 2, 1960). Copyright © 1960, 1962 by Gore Vidal.

young contemporary who had set out to write the big war novel and who had pulled it off would one day be in the same fix I was. Not safe. Not wise. Not admired. A fellow victim of the Great Golfer's Age, then no more than a murmur of things to come in the Golfer's murmurous heart.

My first reaction to *The Naked and the Dead* was: it's a fake. A clever, talented, admirably executed fake. I have not changed my opinion of the book since, though I have considerably changed my opinion of Mailer, as he himself has changed. Now I confess I have never read all of *The Naked and the Dead*. But I read a good deal of it. I recall a fine description of men carrying a dying man down a mountain. Yet every time I got going in the narrative I would find myself stopped cold by a set of made-up, predictable characters taken, not from life, but from the same novels all of us had read, and informed by a naïveté which was at its worst when Mailer went into his Time-Machine and wrote those passages which resemble nothing so much as smudged carbons of an early Dos Passos work.

Sourly, from a distance, that year I watched the fame of Mailer quite surpass John Horne Burns and myself, as well as Truman Capote, who had made his debut earlier the same year. I should explain for those who have come in late or were around then but inattentive that the OK List of writers in 1947 and 1948 was John Horne Burns, Calder Willingham and myself. Capote and Mailer were added in 1948. Willingham was soon dropped; then Burns (my own favorite) sank, and by 1949 in the aftermath of *The City and the Pillar* I too departed the OK List.

"I had the freak of luck to start high on the mountain, and go down sharp while others were passing me"—so Mailer wrote, describing the time after *Barbary Shore* when he unexpectedly joined the rest of us down on the plain. Now the descent, swift or slow, is not agreeable; but on the other hand it is not as tragic as Mailer seems to find it. To be demoralized by the withdrawal of public success (a process as painful in America as the withdrawal of a drug from an addict) is to grant too easily a victory to the society one has attempted to criticize, affect, change, reform. It is clearly unreasonable to expect to be cherished by those one assaults. It is also childish, in the deepest sense of being a child, ever to expect justice. There is none beneath our moon. One can only hope not to be destroyed entirely by injustice and, to put it cynically, one can very often flourish through an injustice obtaining in one's favor. What matters finally is not the world's judgment of oneself but one's own judgment of the world. Any writer who lacks this final arrogance will not survive very long, especially in America.

That wide graveyard of stillborn talents which contains so much of the brief ignoble history of American letters is a tribute to the power of a democracy to destroy its critics, brave fools and passionate men. If there is anything in Mailer's new book [*Advertisements for Myself*] which alarms me, it is his obsession with public success. He is running for President, as he puts it. Yet though his best and most interesting works have been unjustly attacked, he should realize that in this most inequitable of worlds his one worldly success was not a very good book, that *The Naked and The Dead* is redolent of "ambition" (in the Mary McCarthy sense of the word—pejorative, needless to say) and a young man's will to be noticed. Mailer himself nearly takes this view: "I may as well confess that by December 8th or 9th of 1941 . . . I was worrying darkly whether it would be more likely that a great war novel would be written about Europe or the Pacific." Ambition and the day coincided and a success was made. Yet it is much less real a book than Burns's *The Gallery*, or even some of the stories of Robert Lowry, works which had the virtue of being felt, possessed entirely by the men who made them, not created out of stern ambition and dogged competence. But, parenthetically, most war books are inadequate. War tends to be too much for any writer, especially one whose personality is already half obliterated by life in a democracy. Even the aristocrat Tolstoi, at a long remove in time, stretched his genius to the breaking point to encompass men and war and the thrust of history in a single vision. Ernest Hemingway in *A Farewell to Arms* did a few good descriptions, but his book, too, is a work of ambition, in which can be seen the beginning of the careful, artful, immaculate idiocy of tone that since has marked both his prose and his legend as he has declined into that sort of fame which, at moments I hope are weak, Mailer seems to crave.

But it is hard for American writers not to measure themselves according to the standards of their time and place. I recall a conversation with Stephen Spender when I lapsed, unconsciously, into the national preoccupation. Some writer had unexpectedly failed, not gone on, blown up. Spender said rather pointedly, "The difference in England is that they *want* us to be distinguished, to be good." We order things differently; although our example is contagious, for in recent years the popular British press has discovered writers in a way ours never has. Outside the gossip column and the book page no writer except Hemingway is ever mentioned as news in the American press, but let the most obscure young English novelist attack the Establishment and there are headlines in London. Mailer can denounce Eisenhower as much as he likes in *Dissent* but the readers of the *Daily News* will never know the name of Mailer, much less the quality of his anger. Publicity for the American writer is of the "personality" kind: a photograph in *Harper's Bazaar*, bland television appearances . . . the writer as minor movie star, and as unheeded.

Mailer and I finally met in 1954. I had just published my last, or perhaps I should say latest, novel, *Messiah*, and it had sunk quietly into oblivion in America. (If it were not for the continuing interest of Europe, especially England, a great many of our writers would not survive as well as they do their various seasons of neglect.) I liked Mailer, though I am afraid my first impression of him was somewhat guarded. I am suspicious of people who make speeches at me, and he is a born cocktail-party orator. I have not the slightest recollection of what we talked about. I do recall telling him that I admired *Barbary Shore*, and he was shrewd enough to observe that probably I had been driven to read it to see if it was really as bad as everyone thought. Which it was not. Of his three novels I find it the most interesting and the least diffuse, and quite literally memorable. It is hallucinatory writing of a kind Mailer tried, as far as I know, only that one time; and though I think his talents are essentially naturalistic, he does seem again in his new novel (judging from the advance samples he displays in *Advertisements for Myself*) to be trying for that revelation through willful distortion which he achieved in *Barbary Shore*. One is curious to see the result.

I have gone into the chronology of Mailer's days and mine because they run parallel, occasionally crossing, and because the book he has just published is, in effect, an autobiography covering more or less his entire career with particular attention to the days of the Golfer's dull terror. Mailer gives us his life and his work together, and therefore it is impossible to review the book without attempting to make some estimate of both his character and the corpus of his work, the tension of his present and the shape of his future. Mailer is sly to get himself all this attention, but I must point out that it is a very dangerous move for an artist to expose himself so completely. Indeed, in other times it would have been fatal for an artist not yet full grown to show us his sores and wounds, his real and his illusory strength. Until very recently the artist was a magician who did his magic in public view but kept himself and his effects a matter of mystery. We know *now* of Flaubert's suffering, both emotional and aesthetic, during the days of his work, but it is hard to imagine what would have happened if the court which prosecuted *Madame Bovary* could have presented as evidence a volume of his letters. In effect, Mailer has anticipated his own posterity. He is giving us now the storms and the uncertainties, private and public, which he has undergone. He has armed the enemy and not entirely pleased his allies.

However, it may be possible to get away with this sort of thing

today, for we live in the age of the confession. What Mailer has done is
no different in kind from what those deranged and fallen actresses have
accomplished in ghost-written memoirs where, with a shrewd eye on the
comeback trail, they pathetically confess their sins to Demos, receiving for
their tears the absolution of a culture obscenely interested in gossip. I
suspect Mailer may create more interest in himself by having made this
"clean breast of it" than he would have got by publishing a really distinguished novel. The audience no longer consumes novels, but it does
devour personalities. Yet what happens after one is eaten? Is one regurgi-
tated? Or does the audience move on to its next dinner of scandal and
tears, its previous meal absorbed and forgotten?

Nevertheless, I am fairly certain that Mailer will survive everything. Despite a nice but small gift for self-destruction, he is uncommonly
adroit, with an eye to the main chance (the writer who lacks this instinct
is done for in America; excellence is not nearly enough). I noted with
some amusement that, despite his air of candor, he makes no new enemies
in this book. He scores off those who are lost to him anyway, thus proving
that essentially the work is politic. His confessions, when not too disin-
genuous, are often engaging and always interesting, as he tries to record
his confusions. For Mailer does not begin to know what he believes or is
or wants. His drive seems to be toward power of a religiopolitical kind. He
is a messiah without real hope of paradise on earth or in heaven, and with
no precise mission except that dictated by his ever-changing temperament. I am not sure, finally, that he should be a novelist at all, or even a
writer, despite formidable gifts. He is too much a demagogue; he swings
from one position of cant to another with an intensity that is visceral
rather than intellectual. He is all fragments and pieces. He appears to be
looking for an identity, and often it seems that he believes crude celebrity
will give it to him again. The author of *The Naked and the Dead*, though
not the real Mailer, was at least an identifiable surrogate, and duly
celebrated. But Mailer was quickly bored with the war-novelist role, and
as soon as possible he moved honorably to a new position: radical politics,
in the hope that through Marxist action he might better identify himself
to us and to himself. But that failed him, too. Nor is it the new Mailer,
prophet of Hip and celebrator of sex and its connection with time, apt to
interest him or us for very long.

I also noted at moments toward the end of this book, that a
reaction was setting in: Mailer started using military allusions. "Back in
the Philippines, we . . ."—that sort of thing. And there were references
to patrols, ambushes. It was startling. Most of our generation was in the
war, usually ingloriously, yet I have never heard a contemporary make any

reference to it in a personal way. The war to most of us was a profound irrelevance; traumatic for some, perhaps, but for most no more than an interruption. When the 1959 Mailer reminds us that he was a rifleman on Luzon, I get embarrassed for him and hope he is not going back to his first attitude to get the attention he wants.

Now for the book itself. It is a collection of stories, essays, notes, newspaper columns, and part of a play. It begins with his first story at Harvard and ends with part of his new novel. The play, which I read in an earlier version, could be remarkable onstage. But the best work in this volume is two short stories. "The Language of Men" tells of the problems of an army cook who has an abstract passion for excellence as well as a need for the approbation of the indifferent men who eat his food. His war with them and himself and his will to excel are beautifully shown and in many ways make one of the best stories of its kind I have read, certainly preferable to Hemingway's *The Old Man and the Sea*, which it resembles in theme. But where Hemingway was pretentious and external, Mailer is particular and works with gentle grace from within his characters. The other story, "The Patron Saint of Macdougal Alley," is a wildly funny portrait of an archetypal drifter, and I think it is of permanent value: we have had this sort of fool in every age (Catullus and Juvenal each dealt with him), but I have not seen him done quite so well in our day.

By and large, excepting "The White Negro," I did not like the essays and the newspaper columns. Mailer is forever shouting at us that he is about to tell us something we must know or has just told us something revelatory and we failed to hear him or that he will, God grant his poor abused brain and body just one more chance, get through to us so that we will *know*. Actually, when he does approach a point he shifts into a swelling, throbbing rhetoric which is not easy to read but usually has something to do with love and sex and the horror of our age and the connection which must be made between time and sex (the image this bit of rhetoric suggests to me is a limitless gray sea of time with a human phallus desperately poking at a corner of it). He is at his best (who is not?) when discussing his own works and days. The piece about getting *The Deer Park* published is especially good, and depressing for what it reveals about our society. But, finally, in every line he writes, despite the bombast, there is uncertainty: Who am I? What do I want? What am I saying? He is Thomas Wolfe but with a conscience. Wolfe's motive for writing was perfectly clear: he wanted fame; he wanted to taste the whole earth, to name all the rivers. Mailer has the same passion for fame but he has a good deal more sense of responsibility and he sees that the thing is always in danger of spinning down into meaninglessness. Nothing is quite enough: art, sex, politics, drugs, God, mind. He is sure to get tired of Hip very soon. Sex will be a dead end for him, because sex is the one purely existential act. Sex is. There is nothing more to be done about it. Sex builds no roads, writes no novels, and sex certainly gives no meaning to anything in life but itself. I have often thought that much of D.H. Lawrence's self-lacerating hysteria toward the end of his life must have come out of some "blood knowledge" that the cruel priapic god was mad, bad and dangerous to know, and, finally, not even palliative to the universal strangeness.

Perhaps what has gone wrong in Mailer, and in many of our fellow clerks, is the sense that human beings to flourish must be possessed by one idea, a central meaning to which all experience can be related. To be, in Isaiah Berlin's bright metaphor, hedgehog rather than fox. Yet the human mind is not capable of this kind of exclusivity. We are none of us hedgehogs or foxes, but both simultaneously. The human mind is in continual flux, and personality is simply a sum of those attitudes which most often repeat themselves in recognizable actions. It is naïve and dangerous to try to impose on the human mind any system of thought which lays claim to finality. Very few first-rate writers have ever subordinated their own apprehension of a most protean reality to a man-made system of thought. Tolstoi's famous attempt in *War and Peace* nearly wrecked that beautiful work. Ultimately, not Christ, not Marx, not Freud, despite the pretensions of each, has the final word to say about the fact of being human. And those who take solemnly the words of other men as absolute are, in the deepest sense, maiming their own sensibilities and controverting the evidence of their own senses in a fashion which may be comforting to a terrified man but is disastrous for an artist.

One of the few sad results of the collapse of the Judeo-Christian ethical and religious systems has been the displacement of those who are absolutists by temperament and would in earlier times have been rabbis, priests, systematic philosophers. As the old Establishment of the West crumbles, the absolutists have turned to literature and the arts, and one by one the arts in the twentieth century have become hieratic. Serious literature has become religion, as Matthew Arnold foresaw. Those who once would have been fulfilled in Talmudic debate or suffered finely between the pull of Rome and the Church of England have turned to the writing of novels and, worse, to the criticism of novels. Now I am not sure that the novel, though it is many things, is particularly suited to didacticism. It is certainly putting an undesirable weight upon it to use it as a pretext for sermons or the resuscitation of antique religious myths. Works of fiction, at best, create not arguments but worlds, and a world by definition is an attitude toward a complex of experience, not a single argument or theme, syllogistically proposed. In the nineteenth century most of our critics (and many of our novelists) would have been writing books of sermons and quarreling over points of doctrine. With religion gone out of the intellectual world they now write solemnly and uneasily about novels; they are clearly impatient with the vulgar vitality of the better novels, and were it not that they had one another's books about books to analyze, I suspect many of them would despair and falter. The novelists don't seem very bright to the critics, while their commentaries seem irrelevant to the novelists. Yet each affects the other; and those writers who are unduly eager for fame and acceptance will write novels which they hope might interest "religious"-minded critics. The results range from the subliterary bleating of the Beats to Mailer's portentous cry which takes the form of: "I am the way and the life ever after, crucify me, you hackers, for mine is a ritual death! Take my flesh and my blood, partake of me and *know* mysteries . . .!" And the curious thing is that they will crucify him; they will partake of his flesh; yet no mystery will be revealed. For the priests have created the gods, and they are all of them ritual harvest gods.

I was most struck by this remark of André Gide in the posthumous *Ainsi Soit-il:* "It is affectation that makes so many of today's writings, often even the best among them, unbearable to me. The author takes on a tone that is not natural to him." Of course it is sometimes the work of a lifetime for an artist to discover who he is, and it is true that a great deal of good art results from the trying on of masks, the affectation of a persona not one's own. But it seems to me that most of my contemporaries, including Mailer, are—as Gide suggests—desperately trying to convince themselves and the audience that they are something they are not. There is even a certain embarrassment about writing novels at all. Telling stories does seem a silly occupation for one fully grown; yet to be a philosopher or a religious is not easy when one is making a novel. Also, in a society such as ours, where there is no moral, political or religious center, the temptation to fill the void is irresistible. There is the empty throne, so . . . *seize* the crown! Who would not be a king or high priest in such an age? And the writers, each in his own way, are preoccupied with power. Some hope to achieve place through good deportment. Universities are filled with poets and novelists conducting demure and careful lives in imitation of Eliot and Forster and those others who (through what *seems* to have been discretion) made it. Outside the universities one finds the buccaneers who mean to seize the crown by force, blunt Bolingbrokes to the Academy's gentle Richards.

Mailer is a Bolingbroke, a born usurper. He will raise an army anywhere, live off the country as best he can, helped by a devoted underground, even assisted at brief moments by rival claimants like myself. Yet when all is said, none of this is the way to live. And it is not a way (at least it makes the way harder) to create a literature that, no doubt quixotically, remains the interest of each of us. I suppose if it helps Hemingway to think of literature as a Golden Gloves Tournament with himself pounding Maupassant to the mat or fighting Stendhal to a draw, then no doubt the fantasy has been of some use. But there is also evidence that the preoccupation with power is a great waste of time. Mailer has had the honesty to confess that his own competitiveness has wasted him as he worries about reviewers and bad publicity and the seemingly spiteful successes of other novelists. Yet all the time he knows perfectly well that writers are not in competition with one another. The real enemy is the audience, which grows more and more indifferent to literature, an audience which can be reached only by phenomena, by superior pornographies or willfully meretricious accounts of the way we live now. No serious American novelist has ever had any real sense of audience. C. P. Snow made the point that he would, given a choice, prefer to be a writer in England to a writer in America because, for better or worse, the Establishment of his country would read him and know him as he knew them, as the Greek dramatists knew and were known by their city's audience. One cannot imagine the American President, any American President, reading a work by a serious contemporary American writer. This lack of response is to me at the center of Mailer's desperation. He is a public writer, not a private artist; he wants to influence those who are alive at this time, but they will not notice him even when he is good. So each time he speaks he must become more bold, more loud, put on brighter motley and shake more foolish bells. *Anything* to get their attention, and finally (and this could be his tragedy) so much energy is spent in getting the indifferent ear to listen that when the time comes for him to speak there may be not enough strength or creative imagination left him to say what he *knows*. Exhausted, he becomes like Louis Lambert in Balzac's curious novel of the visionary-artist who, having seen straight through to the heart of the mystery, dies mad, murmuring: "The angels are white."

Yet of all my contemporaries I retain the greatest affection for Mailer as a force and as an artist. He is a man whose faults, though many, add to rather than subtract from the sum of his natural achievement. There is more virtue in his failures than in most small, premeditated successes which, in Cynic's phrase, "debase currency." Mailer, in all that he does, whether he does it well or ill, is honorable, and that is the highest praise I can give any writer in this piping time.

RICHARD FOSTER

The Early Novels

W hen Norman Mailer's *The Naked and the Dead* was published in 1948 it was all but universally acclaimed as a major novel marking the appearance of a new American writer destined for greatness. During the next twenty years, however, though he had some warm defenders, the negative judgments among critics substantially outnumbered the positive as book after book appeared: novels, a play, collections of stories and poems, and gatherings of essays and other fugitive pieces. And yet, unlike most of his generation of novelists—the "war novelists" and the urban Jewish writers—he has pursued a course of individualistic development and change which has continued to command the attention of peers, critics, and public; if his readers have sometimes been baffled and frequently hostile, they have grown ever more interested. To use a Maileresque analogy, he has rather resembled an overmatched boxer who, floored in the second round, springs back and sustains the fight far beyond expectations through variety and inventiveness of footwork and temporizing punches.

The match is still not decided. But however it finally comes out, there can be no doubt that the overmatched boxer will at the very least be remembered for his remarkable performance. Mailer's adversary through the 1950's and 1960's has been the current embodiment of operative cultural and literary norms, that plodding but powerful opponent of idiosyncrasy and innovation which Eliot long ago dubbed "the tradition." Mailer had won his first round with a skillful and moving but conventional novel in the realist-naturalist vein. Everything since *The Naked and*

From *University of Minnesota Pamphlets on American Writers, No. 73.* Copyright © 1968 by University of Minnesota.

the Dead, with the exception of a handful of stories from the late forties and early fifties, has been radically innovative in both substance and essential form—without satisfying current conceptions of what constitutes serious literary experimentation.

It has been Mailer's apparent lack of artistic "seriousness" that has troubled his serious critics most. When they were not either ridiculing or dismissing him, their main cry was the lamentation that a major talent was being wasted on trivial material or debased by sloppy craftsmanship. F. Scott Fitzgerald, whose work and career were in many ways similar to Mailer's, was criticized during his lifetime on much the same grounds. But what needs to be stressed in Mailer's case, as in Fitzgerald's, is that he is indeed a serious "experimentalist" writer, though an experimentalist of a different order than our moment in the history of "the tradition" allows us easily to recognize, accept, and understand.

James Joyce was the kind of experimentalist who applied innovative techniques to conventionally "realistic" fictional material. He sought out and found new routes to the old novelistic destinations. D. H. Lawrence, on the other hand, was the kind of writer who discovered new destinations—new materials and knowledge, and thus new obligations for fiction. His technical innovations, always less sophisticated, formal, and predominant than Joyce's, were functional consequences and by-products of what can only be called an experimentalist approach to the *subject matter* of fiction. In the course of writing *The Rainbow* and *Women in Love*, Lawrence discovered, as he told Edward Garnett, that his subject was no longer "the old stable *ego*" of human character, no longer the "diamond" but rather the "carbon" which is the diamond's elemental substance:

> There is another *ego*, according to whose action the individual is unrecognisable, and passes through, as it were, allotropic states which it needs a deeper sense than any we've been used to exercise, to discover are states of the same single radically unchanged element. . . . Again I say, don't look for the development of the novel to follow the lines of certain characters: the characters fall into the form of some other rhythmic form, as when one draws a fiddle-bow across a fine tray delicately sanded, the sand takes lines unknown.

These metaphors describing the substantive nature of Lawrence's experimentation with both matter and form after *Sons and Lovers* might as easily apply to Mailer, whose work after *The Naked and the Dead* has been similarly concerned with the "allotropy"—the changing "rhythmic form" and "lines unknown"—of the "carbon" of human character under complex stress. And like Lawrence, Mailer seems to have become aware of his new departure only after standing away from the new work in hand to see what he was doing and why he was doing it. While working on *Barbary Shore*, he has recalled in an interview, he found his Marxist intellectual convictions continually distracted by compulsive preoccupations with "murder, suicide, orgy, psychosis." "I always felt as if I were not writing the book myself." Other statements by Mailer indicate that much the same creative pathology also ruled the composition of *The Deer Park*, his third novel. The personal stresses and anxieties that underlay the writing of these two novels, and the stories that were spun off from them, found confessional expression in Mailer's fourth book, a compilation of fiction and nonfiction pieces with unifying connective additions called *Advertisements for Myself*, which is the author's intense, immediate, and unabashedly public reappraisal of himself, in 1959, as both artist and human being. Anxiety, compulsion, and hints of psychosis had been the disruptive and only half-conscious creative causes behind *Barbary Shore* and *The Deer Park*. Following the purgation and illumination represented by *Advertisements*, they become, in the later novels *An American Dream* and *Why Are We in Vietnam?* and the related pieces in *The Presidential Papers* and *Cannibals and Christians*, the consciously molded substance of Mailer's hypertrophic images of life in America at mid-century.

A detailed account of this course of change and growth must be left for later. The important fact is that after several more books, plus a string of other accomplishments—including play-producing, movie-making, a fling at architectural design, and a great deal of moral, social, and political punditing, both on paper and on the hoof—the author of *The Naked and the Dead* emerged in the mid-sixties, despite his still uncertain reputation among serious literary people, as decidedly the most active and vivid public figure on the American literary scene.

Like his first published novel and stories, Mailer's early life was at least conventional enough not to foreshadow with any definiteness the panoply of idiosyncrasy that was to come later. Born January 31, 1923, in Long Branch, New Jersey, to Isaac and Fanny Mailer, Norman Mailer was raised and schooled in Brooklyn, graduating from Boys' High School in 1939. While at Harvard, where he earned a B.S. degree in aeronautical engineering in 1943, Mailer began writing in earnest, contributing to the *Advocate*, working at his first two (and still unpublished) novels, and winning in 1941 *Story* magazine's annual college fiction contest. In 1944 he married his first wife and was drafted into the Army, serving in the Pacific theater until 1946. During the next year and a half, part of which was spent in Europe, where he was enrolled as a student at the Sorbonne, Mailer wrote *The Naked and the Dead*, which was published with immediate and dramatic success. The public purchased it in such numbers that it held at the top of the best-seller lists for nearly three months. A movie contract was soon in the works; Lillian Hellman was slated to adapt it for the stage; and Sinclair Lewis was moved to dub Mailer "the greatest writer to come out of his generation."

Though Mailer himself once half dismissed his first novel as a "conventional war novel," and though it was conceived and composed in a manner that Mailer was not to use again in a major work, *The Naked and the Dead* is much more than a "war novel." The embracing action of the novel—the taking of a Japanese-held Pacific island in World War II—is rendered with the skilled realist's commitment to the truthful and vivid depiction of actuality. But in the year of its publication Mailer put on record his view that *The Naked and the Dead*, though cast in the realist mold, is "symbolic," expressive of "death and man's creative urge, fate, man's desire to conquer the elements—all kinds of things you never dream of separating and stating so baldly." And there is no mistaking that the island itself, and the mountain at its center which Sergeant Croft commits himself and his platoon to conquering, acquire an almost Conradian symbolic significance in the eyes of their chief beholders. Here is the soldiers' vision of the setting of their destruction:

> It was a sensual isle, a Biblical land of ruby wines and golden sands and indigo trees. The men stared and stared. The island hovered before them like an Oriental monarch's conception of heaven, and they responded to it with an acute and terrible longing. It was a vision of all the beauty for which they had ever yearned, all the ecstasy they had ever sought. For a few minutes it dissolved the long dreary passage of the mute months in the jungle, without hope, without pride. If they had been alone they might have stretched out their arms to it.
>
> It could not last. Slowly, inevitably, the beach began to dissolve in the encompassing night. The golden sands grew faint, became gray-green, and darkened. The island sank into the water, and the tide of night washed over the rose and lavender hills. After a little while, there was only the gray-black ocean, the darkened sky, and the evil churning of the gray-white wake. Bits of phosphorescence swirled in the foam. The black dead ocean looked like a mirror of the night; it was cold, implicit with dread and death. The men felt it absorb them in a silent pervasive terror. They turned back to their cots, settled down for the night, and shuddered for a long while in their blankets.

In an interview three years later, just after completing *Barbary Shore*, Mailer made this interesting disclosure about *The Naked and the Dead*:

> I don't think of myself as a realist. That terrible word "naturalism." It was my literary heritage—the things I learned from Dos Passos and

Farrell. I took naturally to it, that's the way one wrote a book. But I really was off on a mystic kick. Actually—a funny thing—the biggest influence on *Naked* was *Moby Dick.* . . . I was sure everyone would know. I had Ahab in it, and I suppose the mountain was Moby Dick. Of course, I also think the book will stand or fall as a realistic novel.

This last qualification would also apply, of course, to *Moby Dick.* For Melville saw in the actual hazard and struggle of whaling, as Mailer did in war, the revealed pattern of the grandeur and tragedy of the whole human enterprise. Combat, for Mailer, is the chief means by which the higher laws of life become incarnate in human experience. War is his external subject matter in *The Naked and the Dead;* but his internal theme is the "crisis in human values"—identity, humanity, man, and the nature of their enemies in our time.

With war as the background typification of generalized external crisis, Mailer develops his internal themes by two principal means: first, extensively, through a number of Dos Passos-like diagnostic biographical portraits of a cross section of the fighting men; and second, intensively, through the protracted psychic struggle of mind and personality that takes place between Major General Cummings, the crypto-fascist commanding officer of the invading American forces, and his aide, a questioning liberal named Hearn. Both men have been shaped, though in opposite ways, by reaction against the privileged sterility of their Midwestern bourgeois backgrounds. Cummings is the self-created prophet of a new totalitarianism who commands, in the name of his faith in order and authority, the breaking of men's spirits and the destruction of their wills. Hearn, bitter in his discontent, by nature a loner and yet tenderly humane in his half-guilty identification with the men he commands, is the uncertain voice of the liberal ideal of free man. Most of the fighting men are portrayed as already deprived, twisted, or stunted by the disintegrative and totalitarian forces and counterforces at work in their world, the forces whose contention has culminated in the war which now envelops them all. These men are the data of the dialectical contest which is taking place between Cummings and Hearn. That contest, the original of similar recurring patterns of individual contest, including sexual, in most of the rest of Mailer's work, ends in a kind of draw. Hearn and his convictions are wasted when he dies as a casual accident of war on an irrelevant mission. And though the campaign is won, Cummings is in essence defeated because the agency of victory is not his active military intelligence but rather a chain of chance accidents beyond his control.

One notices not only that a true hero is lacking from the novel's epic-like action, but that his opposite, a forceful antagonist, is lacking too. And yet a large enveloping energy has gathered, thrust forward, and come through to significant issue. A great spasm of nature, an inevitable motion of history, has superseded the efficacies of individual men in a world that has begun to move across Yeats's threshold of apocalypse where "the best lack all conviction" and "the worst/are full of passionate intensity."

But at the core of this vast action, his presence stressing the hero's absence, is Sergeant Croft. After the death of Hearn, he leads the platoon on its doomed assault upon the mountain, dominating his men by the sheer intensity of his undefined "hunger" for the mastery of life. A rough prototype of D. J. Jethroe of *Why Are We in Vietnam?*, Croft has been sired by a tough Texas dirt farmer and a woman conventionally "weak . . . sweet and mild." His father encourages in him a predator's taste for hunting, and he is by nature "mean." Why? "Oh, there are answers. He is that way because of the corruption-of-the-society. He is that way because the devil has claimed him for one of his own. It is because he is a Texan; it is because he has renounced God." The author interprets Croft in an aside as follows: "*He hated weakness and he loved practically nothing. There was a crude unformed vision in his soul but he was rarely conscious of it.*" This embryonic "vision" is different from Hearn's superannuated liberalism and Cummings's authoritarian calculus because it is an animal thing—an energy with fierce tendencies but no "form." Croft represents the kinetic life-substance upon which such alternative ideologies as those of Hearn and Cummings must depend for their unforeseeable realizations. In his irrational will and passion, he is the human microcosm of the vast upsurge of inhuman forces in history which express themselves in the ironic irresolutions of the total action of *The Naked and the Dead*.

The Naked and the Dead, then, even if substantially conventional in form and style, is nevertheless one with the rest of Mailer's work in the apocalyptic energies of its vision. Those energies begin to find their requisite new form, and with that a new sort of voice, in the first of Mailer's "experimental" novels, *Barbary Shore*, published in 1951. *Barbary Shore* was the product, as Mailer has written in retrospect, "of intense political preoccupation and a voyage in political affairs which began with the Progressive Party and has ended in the *cul-de-sac* (at least so far as action is concerned) of being an anti-Stalinist Marxist who feels that war is probably inevitable." The omniscient authorial point of view of *The Naked and the Dead* is abandoned in *Barbary Shore* for first-person narrative, which is to continue as the preferred narrative form for Mailer's books thereafter. ("Memory is the seed of narrative, yeah," says D. J. Jethroe, narrator of *Why Are We in Vietnam?*.) The book becomes, thus, an adaption of *Bildungsroman*; its narrative substance is the hero's education for life in our time—or re-education, since he is suffering from amnesia somewhat inexplicitly induced by war and the breakdown of traditional political idealism. The setting is a Brooklyn rooming house operated by a sexually promiscuous and morally neuter proprietress named, with an irony appropriate to her role as life's presiding norm, Guinevere. In this setting, the case histories of three roomers are presented: an impotent, betrayed, and self-betraying idealist of the old revolutionary left; his demon, a stolid and perverted interrogator for the rightist "totalitarian" establishment; and a mad Cassandra-like girl whose derangement is a consequence and expression of history, and whom, as an exacerbated mirroring of his own distressed psyche, the hero half loves.

The heaviness and inertia of the novel—its garrulous expositions of ideological conflict and the dazed passivity and blankness of Lovett, the hero-narrator, before all he sees and hears—is only a little relieved when at the end he sprints into an inchoate future with a mysterious small object entrusted to his keeping by the failed leftist before his death. The precise nature of the object, which is hotly coveted by the furies of the right, is never specified. But what it means is perfectly clear. It is a symbol or talisman of the sacred idea of man free and whole; and in the moment of the narrator's active commitment to it in the face of the terrible odds and enemies ranged against it and now against him as well, we are meant to feel that it has taken existential power of life itself.

Even this early in his career—after only two novels—it is clear that Mailer's imagination, unique in his generation, is cast in the epic mold. As bard and prophet to an age in which history is at odds with nature or "destiny," he tells in a fevered voice of the permutations of the heroic imperative in a postheroic world. His theme is the struggle of life and form against death and chaos. But his subject matter is history. And as he pursues the theme of the ideal through the matter of the actual he makes a discovery: in our time the sources and resources of life have shifted, to use the shorthand of Mailer's own symbology, from "God" to "the devil." The vision of life at stalemate in *The Naked and the Dead* and *Barbary Shore* is explained by this discovery, a discovery whose fullness of realization in a changed imaginative vision comes clear in *The Deer Park*, published in 1955.

Desert D'Or, a resort of the rich and powerful modeled on Palm Springs, is the principal setting of *The Deer Park*. It is a denatured interior world of concrete and plastic, of harsh light and blinding shadow, thrown up in defiance of the encircling desert outside. This pattern of division between natural and unnatural that is established in the setting extends also to the characters, in whom desire and will, feeling and thought, the wellsprings of motive and motive's fulfillment in action, have been stricken apart. The natural current of the life-force has somehow been broken. And the inhabitants of this world of trauma and aftermath constitute a gallery of parodies of the human image ranging from the absurd to the piteous to the monstrous. They are, as Mailer wrote in a note to his adaptation of *The Deer Park* for the stage, "in hell."

Sergius O'Shaugnessy, the hero-narrator of *The Deer Park*, is both an orphan and, like Lovett of *Barbary Shore*, a symbolic waif of historical disaster. His surrogate home in the Air Force and fulfillment in the exercise of the war pilot's impersonal skills of destruction have been snatched from him in a sudden accidental revelation that he is a killer: "I realized that . . . I had been busy setting fire to a dozen people, or two dozen, or had it been a hundred?" In recoil from such horrors of the "real world" he suffers a breakdown, is discharged, and on the winnings from a prodigiously lucky gambling venture, he comes to Desert D'Or, retreat of the gods of the "imaginary world," to rest, drift, gaze, and spend. A blank slate to be written on, an empty vessel to be filled, and—his vision of the burned flesh of his victims having rendered him sexually impotent—a low flame needing fuel, Sergius O'Shaugnessy is the framing consciousness of an ample world crowded with people exhibiting versions of his own predicament. Among the most important of these are Charles Francis Eitel, a gifted and formerly powerful Hollywood director, and Marion Faye, dope pusher, impresario of call girls, and connoisseur of the moral nuances of sadism. Both of these men become friends of O'Shaugnessy and objects of his studious moral attention.

Eitel has had a golden age, a brief heroic period in the thirties when as a true artist he made courageous movies on contemporary social themes, and when as a man of integrity he put his life on the line in behalf of the fated struggle for democracy in Spain. In reflexive response to the corruption of integrity which has overtaken his art as he has risen to power in Hollywood, Eitel rebuffs a congressional investigating commitee seeking from him incriminating political testimony against his colleagues. In consequence, the industry blackballs him; and his loss of power and identity in the "imaginary" world is measured in personal terms by his loss of potency as both artist and lover. This sequential pattern of aspiration, action, corruption, moral illumination, renunciation, exile, and impotence precisely parallels the pattern of Sergius's life. Eitel is the distillate of the best values of the past by which Sergius has been fathered and orphaned, and for Sergius, consequently, the question of Eitel's destiny— the question of his potential for rebirth and self-renewal—has crucial moral significance.

Eitel stumbles upon a "second chance" in the form of Elena Esposito, and he muffs it. Another man's castoff, she is soiled, tawdry, and simple. She is a poor dancer and a worse actress, and her manners are absurd. And yet she has the dignity and courage, and finally the beauty, of a being wholly natural. Eitel's affair with her becomes the nourishing ground of a new life for him. His sexual potency is restored, and with it his creative potency as he begins to work on a script which he imagines will be the redemption of his integrity as artist and man. But this new access of life fills him with fear; it is the stirring in him of the heroic imperative, with its attendant commitments to solitary battle, lonely journeyings in the unknown, and the risks of failure and defeat. The doors of Hollywood begin to open again, and the thrones and dominations of the "imaginary" world solicit his return: all he must do is confess and recant before the committee, and he may pass back through those doors. Half because of fear, half because of old habit, Eitel takes the easy way of surrender, shunning the hazardous alternatives (as Elena, significantly, does not) represented by those dark angels of life and truth, Don Beda, high priest of satyrism and orgy, and Marion Faye, the hipster prophet of criminal idealism. His harvest is the life-in-death of security through compromise, the corruption of his script and his talent, and eventual marriage to a broken and exhausted Elena, which is possible now that they are no longer "wedded" in a sacramental sense.

Elena is a noble figure—defeated, but honorably so, in her fated but heroic contest with time and what Hardy calls "crass casualty." Eitel's enemies have been lesser ones—history and social circumstance—and his defeat is pitiful rather than noble, because he has "sold out." But he has at least the saving grace of his ironic intelligence, which enables him to understand, when she proudly refuses his first offer of marriage, the principle of Elena's nobility: "the essence of spirit . . . was to choose the thing which did not better one's position but made it more perilous." Later on, when she has no more resources of refusal and he nourishes upon her defeat by "sacrificing" himself in marrying her, he understands his own corresponding cowardice: "there was that law of life so cruel and so just which demanded that one must grow or else pay more for remaining the same."

Eitel is Mailer's version of the traditional hero in his last historical incarnation. Vision, passion, and courage have dwindled in Eitel to intelligence, compassion, and guilt—the "cement" of the world, as Marion Faye contemptuously labels the last two, which binds men, enfeebles them, and turns them into spiritual "slobs." Eitel's very strengths are weaknesses, his virtues are faults, in a world where the apocalyptic beasts of anxiety and dread are raging in prisons of compromise and falsehood. And as the novel draws to its close and Eitel begins to fade into the penumbra of Sergius O'Shaugnessy's memorializing imagination, we are aware that the passing of the man is also the passing of the values he represented. Flanked by comic Lulu Meyers, a movie sex goddess who on impulse marries for "love" rather than career, and by tragic Marion Faye, whose anarch's code of black moral reason leads him behind prison bars, the now enlightened Sergius is the chief chalice-bearer of new human values. He becomes a bullfighter, stud, and teacher of both arts. And he begins to write, his books presumably fired by the existential perils and ecstasies of combat and sexuality. Though the novel ends on a cheerful note of metaphysical exhilaration, Sergius, both as a character and as an archetype of new styles of human value, is vague and inchoate as well as faintly absurd. Sergius has survived all sorts of traumas and temptations and come through to freedom, but he is not very much more fully realized as an examplar of new values in action than was his predecessor, Lovett. He has come to terms with the world that has wounded him, and like the good Emersonian "fatalists" that all such Mailer heroes are, he affirms it as his destined inheritance from nature and history. But neither he nor his author has yet found the requisite lifestyle, the new heroic mold through which to turn understanding and affirmation into creative, perhaps re-demptive action.

Life threatened in our time by the forces of death is Mailer's subject everywhere. When he writes as a realist, as in *The Naked and the Dead*, life is stalemated and defeated by the forces of death. In the next two novels the intensities of anxiety and dread underlying Mailer's subject matter begin to dominate the rational, circumjacent forms of the realist, distorting them in the direction of the expressionistic and the surreal. And with this modification of form comes a coordinate modification of the heroes in whom the issue of the life-death struggle is finally centered. The narrator-hero of *Barbary Shore*, for whom the action encompassed by his consciousness is an elaborately instructive morality play, in the end escapes paralysis and spiritual death. The similarly educated narrator-hero of *The Deer Park* not only escapes but, as he bids fond farewell to the memories of the defeated and destroyed, discerns in the very chemistry of the disease and decomposition all around him the flicker and spur of new possibilities for life. "Think of Sex as Time," says "God" in a final dialogue with Sergius, "and Time as the connection of new circuits."

JACK RICHARDSON

The Aesthetics of
Norman Mailer

There have been times when writing was considered an act of grace, a form of almost supernatural intervention in the ordinary affairs of the human imagination. The modern masters, however, have made it clear that the merely inspired soon perish and that the writer and his book are best, if not entirely, sustained by an act of will. James, Flaubert, Joyce, Mann—their testament can be seen as much in the persistent struggle to create a disciplined and meaningful language as in the worlds and characters that they left us. One need not be acquainted with their biographies to understand that a long battle of attrition once took place to ferret out of the rough matter of inspiration a strong, polished, personal idiom. Indeed, again and again readers have discovered that, at its best, the modern novel often deals with the adventure of its own making and that, while celebrating itself, it more than insinuates that its real hero is its creator, whose passion and agony we, for convenience, simply call his "style."

To many, Norman Mailer may seem far removed from these aesthetic preoccupations, but he is in fact one of the very few writers in the last decade or so who has really understood the hard lesson that the modern masters have taught. He has certainly grasped the act of will—the style—necessary to the writer-as-protagonist, and he has insisted stubbornly on exercising it again and again for its own sake as well as for the periodic re-creation of himself as a writer. He has done this, of course,

From *The New York Review of Books* (May 8, 1969). Copyright © 1969 by the New York Review.

without the aid of the faith in aesthetic form which sustained his predecessors; nor does he conceal his literary strategy and self-awareness by using an ironic and formal mode of expression. Rather he spreads everything out for us so that we may see to the bone and muscle of the writer's determination to survive. For all his pose as an activist and his well-advertised involvement in public life, Mailer's response to the controversy in which he is so much engaged is almost completely stylistic, and one soon realizes that his literary manner is in itself a dramatic dialectic. Mailer seems to be intellectually exhilarated by language, and I honestly believe he would much rather narrate for us the way he has tracked down the proper, self-revealing adverb than give us sagas of how wars are won or analyses of the tactics of political revolution.

Many of his critics have misunderstood the purely literary quality of Mailer's work, its unabashed, almost precious, obsession with itself. They have taken part of the author's public style as a clue to his intentions and have been pleased or exasperated accordingly. But no matter how diligently Mailer insists on creating a persona in the thick of political and social joustings, a persona part demagogue, part clown, part visionary, one cannot help feeling that his forays into the community are little more than intentionally self-lacerating experiences meant to sharpen the nuance and the tone of what he knows will finally be their literary reenactment.

His last novel, for example, *Why Are We in Vietnam?*, clearly displays Mailer's method of digesting experience. Taken as a collection of social insights into Corporate America, it is an outlandish caricature; taken as a narrative of the American spirit coming upon its pagan god at the end of a man's hunting trip, it is simple and familiar stuff; but, considered as the re-creation by means of language of the notions Mailer has about America, it is brilliant. The monologues of the narrator, D.J., are as superbly monstrous, as tortured with vernacular fustian as are the forms of our national existence which he both comments on and embodies. The novel, to be sure, is an indictment, "J'accuse," but it is, in every way, the "J'accuse" of a writer obsessed with language—the "J'accuse," finally, of a belletrist. The oblique title of the novel has its purpose: it is as if Mailer has said, "These words are my politics. Think of this semantic *Walpurgisnacht* the next time the Secretary of State speaks statistically about our war."

The ability to make convincing resolutions almost entirely through literary style is Mailer's major gift. However, finding occasions for the exercise of this gift seems always to have been a problem for him. Though he is what many consider an almost too personal writer, he has produced very little about small, isolated experiences. Everything he writes seems at first glance, to be occasional, to be encased in some prevalent mood, some new philosophy, some general current phenomenon. Again, his critics have seen him as always ready to attach himself and his prose style to any event that is fashionable and guarantees a certain amount of public attention. Indeed, it is true that Mailer's work often seems propped up by the styles of the times. Beat literature, pot, the Black Rebellion, urban planning, sexual freedom—one can wonder if there has been any cult in the last twenty years that he has not used as fuel. Anti-Mailer moralists see this as a sinister form of exploitation, and even his fans talk about the novel he could and should be writing, as though there were some special excellence attached to this particular literary form. Mailer himself admits, in the swaggering boxing metaphors he occasionally uses, to being a counter-puncher, and it appears that only when he is struck by something on the scale of a social movement is he moved to hit back, to draw on the literary energy he apparently keeps ready for all occasions he considers to be in his weight class.

Still, no matter how grand the subject he decided to challenge, it often seemed that his literary sensibility was too well-trained and dazzling to give it a fair fight. One would watch fascinated as Mailer transformed a public event into private expression, but, while grateful for his surprising reflections, one somehow missed the old, recognizable outlines of that event once he was through with it. The aspic of Mailer's prose often covered over events a bit too easily, turning them into grotesque and fascinating semi-philosophical bursts of rhetoric.

Yet so pugnacious a literary will as Mailer's seemed always to be searching for the tougher adversaries he deserved; and in his frequent restive appearances in print he was like some Jacob in extreme need of an angel to wrestle with. Now the 1968 Republican and Democratic conventions hardly suggest angels, but they, along with the Pentagon Peace March of the previous year, have proven to be for Mailer the agents for the action he understands best, the adventure of literary art in the world. He had often before matched himself against a historic moment, but this time history, while not exactly forcing an accommodation, at least succeeded in winning the right of coexistence.

The result is a tense balance between social and literary observation which often reads like a good old-fashioned novel in which suspense, character, plot revelations, and pungently describable action abound. Indeed, I am certain that one of the main reasons *The Armies of the Night* and *Miami and the Siege of Chicago* have been so widely praised is that they permit the well-worn, comfortable habits of reading. Here, after all, the writer-as-hero has come out from behind his aesthetic camouflage and placed himself and the gestation of his work into an arena nicely suited to his battle between public and private style, an arena where no architectural details get in the way of an open, entertaining view. As he proved by his earlier study of the nomination of Barry Goldwater, Mailer has few equals at describing the national rituals of American life; and these last two works demonstrate that he has no equal at all when it comes to matching one's personality against these rituals.

These virtues have been duly celebrated, and certainly Mailer has an eye for and on the souls of his compatriots. He can pin down the immaculate WASP, in town from Iowa to give his polite, Christian consent to Richard Nixon, as well as, with a certain reserved affection, the Yippie who consents to nothing but the half-hearted practice of Japanese riot techniques. Mailer is also an extraordinary synthesizer, a reporter who can sense moods and the subtler vibrations of political performance, and who can turn often tedious and random happenings into interesting, cohesive speculation. Finally, one must mention his ego and his honesty, a combination which permits him to confront events and personages as their antagonist and their equal, certain that it will be *he* who will illuminate *them*.

Still, it is not simply the extraordinary personal journalism that is most impressive about *The Armies of the Night* and *Miami and the Siege of Chicago*. The peculiar power of these books comes not from the fact that Mailer offers us better writing than that to which we are generally accustomed in politics, but, rather, from the uncanny way in which he has managed to maintain in these works the stylistic play and form of the most complex literary fiction. One should never forget the allegiance Mailer feels to fictional truth and judge these two books as showing an elementary split between confessional data on the one hand and public facts on the other.

Consider, for example, the first part of *The Armies of the Night*, the section which is entitled "History as a Novel: The Steps of the Pentagon." Here we have Mailer as character observing himself perform, preparing those observations for the Mailer who is relating to us as we read what he has observed about those observations. And, too, at most times, there is yet another watchful instrument, a television camera, on hand to effect one more layer of awareness. The whole sequence is an elaborate orchestration in which tones merge and blend in a manner which forces one to listen very carefully for the truth of things shaded by style, moments caught in an expressive reality which Mailer sets against the banalties of a *Time* reporter. Mailer has used here the apperceptive techniques of the modern novel, and used them to make a heavy literary assault on the common notions about history. It is not simply a question of the oddities of a single personality brought to bear on a subject that is generally dealt with "objectively." Rather, what Mailer does is to tinker consciously with the ways through which we are used to receiving information and reflection about certain areas of national experience. In short, for three quarters of *The Armies of the Night* Mailer is a literary modernist, juggling forms and experimenting with the narrative voice, teasing our sensibility which insists on getting quickly to the heart of the matter, forcing it to put up with dissertations on rhetoric, and surreal and pedestrian asides, until we admit that we are in a special terrain and must proceed with caution.

However, as I have said, history has made its own demands on Mailer's style, and these have kept him from being too much a formalist, from being a self-indulgent verbal speculator. The historic voice has its own traditions, and these have impressed themselves on Mailer and kept him finally within the boundaries of readability. Taken together, *The Armies of the Night* and *Miami and the Siege of Chicago* form a stylistic argosy from one form of awareness which is antic and novelistic to another which, with some melancholy, admits the strength of a simpler and more brutal actuality. In his reports on the conventions, Mailer seems at times completely overwhelmed by the deep ruptures he senses in America and by the final incapacity of even the most disciplined artistic will to force an adhesion. He becomes less and less concerned with maintaining a literary center to the second work, and allows the sequences from Miami to Chicago to unfold for the most part unchallenged by his imagination.

Whereas in *The Armies of the Night* he was in every sense a participant, in its sequel he is more detached, more wary, as tentative in his verbal manner as he is in his role of Old Guard Revolutionary. Between the quiet inexorability of Miami and the porcine hysteria of Chicago, there seemed less and less room for aesthetic sportiveness, and, as the pressure of these events increased, one felt Mailer's constriction of spirit, a slow sentence-by-sentence admission that there are forces of obliteration uncowed by even the most intricate artifice.

Miami and the Siege of Chicago is like the second part of an artistic *Bildungsroman* in which the hero finally allows the social order its right to a reality of its own. As the book slips into a glum catalogue of events, such as trips to a Hugh Hefner party and missed opportunities to be on hand when the police charged the formidable band of McCarthy supporters, it is as though the end of some passion were being described in a purposefully flat and muted way, as though history and art had worn themselves out in a magnificently equal encounter.

The last few years have produced much talk about the new "creative journalism" and the use of novelistic techniques in reporting. Whatever these phrases meant before—and it is my impression that they meant very little—they have now acquired a definition after the vent of these two books. Mailer has created a fresh entente between the personal mode and the public record, and, at a time when it is badly needed, he has reaffirmed the rights of the individualistic idiom to move in any social sphere. Simply, he has enlarged the territories of language, something the very best writers have always done for us.

TONY TANNER

On the Parapet

Every hundred yards Cummings steps up on the parapet, and peers
cautiously into the gloom of No Man's Land.
— The Naked and the Dead

. . . and I was up, up on that parapet one foot wide, and almost
broke in both directions, for a desire to dive right on over swayed
me out over the drop, and I nearly fell back to the terrace
from the panic of that.
— An American Dream

Since the Second World War Norman
Mailer has demonstrated an unflagging ability to convert environmental
pressures into lexical gestures which makes him one of the most resilient
of recent American novelists. In this study of his novels I want to suggest
why the image of a man standing on a parapet which appeared fleetingly
in his first novel should become the crucial situation in a novel he wrote
seventeen years later. But first we may make a more general approach to
the subject which has obsessed him since he began writing. At the end of
Saul Bellow's The Victim, Asa Leventhal cries out one last question to
Albee: ' "what's your idea of who runs things?" ' It is an apt question with
which to conclude a book in which the persecutor and the paranoid are
never quite sure which role they are in at any particular moment. But
more generally it could be said to be the question which occupies a large

From Critical Quarterly 2, vol. 12 (Summer 1970). Copyright © 1970 by Critical Quarterly.

number of American novelists who, in one form or another, are obsessed with the problems and mysteries of power. It is certainly Mailer's main concern, and his first three novels can be seen as studies of three different kinds of power and their distinctive manifestations or modes of operation. In each, the geographic setting suggests an extra dimension of power outside the particular human power-situation being studied. *The Naked and the Dead* (1948) is about men and war, and the temporary military installations are set in the jungle and surrounded by the sea. *Barbary Shore* (1951) is about men and politics, and the run-down boarding house in Brooklyn which contains most of the action is surrounded by the unfathomable density of the modern megalopolis. *The Deer Park* (1955) is about men and sex, and it takes place for the most part in an unreal annex of Hollywood called Desert D'Or. More real is the actual desert all around it. When he came to write *An American Dream* (1965), Mailer brought together these different geographies (either as actual settings or as metaphors) to make his most comprehensive exploration of the operations of power on many levels. . . .

The Deer Park is set in the town of Desert D'Or, close to the capital of cinema in Southern California. Hollywood, and California in general, are situated on the edge of the Pacific. Desert D'Or is on the edge of the desert. In the last century it was a shanty town round an oasis from which prospectors set out to look for gold. They called it Desert Door. Now it has been completely rebuilt. It is 'all new'. In giving us these details of the setting on page one, Mailer outlines the main subject of his novel. People come West searching for dream gold; every age will define the dream gold it seeks. The quest brings many people to some kind of extreme edge, where they may be confronted with a door through which they might push to some new dimension of experience. Or they may discover that dream gold is fool's gold, and wake up to the actual mess of their lives which becomes clear as the power of fantasy wanes. Once again, the location of the Hollywood dream factory on the western edge of the continent has struck an American novelist with its irresistible suggestiveness.

On the narrative level, the novel is an account of an ex-serviceman named Sergius O'Shaugnessy who plunges into the life of Desert D'Or. He not only has problems about his own identity, but some temporary blocks in the creative realm—both sexual and literary. After various adventures or entanglements—mainly in the rather unreal area in which sex is inextricable from cinema—he finally leaves Desert D'Or for Mexico where he recovers sufficient potency to learn some of the rudiments of bull-fighting, and sleep with a bull-fighter's mistress. From there he goes to

New York, where he achieves full literary potency and writes his book—which is *The Deer Park*. In turning to a study of the corrupting influence of the atmosphere of sex and films which prevails in Desert D'Or, Mailer had not entirely forgotten about politics. There is a film director in the book called Charles Eitel who on two occasions is summoned before a Congressional investigating committee to answer questions about his left wing and communist acquaintances in the past. Out of self-respect, and not from any political convictions or personal affections, he refuses to name names on the first occasion. Even then it seemed ridiculous indirectly to be 'defending a political system which reminded him of nothing so much as the studio for which he worked'. When he does refuse to give evidence he is excluded from the film world, and leaves the studio to 'act a script of his own'. For various reasons he cannot finally endure this state, since film directing is the thing he can do best. At a second hearing he is as forthcoming as his surname suggests, and by the end of the book he is back at work with a series of somewhat mediocre, not particularly successful films to his credit. The implications of Eitel's career seem to be as follows. Political systems seem to have become as unreal as the fabrications put out by the cinema—a suggested conflation of political reality and film which can also be found in the work of William Burroughs. As Burroughs says in one of his novels, the man who offends the people in charge of the elaborate film called society will be punished by being excluded from the film. This is what happens to Eitel. Whereas such a state may be sought for by the artist—so Sergius leaves Desert D'Or for Mexico—for Eitel it is unendurable since for him reality has become a matter of film. In gaining readmittance to the studio set by going along with the tawdry theatricals of the Congressional investigating committee, Eitel is in effect succumbing to the agreed version of things, returning to participate in (and perpetuate) the dominant fantasy which the majority call reality. He could not, after all, write his own script. It is Sergius O'Shaugnessy, and Norman Mailer, who manage to do that.

Another important inhabitant of Desert D'Or, who takes a different way from those suggested by the movements of Eitel and O'Shaugnessy, is Marion Faye. A pimp and drug addict who seems to go in for deliberate degradation of self and others, he is in his own way a quester. He is interested in the extremes of vice or nobility—he himself searching for the former in a way which makes Sergius remark that he is simply a religious man turned inside out. He wants to 'push to the end . . . and come out—he did not know where, but there was experience beyond experience, there was something. Of that, he was certain'. He seeks to break old limits and in an almost experimental way he sees how near to the edge he can push people—in one case he coaxes a girl to the edge of suicide, only to find that he has certain ineradicable compassionate instincts after all. The nature of his quest is perhaps best indicated by his deliberate act of not locking his door, thus metaphorically leaving himself open to the dreads which come in from the desert and the more literal threats of his many enemies in town. Most people in Desert D'Or live with their doors locked in every sense. The houses have walls round them to keep out the sight of the real desert. At the same time they have extravagant interior settings and extensive mirrors inside, so that life achieves the sustained unreality of prolonged narcissism in theatrical conditions. The bars are made to look like jungles, grottos, cinema lounges—life becomes an indefinite extension of the film sets close by. In these conditions people can only play roles and sex becomes a desolate game; where fantasy is everywhere, there is no chance for truly productive relationships. It is not surprising that more than one character, including Sergius, gets locked up sexually, unable to perform the creative act.

Such a world is, to Marion Faye, a world of 'slobs'. He is trying to find the door which opens to some authentic experience which he feels can only be had at the extreme edge of reality. It is one of his pleasures to drive with great speed out into the desert to a small summit from which he can look out, not only over the desert, but also to the gambling city and the atomic testing grounds which are both situated out there. He feels contempt and distaste for the way politicians and army officers produce verbal justifications for these great experiments with destructive power— 'for the words belonged to the slobs, and the slobs hid the world with words'. Language is just another false structure to be broken through. But Marion Faye does not regret the coming destruction which he foresees; rather he longs for it. He yearns for the great explosion which will erase the rot and stench of civilization as he knows it—'let it come for all of everywhere, just so it comes and the world stands clear in the white dead dawn'. It is an authentic nihilistic vision, but its purity is negative: it seems appropriate that Marion Faye should finally involve himself in a nasty road accident. It is obviously imperative somehow to exit from the unreality of Desert D'Or, but the book suggests that Marion Faye has taken the wrong door out. Is there a right one?

This of course is the problem for Sergius O'Shaugnessy. In Desert D'Or he has rented a house 'on the edge of the desert', and, like many other American heroes, he has good reason for pitching his habitation in such a border area, for his experience has taught him that there are two worlds and he has seen enough of both to realise that one has to negotiate a perilous existence somewhere between them. Brought up as an orphan, his identity is problematic for him. Wherever he has been, from the orphanage to Desert D'Or, he has felt like 'a spy or a fake'. After the death of the father he hardly ever saw, he feels in a position to create a new character for himself. He is a recognizable hero—the alienated existentialist, who is not sure where reality is to be found, nor of his relationship to it. He has seen action as a pilot in the Second World War, and the novel starts at the point at which he left the world of war where people burn other people, for the world of illusion in which people employ people as adjuncts to their fantasies—i.e. Desert D'Or. 'I had the idea that there were two worlds. There was a real world as I called it . . . and this real world was a world where orphans burned orphans. It was better not even to think of this. I liked the other world in which almost everybody lived. The imaginary world'. What his experience in Desert D'Or teaches him is that the imaginary world can have its own ruination and destructiveness.

At the end of the novel, Sergius imagines Eitel sending a silent message to him. In it he confesses that he lost the true drive and desire of the artist, which is the conviction that whatever happens ' "there still remains that world we may create, more real to us, more real to others, than the mummery of what happens, passes, and is gone" '. He then urges Sergius to ' "try for that other world, the real world, where orphans burn orphans and nothing is more difficult to discover than a simple fact. And with the pride of the artist, you must blow against the walls of every power that exists, the small trumpet of your defiance." ' This is potentially ambiguous, but the feeling that emerges is as follows. From the world of brutal facts—wars and orphanages—Sergius has moved into the realm of technicoloured air-conditioned fantasies. But there is a further move to make. The imaginary world not only covers the world in which people live isolated in their own dreams and illusions; it also points to the truly creative world of art through which the artist may find a way into the secrets of reality. For Sergius, writing is the right door out of Desert D'Or—and all the puns are functional.

Having touched bottom, Sergius finds the strength to leave Desert D'Or and his subsequent travels in Mexico and then to New York mark stages in his liberation. At the very end he seems to have arrived at a point at which he has moved beyond all politics and religions to put his trust in sex, for he hears from God that sex is time and time is 'the connection of new circuits'. The important transferences and linkings of power will in future be a very private affair, with the ostensibly important power circuits of society counting for less than the mysterious forces which work behind and through them. This it seems to me is one of the terminal suggestions of the book.

The other important resolution concerns Sergius' future as a writer. Back in the American east, he studies a wide range of philosophy, religion, politics, psychology, literary criticism and literature. But he studies only to reject, or at least to advance beyond what he has read. For he discovers that none of the authors he reads 'could begin to be a final authority for me, because finally the crystallization of their experience did not have a texture apposite to my experience . . . and I had the intolerable conviction, that I could write about worlds I knew better than anyone alive'. As so often happens, the American hero decides that no one else's style, no one else's pattern, will do to describe or contain his own experience. Furthermore he discovers that 'there is no point in experience, nor any word, from which one cannot set out to explore the totality of the All, if indeed there be an All and not an expanding mystery'. Not only may the individual find his own terms for describing the worlds through which he himself has moved; using his own experience as a point of departure he may embark on an exploration of the larger pattern, or patternlessness, of Existence. At which point, Sergius effectively hands over his pen to Norman Mailer.

In the ten years before he published his next novel, Mailer spent much of his time writing the various essays which he gathered together with some fragments of fiction in the two books, *Advertisements for Myself* (1957), and *The Presidential Papers* (1963). One may note in passing that the two titles suggest a range of interest which reaches from the self-assertive power of the writer's own ego right up to the most powerful man in America. In a famous essay entitled 'The White Negro' Mailer wrote that no matter how horrifying the Twentieth Century is, it is very exciting 'for its tendency to reduce all of life to its ultimate alternatives'. When Sergius started to find his feet as a writer he tells us that he started to think in 'couples' such as love and hate, victory and defeat, and so on, and this binary reduction or schematisation of life is much in evidence in Mailer's own subsequent journalism and occasional writing. 'Today the enemy is vague', he also said in an early essay, and one can see that throughout his work he has tried to dissipate that vagueness by postulating pairs of opposed extremes—assassins and victims; conformists and outlaws; the cancerous forces of malign control resisted by the bravery and health of the hero and hipster; the black magician versus the good artist (see his classic account of the Liston-Patterson fight); love and death; being and nothingness; cannibals and Christians—and finally God and the Devil. These are just some of the 'couples' that Mailer has deployed in his essays, and obviously he feels the excitement of going after extreme alternatives.

Looking back at those essays one can detect an increasing preference for images drawn from biology, from diseases, and from primitive superstitions. Like Burroughs he sees cancer as an appropriate symbol of the forces of death which are gaining on us. He refers to the 'cancer of the power that governs us'; the FBI is a faceless 'plague-like' evil force; totalitarianism is a spreading disease; the nation is 'collectively sick'. Few people resist this spreading disease, 'the slow deadening of our best possibilities'. There are just a few individuals—Kennedy, Castro, beats, hipsters, Negroes, psychopaths, who can assert their own inner energy and independent vision of reality against the prevailing forces. Such figures are resisting the overall drive towards death which is the dominant conspiracy. Mailer has a 'dynamic view of existence' which sees every individual as 'moving individually through each moment of life forward into growth or backward into death'. And what is going on in the universe as a whole is a battle between an existential God and a principle of Evil 'whose joy is to waste substance'. The confrontation is comparable to that outlined by Burroughs. What Mailer feels is that somehow we have lost the ability to respond to this awesome confrontation. 'The primitive understanding of dread—that one was caught in a dialogue with gods, devils, and spirits, and so was naturally consumed with awe, shame, and terror has been all but forgotten'. Among other things, his next novel was to be about a man who seeks to recapture an adequate sense of dread.

Before examining *An American Dream* (1965), it is worth bringing forward one more of his couplings, from one of the Presidential papers. Mailer suggests that Americans have been leading a double life: 'our history has moved on two rivers, one visible, the other underground; there has been the history of politics which is concrete, practical, and unbelievably dull . . . and there is the subterranean river of untapped, ferocious, lonely and romantic desires, that concentration of ecstasy and violence which is the dream life of the nation'. His notion is that while the western frontier was still a reality, heroic and violent action was possible; but since the closing of the west 'the expansion turned inward, became part of an agitated, overexcited, superheated dream life'. He talks of 'the unstated aristocracy of the American dream' and suggests that the American artist's talent is 'related directly to the dream and ambitions of the most imaginative part of the nation'. The writer must be in touch with both, with all levels of American life, and able to swim in all its rivers: it is almost a direct prescription for Mailer's next novel. Having complained that 'the life of politics and the life of myth had diverged too far' he would create a character who experienced their point of convergence—and separation.

The title, *An American Dream*, might suggest that in this novel Mailer decided to leave the surface river of American life and plunge into the subterranean river to explore 'that concentration of ecstasy and violence which is the dream life of the nation'. And it is true that the hero of the book, Stephen Rojack, is twice very close to a literal plunge from lighted rooms in high buildings to dark streets below. Early in the book during the course of a party, he goes to the balcony to vomit out his rising nausea (an act which he performs more than once, well aware of its ritual cleansing significance). The moon seems to be calling to him to jump from the balcony, and he does in fact start to climb over. He is 'half on the balcony, half off' when 'the formal part' of his brain tells him that he cannot die yet as he has work to do. Outside—the moon, strange influences in the darkness, superstitious promptings, the possibility of a descent which confusingly suggests itself as an ascent, an ambiguous summoning to liberation which may be death. Behind—the constructing and debased routines of a society out of love with itself and engaged in petty power plays and empty sexual games. Poised between them—the Mailer hero, caught in the paradox that while the summons from the moon seems more authentic and important than the voices from the party, to obey the moon would be to abandon form for formlessness, consciousness for unconsciousness, life for death. In this little incident Mailer adumbrates the subject of the whole novel, and anticipates the crucial scene when Rojack walks round the parapet of a high balcony, later in the book.

If you regard this novel simply as a narrative of incidents—as some critics did, and found it outrageous—what happens is this: Stephen Rojack, an ex-war hero, had wanted to get into politics and, partly with this in mind, he had married Deborah Kelly, who was socially influential and whose father wielded extraordinary, and nameless, powers. But having had a very intense experience of the mystery of death during the war when he killed some Germans in a desolate moonlit landscape, Rojack finds that the political game comes to seem like an unreal distraction in which the real private self is swallowed up in a fabricated public appearance. Rojack departs from politics to continue his 'secret frightened romance with the phases of the moon'. By the same token he is leaving the mental enclosures of bourgeois society and venturing into a new kind of power area in which the supernatural, the irrational, and the demonic hold sway. This step out of society is marked by his murder of Deborah. He manages to make the murder look like suicide, and now he finds that he has dropped out of respectable society and has entered a strange underworld. The geography shifts from fashionable uptown New York to the Village, Harlem, the lower-East Side; the atmosphere becomes darker and more confused; he is pursued by police and criminals and is involved in power manoeuvres which he cannot fathom. He has to fight for his life—psychically with a gang of hoodlums; physically with the Negro Shago Martin. He has, in effect, taken that plunge to the lower level of American life.

On that lower level he finds true love with a singer named Cherry, an authentic, utterly private passional relationship which had not been possible in the confines of society. But that lower level is also the place of death, and Cherry is pointlessly and brutally murdered. It is done in error, but there is no clear light at this level and everyone is prey to confusions. After this Rojack leaves New York, first of all going where he makes a lot of money in Las Vegas, and at the very end of the book heading for the jungles of Guatemala and Yucatan, away from the United States and towards the most primeval area left on the whole American continent. He is by this time well beyond the constituted power of the law, and the unconstituted powers of the lawless inhabitants of the lower level—indeed it might be said that he is beyond the United States of America al-together. It would seem that his apparent escape from the powers of retribution was very upsetting for some reviewers who felt that wife-murderers should not get off so easily. But taken as a vivid exploration of a man's relationship to the different orders of American reality, the novel is much more interesting and complex than any gesture of *épater le bourgeois*—which many reviewers took it to be.

Although the novel takes place in contemporary America, through the use of metaphor it opens onto every kind of pre-social reality—the jungle, the forest, the desert, the swamp, the ocean-bed. This metaphori-cal activity in the writing is so insistent that it provides a dimension of experience as real as that provided by the very detailed documentation of settings and scenes in contemporary New York. People are described in animal terms throughout. In addition the constant emphasis on all sorts of odours emanating from people, places, things, bespeaking growth or, more usually, decay, suggests a regression to a more primitive mode of percep-tion and orientation. Language is efficient only on one level; elsewhere it is often safer to follow your nose.

In addition to touching on those powers and drives which operate on the many natural levels below society, language, and consciousness (the three are obviously linked), the book tries to point inclusively to those supernatural powers which transcend this distinctively human trilogy. Starting with the moon, we encounter a widening range of references to evil spirits, vampires, demons, voodoo, magic, Zen, grace, and all those strange powers which the individual experiences as an 'it' working *through* him, but not originating within him (this makes the world of the book in some respects like Burroughs' universe). The thesis of Rojack's great work—for he is in effect the writer Sergius set out to become—is that 'magic, dread, and the perception of death were the roots of motivation'. As he says, he has come to believe in witches, spirits, demons, devils, warlocks, omens, wizards, fiends, incubi and succubi—'in grace and the lack of it, in the long finger of God and the swish of the Devil'. One statement imputed to him is that 'God's engaged in a war with the Devil, and God may lose'. The implications of this are potentially pessimistic, for it reduces man to an incidental point of intersection of warring supernatural powers, a helpless pawn in a larger battle, susceptible to voodoo, desperate for grace, Rojack sees civilization itself as a disturbance of two orders. Primitive man had an instictive sense of dread in his relationship with non-human nature; civilized man has disrupted this by believing himself to be permanently elevated above animals and the jungle. As a result that sense of dread which is requisite for psychic and spiritual health has been greatly attenuated. Related to this is civilization's 'invasion of the supernatural' which takes the form of denying powers which it cannot see. The price of this, he thinks, is 'to accelerate our sense of some enormous, if not quite definable disaster which awaits us'. If a man becomes aware of those dimensions of nature and super-nature from which he feels that the rest of society has resolutely closed itself off, where does that leave him standing? By analogy we might say on an edge as precarious as the parapet round a balcony.

I will return to this analogy, but first let us reconsider the plot line of the novel, this time thinking of it as an almost allegorical exploration of different levels of mystery, different areas of power, different orderings of reality. One could simply say that Rojack moves through the three different worlds of Mailer's first three novels—war, politics, and sexual experience, encountering different forms of death in each world. But a little more detail is called for. The world of Deborah Kelly and her father is centred on Park Lane and is connected with all kinds of political power. The Kellys are involved in a power web which reaches not only to President Kennedy, but to the CIA, the Mafia and unspecified spy rings and international agents. Entering this world in an attempt to gain political power Rojack finds himself very much its prisoner: he is manipulated and pre-empted by its far-ranging coercive resources, he is in danger of being trapped in its version of reality. When he murders Deborah, he is breaking free not just from a destructive woman, but from the picture of reality imposed by her world. As he is strangling her he feels he is opening a door, and he glimpses what lies 'on the other side of the door, and heaven was there, some quiver of jewelled cities shining in the glow of a tropical dusk, and I thrust against the door once more . . . and *crack* the door flew open . . . and I was through the door . . . I was floating. I was as far into myself as I had ever been and universes wheeled in a dream'. The image obviously recalls the attempts of Sergius to find the right door out of Desert D'Or, and among other things Rojack has broken out of the conventional novel into a realm of dream—one should take the hint. The question which interests us is what he finds on the other side of that door. Does Rojack find heaven, the jewelled cities, or is he drawn on by a mirage? Is his journey away from society and down finally to the ancient centre of America an analogue for some deep descent into his own self?

He has the vision of a jewelled city on two further occasions, both times as an accompaniment to sexual orgasm. The first occurs with Ruta, Deborah's maid, with whom Rojack has intercourse immediately after the murder. During intercourse, he alternates between vaginal and anal penetration. The detail of this scene was offensive to some, but for Mailer it is quite clearly an analogue to a more metaphysical ambiguity. For just as one kind of intercourse is procreative, the other kind quite the reverse, so Rojack cannot be sure whether he has broken through to some of the true mysteries of creativity after the sterile world of politics; or whether he has unwittingly aligned himself with the Satanic forces of waste. With Ruta the resultant vision of the mysterious city is correspondingly desolate and dead. It seems like a place in the desert or on the moon, and everything in it looks as unreal as plastic.

Having left the political world, Rojack finds himself in a demonised world of invisible powers and strange portents, of rampant superstition and accurate magics. In moving away from Park Lane both to Harlem and to the lower East-Side, Rojack is in effect leaving established society and conventional modes of consciousness for darker areas of experience, hidden at the heart or forgotten at the edge—of the city, of the mind. And in this world Rojack experiences a visionary orgasm with Cherry. This time it is purposefully and successfully procreative (he throws away her diaphragm as a signal of his intent). As a reward the vision is not of an arid, plastic place, but one of rich under-sea mystery. 'I was passing through a grotto of curious lights, dark lights, like colored lanterns beneath the sea, a glimpse of that quiver of jewelled arrows, that heavenly city which had appeared as Deborah was expiring . . .' It scarcely matters whether we feel this to be Jungian or not. In sinking or plunging down to the depths (the second river of American life), Rojack has re-established contact with the secret source of life. It is as near heaven as he gets.

In the depths, authentic passion is inseparable from authentic violence, for this is the sub-conscious (or slum area) in which all the basic intensities are freed from the control of the socialized consciousness (or the uptown authorities). Rojack's intensely private moments of happiness with Cherry are foredoomed, and while Shago Martin is being beaten to death in Harlem, Cherry is being murdered in her lower East-Side hideaway. Rojack does not find it wholly liberating to be in an area in which the older dreads and magics connected both with the jungle and the moon have full play. Here death seems to strike more often than love.

Leaving New York, Rojack comes to Las Vegas and before setting off for Guatemala and Yucatan, he walks out into the desert to look up at the moon and back at the city. 'There was a jewelled city on the horizon, spires rising in the night, but the jewels were diadems of electric and the spires were the neon of signs ten stories high. I was not good enough to climb up and pull them down'. This has various implications. The two kinds of 'jewelled city' he glimpsed while in union with Ruta and Cherry may indicate the two aspects of the creative-destructive dream which man has imposed on the American continent in his continuing loving and raping of the land. Given Rojack's response to Las Vegas it would seem that the destructive element has been realised and the original American 'dream' has turned into this plastic and neon reality in the desert, deceptively brilliant from a distance. In his search for the true heavenly city, Rojack will have to keep on moving. Perhaps it is like Gatsby's green light, the orgiastic future which recedes as it is pursued. Perhaps it can only ever be a private vision, never to be realised but occasionally to be glimpsed in the rich depths of the imagination. In any case, Rojack leaves Las Vegas, which after all is a distillation or extension of the corruptions and violences he has encountered in New York. After talking to Cherry in Heaven on a disused rusty phone—for when a man is standing between the desert and the moon, the customary circuits do not obtain and new kinds of communication are possible—Rojack heads south in space and back in time, aiming perhaps to penetrate the secret centre of his own, and America's, identity.

The crucial last chapter is entitled 'At the Lion and the Serpent'; (Rojack's exodus from society through Las Vegas and towards South America is contained in an Epilogue, which suggests that the critical and decisive moment is passed). In terms of the plot, the situation in the chapter is as follows: Kelly has summoned Rojack to the Waldorf Towers on Park Avenue to question him about the death of his daughter and other matters. Rojack sets out with the conscious intention to keep the appointment. But as he is travelling there he is aware of a subconscious voice telling him to ' "Go to Harlem" ' if he wants to save Cherry. (In addition, Shago Martin's umbrella which Rojack has brought with him seems to be twitching with signals in his lap—telepathy and animism are common in Harlem). He has earlier referred to the magician who lives in the 'gaming rooms of the unconscious' and who sends messages up to 'the tower of the brain', and the irrational summons to the dark depths of Harlem which challenges his more rational resolve to go to the Towers on Park Lane, obviously comes from that source. Once again, the two parts of New York serve as projections for different levels of consciousness. Rojack's uncertainty as to which part of New York he should head for at this moment of crisis, offers an analogue for Mailer's uncertainty as to which part of the psyche he should rely on in trying to cope with the mystery of America—the empirical or the demonic, the formal decisions of reason, or the formless promptings of dream.

In the Waldorf everything suggests death; even the real flowers look plastic. In Kelly's room, the ageing mobster Ganucci seems to reek of the cancer which is devouring him: decay is everywhere in the air. At the same time, the room is a centre of political power, with lines reaching to the White House, the CIA, the Mafia, and other unspecified organisations. Kelly himself, though he works through political agencies, seems like an elemental force or principle to Rojack. His coat of arms was once just a naked baby, but he added the lion (power) and the serpent (cunning), which is perhaps another suggestion of how the original innocence of America has been corrupted, or corrupted itself. Kelly smells of animal power, and although his furniture is composed of expensive antiques and art works, Rojack has the sense of 'vegetation working in the night' and experiences the civilized apartment as being something between a dark corner of the jungle and an ante-chamber of hell. Kelly tells him ' "There's nothing but magic at the top" ' and one is made to feel that all the magic he draws on, as he manipulates the political levels of reality so cynically, is black. The forces he commands serve to extend the empire of death, just as his deepest sexual drive is incestuous (with his daughter), his aides and agents are cancerous (Ganucci), and his cities are plastic (he is a big power in Las Vegas). The power passing through Kelly is on the side of entropy.

Early on during this evening encounter Rojack goes out to the parapet of the balcony. Standing half on the edge, strange intuitions and suggestions come to him: to jump would be a cleansing act after the foulness of the room he has just left; it would be for Cherry; God exists, he suddenly feels, as he looks down. But he also realises that the fall to the street would mean a death as sharp and certain as that threatened by Shago Martin's knife—an important connection of ideas because it relates the notion of the jump to the Harlem side of Rojack's experience. At this stage Rojack climbs down from the parapet and returns for his long conversation with Kelly, but he returns to it at the end of the conversation because—' "I was caught" '. He is caught between the deathly force emanating almost irresistibly from Kelly and the disturbing dreads which seem to be reaching him from Harlem. He is caught up among encircling and opposing demonisms which he cannot control nor clearly understand, or perhaps between the Devil and the Lord who have, however, lost their consolingly familiar theological identities to become names uncertainly applied to gusts and currents of power which drive unpredictably through the air. And at this point Rojack decides—'I wanted to be free of magic . . . But I could not move'. It is at this point that he decides he must walk round the parapet of the terrace. Once up on the parapet he is poised between 'the chasm of the drop' and 'the tower behind me' or, as we might say, between rigid architecture and formless darkness. Both Park Lane and Harlem would destroy Rojack. As in so many contemporary American novels, too much form (fixity) and pure formlessness (the flow) alike threaten to obliterate the identity of the American hero. Both rivers of American life promise drowning.

This is why Rojack has to walk round the parapet. He has to prove that he can negotiate that edge where the worlds meet—capitulating neither to a political nor to a demonised ordering of reality, avoiding the traps of social architecture and the chaotic dissolutions of the pre-social or sub-social dark. To be able to keep his balance is to achieve some degree of liberation from the coercive powers of both worlds—and after his walk Rojack strikes down Kelly and then throws Shago Martin's demon-charged umbrella over the parapet. He is temporarily free from both magics, and in terms of the plot it is this symbolic demonstration of his ability to keep that precarious balance on the edge which frees Rojack and effectively allows him to move beyond the two kinds of power exerted by the tower and the chasm. Earlier in the book he had described himself as feeling like a creature locked by fear to the border between earth and water who finally 'took a leap over the edge of mutation so that now and at last it was something new'. Passing through doors, moving across changing terrains, Rojack feels like a 'new breed' of man and is once described as a 'new soul'. Whether or not he actually becomes a new breed of man, and what the novelty consists of, the book may fairly be said to leave ambiguous. But it does make clear that he is a man who has to live at the edge, trying to hold on to his identity between two threatening realms. In the East these realms are represented by Park Avenue and Harlem; in the West he also moves into 'two atmospheres'—the scorching maddening heat of the desert, and the mortal chill of the air-conditioned rooms which remind him of life in a submarine or on the moon. In each case, the alternatives both portend a form of death. Not for nothing does Rojack attend an autopsy on his journey from the East to the West, for from the beginning he has been studying the different forms of death. If he does finally take a leap, it is not from one realm or atmosphere or river into the other, but rather into some third or new area beyond the existing alternatives formulated by North America. Yucatan is, one feels, a temporary destination. Rojack is really moving out towards some placeless city of his own imagination.

In this connection it is interesting to note the frontispiece of Mailer's next book, *Cannibals and Christians* (1966). It depicts a model of a possible vertical city of the future and was designed by Mailer himself. The whole section in the book devoted to 'Architectural Excerpts' is extremely relevant in considering *An American Dream*, and I will only quote a fragment. 'Perhaps we live on the edge of a great divide in history and so are divided ourselves between the desire for a gracious, intimate, detailed and highly particular landscape and an urge less articulate to voyage out of explorations not yet made. Perhaps the blank faceless quality of our modern architecture is a reflection of the anxiety we feel before the void . . .' Since man is caught between old architecture and the void of space, as Rojack was caught between the tower and chasm, Mailer has designed a sort of dream city which will rise up into the sky and sway there like a ship in oceans of space. This is obviously again a sort of third area, between old architecture and unknown space. It is really the city of his own style.

With the mention of style, we have come to the last aspect of the book I wish to consider. I have stated previously that I think we can often detect a significantly analogous relationship between the situation of the character in the plot and the author in his language. Just so, when Rojack is moving in the world of politics and policemen, Mailer tends to employ a mainly documentary style, full of empirical notations and transcriptions of recognizably realistic dialogue. But when Rojack has broken out of this world into an area in which both the pre-social and the supernatural seem to hold sway, so that life is experienced more as a jungle full of magics, then Mailer calls on every kind of mythic, religious, superstitious reference, and metaphors drawn from every level of existence, to provide a style which is adequate to Rojack's novel experience. The documentary is extended to the demonic. (This extension is often managed by what we might call the 'as if' principle, whereby a narrative fact is amplified by an unsuspected comparison drawn from the rich resources of Mailer's style). A nice example of the confrontation of styles comes when the police are interrogating Rojack about the death of his wife. Rojack, fabricating his version of Deborah's death, explains that she committed suicide because she felt haunted by demons. ' "I don't know how to put demons on a police report" ' says Roberts. The police report is the equivalent of a style which only credits empirically perceived facts, a narrow naturalism. Rojack is quite sure that there are more things in heaven and earth than can be contained in a police report, and his vocabulary (which is Mailer's style) has been enlarged accordingly. One policeman is convinced he knows the facts of the matter. He asserts that Rojack killed her with a silk stocking—that is how it is usually done. Even so-called empirical realism has its own predetermining fantasies which it imposes on the given data. One of Rojack's struggles is against the inadequate fantasy patternings of reality implicit in the policeman's narrow and clichéd terminology; and it reflects Mailer's sense of his own struggle with available, inadequate, literary styles. Rojack's ability to defy the police and to negotiate that haunted violent part of New York connected with his Harlem and lower East-Side experiences, is linked to Mailer's ability to break out of an old style and negotiate that new territory linguistically.

But just as Rojack finds that the second level of American life has its own way of trapping people in its version of the world, and he finally gets away from that area too, so Mailer has no wish to exchange materialism for supernaturalism and commit himself henceforth to a purely demonic mode of writing—for that too is only a version, a fixed reading. He needs his demonology to give some definition to Rojack's confused perceptions of the realities of the dark world of Harlem, dream, chaos and old night. But if he went over to this style exclusively then he would become a prisoner in his own system. Just as Rojack does not want to be caught in any power system, politics or magic, so Mailer does not want to be stylistically restricted to naturalism or supernaturalism. And just as Rojack walks the edge of the parapet to signify his intention to remain unclaimed by both sides, so Mailer walks a stylistic edge. He touches continually on two worlds—the inner and the outer, the demonic and the political, the dreaming and the waking, the structured and the flowing—and tries to be stylistically adequate to all without being trapped by any one. Just as Rojack sways in the wind on the papapet, and just as Mailer's city of the future is designed to sway in the air above old-fashioned cities, so Mailer's style, firmly rooted though it is in a sense of the concrete actual world, seems to sway in the far reach of its metaphors and in its attempts to achieve liberation from more limited and partial modes of depicting the complex nature of reality.

As the plot of the novel thickens, or perhaps one should say multiplies, Rojack experiences that familiar American sense of 'mysteries revolving into mysteries like galaxies forming themselves'. Later, as he is driving through New York, he feels a growing nausea as he realises that although he is aware of plots and mystery revolving around him, 'I did not know if it was a hard precise mystery with a detailed solution, or a mystery fathered by the collision of larger mysteries, something so hopeless to determine as the edge of a cloud, or could it be, was it a mystery even worse, something between the two, some hopeless no-man's land from which nothing could return but exhaustion?' If the mystery is a political, social one then Mailer can meet it with his more naturalistic style and the surface plot—Kelly, CIA, Mafia, and so on. If it is a larger mystery then Mailer will try to meet it with his rhetoric of myth, demons, and dread. It may be a mystery in between, however. In which case, Mailer shows himself grappling with it, tottering on that vertiginous edge where the two kinds of mystery meet, a no-man's land (into which General Cummings timidly peered, seeing nothing) which perhaps only the artist can fathom without falling. Unlike Cummings, Rojack has a sense of the powers on both sides of the parapet. Rojack learns that the secret of sanity is 'the ability to hold the maximum of impossible combinations in one's mind', and Mailer's work represents an attempt to show, stylistically, how this may be done.

ROBERT LANGBAUM

Mailer's New Style

Norman Mailer is a most irritating author to write about. His public image is entirely too powerful and unattractive; and his ideas, as stated in his essays, are often nonsensical (his mystique of the apocalyptic orgasm or of the spiritual significance of cancer) and sometimes intolerable (his glorification of Hip criminality). The result is that people have not taken his recent novels seriously enough. Since his image is by now better known than his novels, people like the Sunday *Times* reviewer of *Why Are We in Vietnam?* are apt to write him off as belonging more to the history of publicity than to the history of literature. And the success of his political writings since the novels—*Miami and the Siege of Chicago* and *Armies of the Night* (1968)—has only made people say he is better as journalist than novelist.

Yet if we forget the public image and read through the five novels, we find that Mailer's ideas are fruitful for his fiction and that he has as much artistic integrity as anyone writing today. First of all he has refused to capitalize on the spectacular success of his first novel, *The Naked and the Dead* (1948). Having at twenty-five triumphed in the received realistic style of American social-consciousness fiction, Mailer has been working ever since at finding a new style. It was not until 1965, the year *American Dream* came out in book form, and 1967, the year of *Why Are We in Vietnam?*, that he finally broke through to a style new enough to offend many of the reviewers.

"The realistic literature," said Mailer in a paper of 1965, "had never caught up with the rate of change in American life, indeed it had fallen further and further behind, and the novel gave up any desire to be a creation equal to the phenomenon of the country itself; it settled for being a metaphor." Novelists were "no longer writing about the beast but, as in the case of Hemingway (if we are to take the best of this), about the paw of the beast, or in Faulkner about the dreams of the beast."

Mailer's whole attempt in his second novel, *Barbary Shore* (1951), is to turn fiction into metaphor, indeed into an allegory of the beast's political dreams. To achieve allegory, Mailer abandons scope. Whereas *Naked* portrays the Pacific campaign of World War II and the American society behind it, *Barbary Shore* takes place in a Brooklyn rooming-house and involves only five adults and a child. The concentration produces an atmosphere of intensity that helps us accept the characters as personifications of political alternatives in the McCarthy era. The liberal hero, Lovett, whose war-induced amnesia makes him forget his old Socialist sympathies, comes out in the end with a Trotskyite position; though Lovett seems to see, in the Trotskyite McLeod's failure with his wife, the failure of Communism to take sex seriously, to make an erotic appeal to the masses.

The Trotskyism didn't last long, as we see by Mailer's next novel *Deer Park* (1955), where the morally sensitive hero is failed by Eitel, his model of political and artistic integrity, as the hero of *Barbary Shore* is not failed by his Communist model, McLeod. The hero of *Deer Park* drifts in the end into that state of thorough disaffection which Mailer, in his famous essay of the period, "The White Negro," calls Hip. But the main subject of *Barbary Shore* accounts for the subsequent novels; for the subject—as Norman Podhoretz suggests in his Introduction to the paperback edition—is the effect on modern life of the failure of the Russian revolution to turn into a world revolution. Because the human spirit failed to take the necessary next step in its evolution, it is dying of stagnation. Mailer's vision of general disease and madness becomes ever more comprehensive and strident with each novel.

Although *Barbary Shore* is Mailer's faultiest novel, it is the seedbed of his new style. *Deer Park*, instead, which is almost flawless, is Mailer's lightest novel. In *Deer Park*, Mailer returns to realism, but uses the restriction of scope learned in *Barbary Shore* to give to his satirical depiction of the small Hollywood world a haunting suggestiveness that makes it vaguely applicable to all America. There are, however, two things in *Deer Park* that point toward Mailer's remarkable breakthrough ten years later. One is the development, toward the end, of the pimp Marian Faye, with his illusionless honesty and courage, as a Hip answer to the self-deceptions of the liberal artist, Eitel. Another is the central importance given to sexuality. For the last two novels are organized by a sexual vision so pervasive that characterization is determined by sexual quality and the very fabric of external reality is sexually charged.

The most obvious sign of breakthrough is the new metaphorical prose that begins in *American Dream*, prose that calls attention to itself as it did not in the earlier novels. Here, for example, is the way Rojack, the hero of *American Dream*, describes a German soldier he shot in the war, a soldier whose eyes he cannot forget.

> He had eyes I was to see once later on an autopsy table in a small town in Missouri, eyes belonging to a redneck farmer from a deep road in the Ozarks, eyes of blue, so perfectly blue and mad they go all the way in deep into celestial vaults of sky, eyes which go back all the way to God is the way I think I heard it said once in the South, and I faltered before that stare, clear as ice in the moonlight. . . . The light was going out in his eye. It started to collect, to coagulate into the thick jelly which forms on the pupil of a just dead dog, and he died then, and fell over.

Here is how Rojack's wife, the beautiful society girl, Deborah Kelly, looks to him in the morgue after he strangled her, then pushed her out the window to make it look like suicide. He caught "a clear view of one green eye staring open, hard as a marble, dead as the dead eye of a fish." Observing the nightclub singer, Cherry, with whom he falls in love a few hours after the murder, he sees in her substantial bottom the loving small-town Southern girl concealed beneath the sophisticated face. Her face he might possess, but not "her bee-hind . . . no one ever had . . . so all the difficulty had gone down to her feet, yes the five painted toes talked of how bad this girl could be." "A sickness came off her, something broken and dead from the liver, stale, used-up, it drifted in a pestilence of mood toward my table, sickened me as it settled in." He retires to the men's room where for the second time that night he vomits, "and thought that if the murderer were now loose in me, well, so too was a saint of sorts, a minor saint no doubt, but free at last to absorb the ills of others and regurgitate them."

Such somatic characterization, reminiscent of Lawrence, makes plausible the events of this American dream, in which the submerged or potential becomes manifest. In Bellow's *Herzog*, which came out a year earlier, the hero wants to kill his wife, but does not because he cannot reconcile with ordinary reality his momentary insights into her supernatural evil. Mailer's hero can do what Bellow's cannot, because his insight into Deborah's evil transforms reality for him. "I had learned to speak," he says, "in a world which believed in the *New York Times*," but he has lost his "faith in all of that," because he has learned from Deborah that the forces that matter are magical. "It was horror this edge of madness to lie beside Deborah in a marriage bed and wonder who was responsible for the cloud of foul intent which lifted on the mingling of our breath. Yes, I had come to believe in spirits and demons."

I would call the style of *American Dream* "hallucinated realism," because I want to differentiate it from the ordinary realism that contrasts subjective feeling with the neutrality of the objective world, and because I want at the same time to call attention to its realism. For nocturnal New York is sketched in superbly, as are the various kinds of New York manners. Here, for example, is a bit of dialogue between Steve Rojack and the producer of his TV show, who has telephoned, after the news of Deborah's suicide, to persuade Steve to resign.

> "Steve, *anxiety* is loose here [in the studio] today. It hasn't been so bad since Kennedy stood up to Khrushchev with the missiles. Poor Deborah. I only met her once, but she's a great woman."
> "Yes. *Was.*"
> "Steve, you must be in a state of shock."
> "I'm a little rocky, kid."
> "I'll bet. I'll bet. These dependencies we feel on women. When they go, it's like losing your mother."
> If Deborah were not dead, but had merely run off to Europe with another man, Arthur would have said, "It's like losing mother's tit."

The surface is rendered in order that it may be psychologically penetrated, imbued with magic. When the psychological penetration is deepest, the hallucinated realism turns, for those moments only, into allegorical romance.

Through a style that talks with the same words about conscious and unconscious levels of existence, Mailer solves his old problem, going back to *Naked and the Dead*, of the conflict between morality and power. Rojack is the first of Mailer's morally sensitive heroes who can compete with people of power like Deborah and her multimillionaire father. But it is only in the course of the novel that Rojack acquires the strength to compete, because he draws out of himself his own bestiality and thus discovers the source of their power and his. The story tells how Rojack finds his courage and therefore his freedom and humanity.

Rojack, who is professor of something called existential psychology, believes that "the root of neurosis is cowardice rather than brave old Oedipus." By Rojack's criteria, Bellow's Herzog is and remains a coward because he is too nice; he never *does* the unspeakable thing that would teach him what he is capable of. Mailer's story takes place way out beyond the moral experience of the Herzogs, the decent, reasonable people who read the *New York Times*.

That's why it takes place at the top, among *big* people, who are rich, famous, extravagant, who are the equivalent of the kings and princesses of fairy tale. "God and the Devil are very attentive to the people at the summit. I don't know if they stir much in the average man's daily stew, no great sport for spooks, I would suppose, in a ranch house, but do you expect God or the Devil left Lenin or Hitler or Churchill alone? . . . There's nothing but magic at the top."

High on a balcony over Sutton Place, Rojack is at the outset tempted to jump by the Lady Moon, who speaks to him with Deborah's voice, urging him to die. Not yet, he thinks, but he knows this was the moment his death began, "this was the hour when the cells took their leap." The middle-aged Rojack is at Dante's "mezzo del cammin," and starts his descent to Hell.

He starts downward by strangling Deborah in the upstairs bedroom of her duplex, which is suspended over the East River and is hung with a fabric of tropical flowers that provides the sense of New York *chic* and the jungle setting appropriate to their moment of truth. Sexually exhilarated by the murder, Rojack descends a flight to vent his hate in intercourse, involving buggery, with Deborah's German maid. This graphically de-scribed bang is a *tour de force*; for it is so thoroughly absorbed in intellectual and moral contemplation that it is transformed—as Coleridge said Shakespeare transformed *Venus and Adonis*—into something other than pornography.

It is only after this further descent into evil that Rojack can reascend to Deborah's room, throw her dead body down to the East River Drive and fabricate the story of suicide. The circle of evil widens at the police station, where we see the criminal mentality of the detectives and learn that one of the cars stopped by Deborah's body contained a Mafia big shot, who has been hauled in with his mistress, Cherry. The Mafia man is released; so finally is Rojack, because of a signal from on high. When the next midnight Rojack ascends the Waldorf Towers to see Deborah's father, he learns who has made the signal. For Kelly is, as he says of himself, " 'a spider. Have strings in everywhere from the Muslims to the *New York Times*.' " He has strings in on the CIA and the Mafia, too. The Mafia man is there; so is the German maid, who turns out to be Kelly's mistress, set to spy on Deborah who had herself indulged in some unspecified political spying. Kelly once had Cherry as mistress, and has even had—this is the climactic revelation of evil—an incestuous passion for Deborah. Kelly has called off the police investigation into the murder, perhaps because he fears exposure, more likely because he has his own plans for Rojack.

As in *Barbary Shore*, the claustrophobic closed circle so intensifies the moral atmosphere as to make allegory believable. The main action is compressed into a nightmarish thirty-two hours; and we come to feel, as all threads wind back to Kelly, that he really is the Devil and that the Devil dwells on top, on top of the power structure. It is God who dwells, if anywhere, on the bottom. That is why when Rojack is on his way to the Waldorf Towers, an inner voice tells him to go to Harlem instead. Although we are not allowed to forget Harlem, Mailer fails to make anything morally substantial of it or of the good girl, Cherry, who comes off as a sentimentalized abstraction.

The Devil comes alive in Kelly because Kelly is magnificently attractive, with his intelligence and forcefulness, and because Rojack smells beneath Kelly's cologned surface something else, some whiff of the "icy rot and iodine in a piece of marine nerve left to bleach on the sand." Because Rojack's apprehension of evil is registered as sensation, we understand how he can *know*, without knowing why, that he must to escape it rush out to the terrace and walk round the parapet thirty stories above the street. This walk round the parapet is the high point of the novel, a triumph of narration. Because we sweat it out with Rojack as wind, rain and psychologically sensed supernatural forces (Deborah's hands, for example) threaten to dislodge him, we believe in the importance of this ordeal, that it is his Purgatory, his penance and way to salvation.

But Rojack does not walk the parapet a second time, as he knows he should for Cherry's sake. Cherry, whom he followed the night before from the police station to her nightclub and her bed, has become his Beatrice, pointing the way to salvation. They experienced with each other their first genuine emotion of love; and it is Cherry who has transformed the Deborah-inspired impulse to jump into the life-enhancing impulse to walk the parapet. Rojack has already had to pass two tests of courage for Cherry—he has had to defy a Mafia thug and fight her Negro ex-lover, Shago Martin. Now, as he rushes off to possess her, hoping he has fulfilled "the iron law of romance: one took the vow to be brave," he is seized with dread. " 'You've gotten off easy,' " he tells himself; and sure enough, he finds Cherry dying, beaten to death by a friend of Shago's. Shago himself has been found beaten to death in Harlem.

Rojack's self-admonition should be answer enough to the reviewers who complained that Rojack does not pay a moral price for the murder. He pays a price in the same way as the Ancient Mariner; and, indeed, Mailer's novel is like Coleridge's poem all about the moral price. The murders in both works are merely the occasions for expressionistic portrayals of the *experience* of guilt, penance and at least partial redemption. The novel, in addition, draws our attention away from the murder to the web of social evil the murder discloses, a web in which Deborah was thoroughly implicated.

In his wartime heroism, Rojack showed a potentiality for courageous action that got squashed in civilian life, where he allowed himself to be used by the Kellys and their like. His marriage went bad because Deborah considered him, and he considered himself, a coward. Now with the murder, an act that disengages him from career and social position, he finds his courage and with it the ability to love. The only really implausible thing in this just plausible novel is the number of Rojack's monumentally long coitions during the night hours that remain after the murder. But this is the American dream—that courage is connected with sexual potency and that a man, when tested, will be found to have infinite supplies of both. The point is that modern American society suppresses the chance of most men to realize this dream by passing—through some traumatic test of courage equivalent to primitive initiation rites—into possession of their manhood. Hence the locked-up seething madness of American life.

In the end, Rojack drifts off to Las Vegas to join "a new breed of men"—presumably a breed recovering the old Wild West virtues by testing their courage at the gambling tables, a breed who if they have not found the good have at least disengaged from the evil. This 'solution' is the Hip equivalent (in "White Negro," Mailer speaks of the Hipster as "a frontiersman in the Wild West of American night life") of the purgatorial wandering in which the Ancient Mariner is finally suspended.

On his way to Las Vegas, Rojack witnesses the autopsy of the old Missouri farmer through whose blue eyes he has evoked the eyes of the German soldier he shot in the war. The old man died of cancer; and we see here how Mailer's psychosomatic theory about cancer seems valid enough when used for symbolic purposes. The old man's terrible smell haunts Rojack's nostrils for the rest of the journey, coming back at him from off the landscape like some quintessential atmosphere of America.

Cancer is the growth of madness denied. In that corpse I saw, madness went down to the blood—leucocytes gorged the liver, the spleen, the enlarged heart and violet-black lungs, dug into the intestines, germinated stench. . . . some of the real madness went into me. The stink of the dead man went along the dry lands of Oklahoma and northern Texas, through the desert bake of New Mexico, Arizona, on into the valleys of the moon—

where sits Las Vegas, described as the volcanic place where the madness erupts.

Does the eruption make Las Vegas beneficial, and has Rojack saved himself from cancer by expressing his madness? There is in Las Vegas another atmosphere and temperature, that of the air-conditioned interiors which seem to contain air brought "through space" from some "pleasure chamber of an encampment on the moon." The moon, which originally symbolized Deborah, seems now to be a good, even a heavenly, thing; for Cherry speaks to him from it, from perhaps (as my colleague Anthony Winner suggests) Dante's lowest circle of Paradise, the lunar circle of nuns who were forced to marry (Cherry conveys regards from Marilyn Monroe). Rojack's madly comic oscillation between the "two atmospheres" (of hell and heaven?) seems to do him good. In the last sentence, he is "something like sane again" as he sets off for the jungles of Guatemala and Yucatán. Why there? His spiritual progress has all along been backward and downward. Hence he feels Harlem is the good place, perceives heaven in the hell of Las Vegas, and sets forth to find what he has earlier called "the beast of mystery" in its jungle habitat. This final chapter is too elliptical to be clear, but the symbolism—moving as it does through smell, somatic imagery, and the unearthly moon, to recall all that was contained in the madly cerulean eyes of the German soldier, who was shot in moonlight—brings to a climax the coherence of vision that accounts for the success of this powerfully imaginative novel.

Why Are We in Vietnam? is even more wildly imaginative in its treatment of the American dream and the American madness. Here the Wild West theme is central, for the characters are all Texans; and though the Texans are satirized, it is clearer than in the earlier book that there is something to be said for the American dream of courage and sexual potency and for the barbaric energies it expresses. In this book, imagination shows itself not in the Gothic nightmare way, but through wit and nature poetry. Narrated by an eighteen-year-old Texas hellraiser, named D.J., the book is, considering its horrendous message, curiously light-hearted and young. One feels in its ease of execution that Mailer has finally broken through, has learned how to speak with one voice about the horror and the glory of, to use his phrase, the American "giant."

The wit is not cerebral; it is the expression of physical exuberance, and employs the word "ass" as an all-purpose intensifier. Mailer has borrowed from Joyce and William Burroughs to create an idiom that is genuine, semi-literate, all-boys-together American, heightened most of the time (sometimes Mailer tries too hard) into wit and poetry. Once you get over the first shock at the unceasing obscenities, they take on (if the book works for you) the quality of metaphor, a way of talking about the whole of life like the somatic images of *American Dream*; and they come to seem the only richly expressive way of talking—the rhythm seems wrong when you leave them out, the expression thin. The obscenities seem necessary for the giant qualities Mailer wants to portray. Mailer has always admired big, strong characters even when they are bastards. In this book, all the major characters are big, strong bastards.

The idiom is D.J.'s; the others do not all or always talk this way, but D.J. shows through the idiom what they are really saying. "If the illusion has been conveyed that my mother, D.J.'s own mother, talks the way you got it here, well little readster, you're sick in your own drool, because my mother is a Southern lady, she's as elegant as an oyster with powder on its ass, she don't talk that way, she just thinks that way." The idiom is also the means of satirizing D.J. and the others. The point of the satire is that these Texas Yahoos, many of them with Indian blood, are living in "this Electrolux Edison world, all programmed out," and are, like D.J.'s daddy, Rusty, who is a big corporation executive, at the center of the non-vital, anti-individualistic, anti-heroic American corporation system. Rusty's God is a G.P.A. or Great Plastic Asshole, excreting "his corporate management of thoughts. I mean that's what you get when you look into Rusty's eyes." The vision is of barbarism equipped with advanced technology.

It is to pit Rusty's God against the vital God of the wilderness, and to pit Rusty against an authentic man like the guide Big Luke, that Mailer sends his Texans to hunt above the Arctic Circle in Alaska. The hunt is being narrated at a Dallas dinner two years later; and to further the satire of our electronic world, D.J. is supposed to be a Disc Jockey broadcasting to the world. He regularly interrupts the action to address us directly in little chapters called Intro Beeps, which are often tiresome. There is entirely too much narrative method for so small a novel; and to confuse us further, Mailer suggests fleetingly that D.J. may himself be a fiction in the brain of a Harlem genius. Mailer cannot get Harlem off his mind.

But the hunt, with its rich recollections of hunts in Hemingway and Faulkner, is the substance of the book and the thing that gives the book its high value. The point of the hunt is explained by Rojack's lecture in *American Dream* on the primitive view of mystery: "In contrast to the civilized view which elevates man above the animals, the primitive had an instinctive belief that he was subservient to the primal pact between the beasts of the jungle and the beast of mystery." The spiritual essence that in *American Dream* is suggested through somatic and animal imagery is evoked here through the rendition of actual animals. The beast of mystery turns out to be more Devil than God.

We are given murderous little pastorals like this:

> You can tune in on the madness in the air, you now know where a pine tree is rotting and festering somewhere out there, and red ants are having a war in its muck, and the bear is listening to those little ant screams and smelling that rotten old pine, and whoong goes his nose into the rot, and he bites and swallows red ants, slap, bap, pepper on his tongue, he picking up the bite of death in each ant and the taste of fruit in the pulp, digging that old rotten tree whose roots tell him where we are.

When D.J. feels himself "up tight with the essential animal insanity of things," we see that the social madness of *American Dream* is now connected with cosmic madness.

Yet there is a difference between the violence of nature and of these Texans. The Texans violate the wilderness. For Rusty the hunt is a status symbol, a gambit in the game of corporation politics. The Texans don't so much shoot the animals as shatter them with overpowered guns. Worst of all, the Texans get Big Luke to break his professional code by transporting them to the various hunting grounds in a helicopter.

The animals seem noble just by contrast. Even the grizzly bear, who epitomizes all the insane force of nature, has when dying a look in his eyes that makes D.J., who shot him, refrain from finishing him off and step up close to see: "something in that grizzer's eyes locked into his, a message, fellow, an intelligence of something very fine and very far away." But Rusty finishes the bear off and later claims possession of the skin, thus disgusting D.J. and bringing to an end the idyllic episode in which the father and son, slipping off from the others, discovered love for each other as hunting companions.

This is the first of two idyllic episodes which are the high points of the book. Both episodes end in failure. In the second, D.J. and his best friend, Tex, slip off in disgust at the moral impurity of the hunting party, and discover for themselves the old Indian purification ceremony. Out of the same instinct that makes Rojack walk the parapet, they advance into the wilderness without any weapons. To protect themselves against a grizzly bear, they climb a tree, and from there enjoy a panoramic view of nature in all her subtly anthropomorphized aspects (Mailer's way with animals reminds me of Isak Dinesen's in *Out of Africa*). They see nature as genial when the bear gorges itself on berries; as terrifying when the bear rips open a living caribou calf to eat her entrails and then, for sheer assertion of power, kills her and excretes around her body; as sorrowful when the caribou mother returns to her dead calf.

She circles about in a dance, but never takes her nose off as if she is going to smell on through to the secret of flesh, as if something in the odor of her young dead was there in the scent of the conception not ten months ago when some bull stud caribou in moonlight or sun illumined the other end of the flesh somewhere between timber slide and lightning there on the snow, some mystery then recovered now, and woe by that mother caribou nuzzled in sorrow from her nose while above blue as a colorless sea went on and sun burned on her, flies came, last of the flies traveling over the snow and now running a shuttle from Baron Bear's pile of bauble to the nappy spotty hide of caribou mother, she twitching and jumping from the sure spite of the sting but not relinquishing her nose and the dying odor of her yearling calf and D.J.'s head full spun with that for new percipience, since could it be odor died last of all when one was dead? and took a separate route.

Even more than in *American Dream*, we are in an intensified Wordsworthian world where smell and the ability to smell is an index of spirit; so that D.J. moves, through his question about odor, into intimations of immortality and divinity. Another index of spirit is the recurring imagery of electro-magnetism, the suggestion that the far North is spiritual because electro-magnetic, because it draws up all the "messages" or secret desires of North America. When the two boys go to sleep together that night, the Arctic lights, Aurora Borealis, are out; and "the lights were saying that there was something up here, and it was really here, yeah God was here, and He was real and no man was He, but a beast." The writing here is mawkish, but the point is important; for it is to merge with this great beast of desire that D.J. puts out a hand to touch Tex and make manifest the latent homosexual feeling between them. "They is crazy about each other," we were told earlier. "But fear not, gentle auditor, they is men, real Texas men."

The satire is directed against their suppression of homosexual feeling. Although Mailer has in the past treated homosexuality as a sign of failure, we have here to follow the story, which seems to suggest that the homosexuality ought to be recognized and outgrown. For the same reason that Rusty kills and claims possession of Griz #1, Griz #2 kills and excretes on the caribou calf, so some demonic will to power (there has been a running satire on Texas will power) causes the boys to vie in an unspoken contest for the male role. Instead of love, "murder" breaks out between them and they make a pact in blood to be "killer brothers." The effect of the hunt has been pernicious, as we see by the near-criminal behavior of the boys during the two years following in Dallas. And we learn in the last sentence of the book that they are now off to "Vietnam, hot damn."

Only here are we finally brought round to the irritatingly odd title. Why are we in Vietnam? Because we are crazy and nature is crazy, but nature's fall is apparently caused by ours (the Arctic animals are being driven crazy by the noise of airplanes). And why are we crazier and more dangerous than other nations? Because we are bigger, more energetic, more heroic. The whole book sings our potential heroism, what we might have been and how terribly we have gone wrong. Through joking references to the pioneer days, we are reminded of the old American dream of heroic fulfillment in nature. In the Arctic wilderness, the Texans have a chance to start over again. They might have found God there; they find instead the Devil, because of a fatal flaw—the need to express their Faustian pursuit of infinite courage and sexual potency through the desire to dominate and possess. I think we are to understand that this flaw goes back to their origins, but has been aggravated by technology.

"The country had always been wild," says Mailer in *Armies of the Night*, a book which, in dealing with the 1967 anti-war March on the Pentagon, incidentally throws light on the last two novels.

> It had always been harsh and hard . . . the fever to travel was in the American blood, so said all, but now the fever had left the blood, it was in the cells, the cells traveled, and the cells were as insane as Grandma with orange hair. The small towns were disappearing in the bypasses and the supermarkets and the shopping centers. . . . Technology had driven insanity out of the wind and out of the attic, and out of all the lost primitive places: one had to find it now wherever fever, force, and machines could come together, in Vegas, at the race track, in pro football, race riots for the Negro, suburban orgies—none of it was enough—one had to find it in Vietnam; that was where the small town had gone to get its kicks.

As an analysis of our political reasons for being in Vietnam, the passage is no less deficient than the novel that asks this question; for both attribute the war to popular bloodthirstiness, when there has never been a war more unpopular. But as a metaphorical vision of our culture, employing a parable about Vietnam, the passage has a certain psychological validity—a validity demonstrated by our unhappy precedence over all other advanced nations in crimes of violence, and by isolated cases of American atrocities in Vietnam. The psychology is only valid non-statistically, however, and at a depth that is best portrayed in fiction, where it need not lead to a doctrinaire position.

Even in his political writings, Mailer cuts through doctrinaire positions—as in *Miami and the Siege of Chicago*, his account of the 1968 nominating conventions, where in preferring the coarsely sensual face of

Chicago, represented by its Mayor, to the "thin nostrils" of McCarthy's supporters, he expresses metaphorically his temperamental though not political antipathy to the liberal academics whom he sees as new men, natural managers of technology land. Complexity of political judgment is especially apparent in *Armies*, where Mailer describes himself as a Left Conservative and reveals the aristocratic bias inherent in the paradoxical cluster of ideas we have earlier associated with the word *culture*, ideas best expressed through forms of imaginative literature. Mailer subtitles *Armies: History as a Novel, The Novel as History* to make us read it as imaginative literature. Nevertheless, his political and cultural vision is expressed most profoundly in the novels, especially the last two.

All Mailer's novels are tied to an outstanding event of the time— World War II, the Korean War, the McCarthy investigations, now Vietnam. In spite of his apparently unrealistic new style, Mailer still adheres to the large realistic tradition of the novelist as a chronicler of his time. He remains political and uses his new style to project those unconscious pathological forces that are, as he sees it, the main determinants of political behavior, especially in America now. Mailer's psychological and social intelligence combines in these two novels with a wild, fantastic, unpredictable quality of mind that touches raw nerves in us because it is so alive. We can pick at faults in the novels, but the important point is this—that we sense Mailer's intelligence as a force, passionate and all-pervading, that sees things through to their ultimate causes and consequences; and this marks him as a major talent.

GERMAINE GREER

My Mailer Problem

It was early on in the career of *The Female Eunuch* as the forever out-of-print English best seller that I heard Mailer wanted to debate with Kate Millett and me in a benefit for the Theatre for Ideas in the New York Town Hall. It seemed such an extraordinary recognition for a new writer that it never occurred to me to refuse, although within days I had heard Kate Millett had done just that. I never did hear her reason, although I privately rejected other people's versions of it: that Kate was afraid of Mailer, that she was gentle and shy, that she was exhausted and disgusted after being long enmeshed in the machinery of publicity. It was not until I acquired a copy of *Harper's* March, 1971, issue that I began to see that there were legitimate and persuasive reasons for having nothing to do with the liberation of Norman Mailer. *The Prisoner of Sex* is itself a counter-offensive in among "the radiation of advancements and awards in the various salients, wedges and vectors of that aesthetic battlefield known as the literary pie." For Mailer, Women's Liberation had become simply another battle of the books in a war in which he had been campaigning all his life. I had already discovered the seedy side of Grub Street, in the curious selection by editors of pregnant women to review my book, in the cursory readings which supported the subjective bias of reviewer after reviewer, especially those who praised me. This squalid arena was where G.I. Joe Mailer liked best to fight; unfortunately he persisted in confusing paper pellets and bullets of the brain with real blood and iron, so there was no telling where this armchair militarism might lead him.

It was this failure in perspective which led him to be so easily

From *Esquire* 3, vol. 76 (September 1971). Copyright © 1971 by *Esquire*.

convinced by no less a guardian of truth than the editor of *Time* magazine, that "he was, as he knew all too well, perhaps the primary target of their [the women's] attacks." The grammar of this idea must have come from Mailer himself. One could hardly imagine anyone actually saying, and on the telephone too, "You are, as you know all too well, perhaps the primary target of their attacks." Even editors of *Time* are not so certain of *perhapses*, one would hope. But if we continue with Mailer's narrative we find him tamping down the masochistic rage to occupy the direct line of fire, and replying demurely, "No, he had not realized." How could he after all realize? With misery, disappointment, frustration, injustice, poverty, helplessness and despair for the women to wage war against, how could a man with a chink of discretion in the massy structures of his ego imagine that *he*, little he, represented a *primary* target (with or without a quaver of perhaps)?

But the editor of *Time* exhorts him to face it like a man and so talks himself plumb out of a cheap story. Mailer instantly twigs that to offer on the telephone the meat of a possible book—to figure as one of a hundred snappy anecdotes which make pre-masticated mass-circulation news—was "improvident. He would be giving up substance—which is to say—not making money. . . ." But stronger than the need for money to run his complicated life and support his ambitions to be a great actor and film maker, was his need to draw the women's fire. Luxuriating in the presumption that "a squadron of enraged Amazons, an honor guard of revolutionary (if we could only see them) vaginas" had ambushed his "ghost-phallus" and were chewing it half to death, he unwittingly betrayed his deepest fantasy, that his talent, alias his phallus, alias "firm strong-tongued ego," three sides of the equilateral triangle which constitute the Mailer godhead, soared above them all. The last temptation was, as far as the women could be concerned, the greatest treason.

Now he was tempted. To be the center of any situation was, he sometimes thought, the real marrow of his bone—better to expire as a devil in the fire than an angel in the wings.

The imagery is drawn from the morality play, and perhaps it applies even better than Mailer was aware, for the devil is a burlesque character, heralded by squibs and crackers, absurdly pretentious and deluded, forever belying his gnawing grief and fury at having lost the love and the sight of God. The battle of the books would also involve a skirmish with the "High Media"; the book would require publicity, publicity means film and television. The pseudo-debate in Town Hall would satisfy all needs. There would be another book in it, perhaps a film too, with luck and good management.

His genius was to mobilize on the instant.

Long before *The Prisoner of Sex* dealt the final stroke to Willie Morris' *Harper's*, Mailer was setting up his own morality play, in which he could enact his own *sparagmos* by being torn apart by a horde of women, for he would not risk being outfaced by a single woman. When Kate Millett refused to join in, I assumed that there would be no debate, for quite other reasons, for I still considered myself too insignificant to provide adequate opposition. Nevertheless I embarked on a needling campaign which committed me to the eventual confrontation long before I ever saw the egregious confessions in *The Prisoner of Sex.* It became a standing joke that I would seduce Norman Mailer and prove to the breathlessly waiting world that he was, as I had opined to Felix Scorpio, the world's worst. When Pierre Berton asked me on his television show why I had such a high opinion of Valerie Solanas despite her attack on Andy Warhol, I minced out a crack about attempting to kill people did not mean that you're a bad person. "Norman Mailer stuck a knife in his wife and no one would deny that he's a great writer." More and more often I was being asked what I thought of Norman Mailer, and my replies became more and more Byzantine. Ultimately, in a rash of alliteration, I announced that I wanted to carry him like a wounded child across the wasted world. In an article for *The Listener* I wrote that I half expected him to blow his own head off "in one last killer come," like Ernest Hemingway. Like Muhammad Ali I was softening up my opposition in advance with rhetoric.

Imagine then my consternation when the New York women asked me to boycott the whole shindig. Kate's refusal had been followed by Ti-Grace Atkinson's, Gloria Steinem's, Robin Morgan's. Robin had said she would come if she could shoot Mailer, citing the particulars of her license to possess a firearm, which is one way of putting a stop to phony revolutionary theatricals. I have always felt rather Nero Wolfeish about my word, given now so long before in ignorance. Moreover the affair was going onward, Diana Trilling and Jackie Ceballos were speaking. My withdrawal would have the certain effect of withdrawing support from them, even if the public was ever to understand my motives, which was doubtful. "But why," argued the women, "should we give an account of ourselves to Norman Mailer? Why should he run the show, he adjudicate?" They might also have asked, if any of us had known what was going on, which we didn't, why Mailer had started considering literary rights and offered to put up money for Don Pennebaker's filming of the night's entertainment. The Mailer-Women's liberation title fight was being set up for maximum exploitation.

Meanwhile I was in training, reading and rereading *The Prisoner of Sex* in an attempt to assess my opponent's form. There was no argument there to discredit the women's cause, although plenty to discredit Mailer, as he obviously knew and did not care, in his divine or diabolical desire to go all the way. Every page bespoke the terrors of the dying king, reaching further and further back beyond morality, beyond Christianity toward the long-dead if not always imaginary age of heroes to which the Prisoner yearned to belong. Mischievously I decided to apply his fine words of compassion for D. H. Lawrence to himself.

> . . . *yet he was locked into the body of a middling male physique, not physically strong, of reasonable good looks, a pleasant to somewhat seedy-looking man, no stud. . . .*

For all I knew he was a silvery-maned bull of a man with electric-blue eyes, and yet I knew that the words would apply, for the tragedy of machismo is that a man is never quite man enough. (I had every intention of using the words against him in Town Hall, indeed I have them written on a file card still, but when I saw how cruelly apt they were, my heart quailed with pity and I thrust the card to the bottom of the pile.)

> *For his mind was possessed of that intolerable masculine pressure to command which develops in sons outrageously beloved of their mothers—to be the equal of a woman at twelve or six or any early age which reaches equilibrium between the will of the son and the will of the mother is all but to guarantee the making of a future tyrant, for the sense of where to find one's inner health has been generated by the early years of that equilibrium—its substitute will not be easy to create in maturity. What can then be large enough to serve as proper balance to a man who was equal to a strong woman in emotional confidence at the age of eight? Hitlers develop out of such balance derived from imbalance, and great generals and great novelists (for what is a novelist but a general who sends his troops across fields of paper?).*

Granting that Mailer himself is a great novelist (for failing to do so merely minimizes the seriousness of the situation and the radicalism of the changes that need to be made), we may safely grant that on his own admission the rest of the syndrome described also applies to him. Certainly his aesthetic imagination is still dominated by war and the imagery of war, whether he be wondering whether women are the aggressors in a primal war between the sexes, or stealing concubines from the potentates of *Time* magazine, or thinking of Bella Abzug's bosom as redolent (among other things) of "the firepower of hard-prowed gunboats." And yet the wars are not real wars—

> . . . *for one senses in his petulance and in the spoiled airs of his impatient disdain at what he could not intellectually dominate that he was a*

momma's boy, spoiled rotten, and could not have commanded two infantrymen to follow him, yet he was still a great writer.

Unlike Hitler, or the great generals of history, the artist is a fantasy achiever. Moving his troops around on paper he achieves in fantasy what he could achieve in no other way: honor, power, riches and the love of women. Only as an Artist could he manage to capture women from Nabobs of the High Media, or from Shago Martin. The man who boasts of the men he stole his women from is still deeply involved with those men. But how to convince Mailer of the element in himself that he exaggerated in his description of Lawrence, his own obliterated and outlawed femininity? How could he bear to hear that his love letters to great pugilists in the columns of the daily press are the outpourings of a boxers' groupie? All the violent men I have known have had a craving for gentleness, but every puny drunk in every bar thought it cute to bait them; to appease their foolish masochism (for fighting and fucking are in their sensibilities so confounded) the strong man must knock down the weak and earn his own contempt. If he resists or allows himself to be beaten he must endure the contempt of others. Mailer's truculence is of the weaker sort, like a drunk ordering the other drinkers in the bar to put up their dukes. In challenging the women's movement he put himself in danger, for theirs is a fight for life, no holds barred. He was more likely to face a tire lever or a broken bottle or Robin Morgan's revolver than the Marquis of Queensberry's rules. He may have no realistic idea of his strength, but the women's movement is very aware of its physical weakness. As long as Mailer sees his spirit as a triumvirate of phallus, ego and talent he cannot discern the fantasy nature of his conquests, he can have no mercy on his own defect in physical competitiveness. His old age threatens to disgust him: perhaps like Hemingway (and Hitler) he will not have the courage to see it through. The women's movement offers Mailer the only escape from his own worries about his thickening waistline and the incipient "humphreys of his ass," not to mention the growing capriciousness of "his fast-rusting barb" (another diabolical image, for only the Devil has a penis of barbed steel).

The concept of the worshiped feminine which holds the Prisoner of Sex in thrall is the Omnipotent Mother. To this day Mailer's relationship with his mother is important: when he confesses that he has never been able to live without a woman, it is not just sex and company that he needs but nurture. The near-equal war, *a brutal bloody war with wounds growing within and the surgeons collecting the profit from either sex* is still the antagonism between the formidable mother and the questing boy-child.

The goat-kicking lust which drove Henry Miller into one woman after another is "man's sense of awe before woman,"

his dread of her position one step closer to eternity (for in that step were her powers) which made men detest women, revile them, humiliate them, defecate symbolically upon them, do everything to reduce them so one might dare to enter them and take pleasure of them. . . . So do men look to destroy every quality in a woman which will give her the powers of a male, for she is in their eyes already armed with the power that she brought them forth, and that is a power beyond measure—the earliest etchings of memory go back to that woman between whose legs they were conceived, nurtured, and near-strangled in the hours of birth.

Memory might more reasonably be expected to go back as far as the giantess who had control of these vengeful satyrs when they were first struggling to discover the world. Mailer's explanation of abuse of the female is only another version of the description of rape as an act of revenge against the oppressive mother. What Mailer will not heed is the cry of the mothering sex that they are depleted by this attritive war of the sexes, by the endless duplication of Oedipal dependencies and hostilities, that they wish no further part in the primal war because, unremarked by their antagonists, they have borne great casualties. To an abused woman it is a bitter blasphemy to explain, as Mailer would, that her humiliation is enacted simply to prove the "power and the glory and the grandeur of the female in the universe," for she feels only the female in her debased self. What does it mean to the woman raped and bashed to learn her assailant did it to show the power of the feminine "can survive any context or any abuse"? Not that it's even unusual—many a rapist says "I love you."

More and more women are refusing to be doting mothers, looming over their children like mountains to be scaled as a first lesson in exploiting the universe. Part of their motivation may be found in Mailer's description of the formative years of the young dictator. The women's defection from the most exaggerated form of motherhood ever to be developed is timely. Next time round Hitler will be a machine, developed by male conquest as the most efficient method of subduing the peoples of the earth. Our only hope is that we have yet time to breed a generation which cannot be ruled in such a way or seek such a way to rule. We have no more need of great generals, for war is no longer fought by men but by machines against men. Machines are not mortal nor do they feel pain, so they must perforce win the war, unless the last of the fantasy heroes can acknowledge his weakness and his terror, and beg pardon. Children in a trance frag their commanding officers these days because their war is waged against the war machine, not Nixon's fabled enemy. The fight for life against the machine is women's fight too, and it is from this essential struggle that Mailer's games seek to divert them. Perhaps after all it is necessary to knock him down and out of the way.

While women are deciding to withdraw their cooperation in the process of developing fiercely competitive children with swollen egos in the interests of ecology, artistic as well as sexual and political, their children themselves are formulating their own critique of competitiveness and acquisition. But Mailer finds the new personality boring and frightening insofar as it rejects power and courage and insofar as its sexuality is inquiring and polymorphous. The rejection of monolithic standards of excellence in university courses has already broken down the tiny sacred society of truly great writers which he lusts to join. Concepts of aristocracy are breaking down all over, and Mailer's chagrin swells when he considers that he was maybe just about to make it, with his Great American Novel. It is ironic that student interest in him was one of the ways in which students pushed courses in American literature out of shape. It is sad that he himself does not realize that the immense pressure that the literary machine brings upon genius has already turned him into Superhack, poet without bays writing the praise of the machine. The young are the only ones who will forgive him for this major prostitution, but Mailer retreats from them into the past and the Right Wing, speaking coldly of

a crowd in the jail of New York with blacks and Puerto Ricans overcrowded in their cells, and ghettos simmering on the American stove, a world of junkies, hippies, freaks, and freaks who made open love at love-ins, be-ins, concerts, happenings, and on the stage of tiny theatres with invited guests . . .

and more coldly still of the new revolution,

that ill-mannered, drug-leached, informer-infested, indiscriminate ripping up of all the roots, yes, spoiled young middle-class heroes with fleas in their beard and rashes doubtless in the groin. . . .

What are these but the same old hot imaginings of the beleaguered Puritan bourgeois? Merely another version of "long-haired, dirty and unwashed," a description that the real McCoy thought applied to Mailer until he paid his dues and bitched the Left Wing on call. Horrible to imagine that these scruffy young folk have no trouble with their erections, that their semen flows like branch water. But most horrible of all to think that they don't care whether Eldridge Cleaver writes better than Mailer or not, they just want to know what both are into, whether they will serve a purpose. Suddenly, wryly, but foreseeably, Mailer abandons the Jewish troublemakers, Hoffman, Rubin and friends (and me) and takes up with Podhoretz and the Jewish Establishment.

This defection kindles a flame of anger in me that will stand me in good stead for our bout together. Those same revolutionaries whom he now reviles as fascists provided him with two books and a film, and of all three he was the hero. With me, on the other hand, he finds that he can agree because I breathe sweet liberalism, Cambridge (England) and Golden Square. My publishers are delighted and I am disgusted. He quotes the worst parts of my book and embeds them in non sequiturs. More than ever I am desirous of drawing him into range so that I can knock him down.

Yet all the time I wonder whether he ought not to face his own wives and old loves on the stage of Town Hall, for Women's Liberation is a personal issue. In supplying spokeswomen we bely the real nature of our activity, for we are not yet another crazy bureaucracy in the making, nor is there ideological orthodoxy among our ranks. We are no pseudo-army issuing dispatches. How shocking and valuable might it be for Mailer to hear the grievances of his women before an impartial observer, without the possibility of overbearing them by the threat of violence or eloquence! What fun it would be to accept all his thrasonical challenges and then unveil to him his own womenfolk, including his dark and velvety daughters, and ask them what they think of him. If only pity, the curse of women, would not tie their tongues! And then, unexpectedly for it was arranged not by me, I met Beverly Mailer. She had driven from Provincetown to New York with a beautiful brown boy who wanted to hear her brother play guitar. She was gallant, a little wry and regretful, mildly astonished that Mailer had been so careless of her actress' talent when he had so much opportunity to indulge it. She smiled and shrugged her shoulders, and I knew that without help now it was likely to prove harder than ever, but she had preferred the prerogative to try. I trembled, wondering if I had the right to present her cause, but afterward Dick Fontaine told me that as we left she winked. I took that as my okay and secretly regretted my covetise of her brown musician.

When at last I met the great man he was sitting in a snot-green dressing room at the New York Town Hall, lit like a matinee idol, being photographed by a very apologetic (and rather plain) professional. Mailer feigned butch embarrassment, while I wondered if the star treatment was altogether normal, for Mailer does not strike one as a great photogenic. I was asked to pose beside him. "You're better-looking than I thought," he said. "I know," said I, remembering his descriptions of Women's Liberationists, and his absurd insistence upon my English lectureship. Later he was to tell me that my picture on the book looked like any other uppity Jewish girl, so he was relieved to see that I was a shiksa (except that that was wrong too—I am like God in his last despairing suspicion, half Jewish). My convent education prevented me from saying how disappointed *I* was. I expected a hard, sort of nuggety man, and Mailer was positively blowsy. I contented myself with saying that his eyes were less blue than certain retouched color photos had led me to believe. Ever since, Mailer has fended off any question about me by some appreciation of my looks, especially my wonderful crooked fang. With him being so gallant, it ought to be difficult for me to explain that my old editor's telegram begging for an option on the story of the Mailer bedroom farce for his underground paper had to go unanswered. I was, after all, defective in Oedipal sentiment. I liked Mailer, but not enough. I disliked him too, and that not enough either.

When we were all assembled before the glittering, turbulent crowd of those who were rich enough to pay twenty-five dollars a head for the stalls and ten dollars a head for the circle, I felt for him right enough, for the devil in the fire is a ridiculous figure. There was almost no way in which he could appear sympathetic. It was evident at once that he was the carnival barker who had drawn in the crowd of diamond-studded radical-chic New Yorkers, and that *The Village Voice* would approve of anything he did, but it was also evident that he would not be able to do anything right. As moderator he was principally timekeeper of the speeches and controller of the audience. He was bored by Jackie Ceballos' speech, and grated his question, after an over-expanded compliment, as to whether there was anything in her and N.O.W.'s program that would give men the notion that life might not continue to be as profoundly boring as it is today.

Then it was my turn. I was so tense traversing the space between the chair and the lectern that I tripped over the air. My fox fur, which I had worn for fun and satire because it cost a pound, I stuffed down somewhere on the floor, thus exposing my ten-shilling dress and the chromium Women's Liberation symbol that Flo Kennedy had given me. This was the ensemble that was so wildly reported as elegance, furs and jewelry, by the humorless and unsophisticated New York press. My Australian/English/American hybrid accent was also taken for the true accent of Cambridge (England), which to the best of my knowledge has not existed since returned soldiers were admitted to the University after the war. Once safe behind the lectern, I clung on tight and launched my shot out over the crowd and (I hoped) into Mailer's sagging bosom. "The creative artist in our society," I wailed, "is more a killer than a creator" (remember, Norman, your notion of the artist as a great general?), "aiming his ego ahead of lesser talents, drawing the focus of all eyes to his achievements, being read now by millions and paid in millions." (How does that grab you, Superhack?) "Is it possible that the way of the masculine artist in our society is strewn with the husks of people worn out and dried out by this ego?" (Will this serve, Beverly?) "The achievement of the male ego is at my expense. I find that the battle is dearer to him than the peace would ever be . . ." (in my quoting voice) " 'The eternal battle with women both sharpens our resistance, develops our strength, enlarges the scope of our cultural achievements.' " And so on. In my convent-bred obedience I did not go beyond my time. Was it my imagination or did Mailer turn to me with clenched teeth, when the applause ended (why did those people applaud I wonder, for they cannot have accepted what I said) and charge me with diaper Marxism? As an old Anarchist I take that as a compliment. The infancy of Marxism is profoundly more relevant than anything since betrayed.

From then on the evening was simply fun, except for the cries of the women who asked what I was doing there, and whether Women's Lib was only for rich bitches and so forth, as if we women were grossing a bent nickel from the whole detestable circus. Jill Johnston's poem was exquisite and outrageous, much the most entertaining thing that had happened, if only the love scene at the end had not been quite such an anticlimax. It served to blow Papa Mailer's cool, though, and that's just as well. Jill promptly vanished, and we had to endure some querulous questioning as to what we had done with her. In New York, paranoia knows no bounds.

Diana Trilling's attack on *The Prisoner of Sex* was careful and beautiful, if only she had not considered it so necessary to dissociate herself from the rest of the women's movement so clearly. How much one might have wished to have said that Mailer's was a "free-wheeling solipsistic fancy to ask for the constant apotheosis of sex in parenthood." (Yes, yes, like an old Olympian whose loves could lenghten the night and always made children!)

And so the evening wore on in skirmishing and foolishness, with some of the best contributions coming from the floor, from Cynthia Ozick and Betty Friedan. The most publicized incident occurred when a cockerel by the name of Anatole Broyard was allowed to ask the last question and he put it to me.

"I would like to ask Germaine Greer as having a peculiar aptitude for this question to describe, perhaps, in the form of a one-act play what would it be like to be a woman and to have the initiation and consummation of a sexual contact so that now we can get down to the particulars of the evening. . . ."

Now if it were possible to strut in one place, he was strutting, and smirking like a popinjay. Mailer's hackles rose at the same instant as mine (and at that moment I lost my rancor toward him) and when I went for

Broyard he murmured, "Attagirl!" or "Sic him!" or something. The dozing columnists were only just aware that something was wrong when I was already furious, so they never did find out what produced the kind of feminist fury they had waited all night to see. The *pappagallo* tried to rescue his question. . . .

"I don't know what women are asking for. Now suppose I wanted to give it to them."

(For God's sake! After a whole night's wrangling. What does one do with these men?)

That night will be chiefly memorable in my life because when I was escaping from the continued interrogations and clamor at Westbeth afterward my cab was being driven by a corrupt child of my own generation, with a white angelic face (marked a little from experiences on the streets and in reform school) who was to become famous on the West Coast as my "bodyguard." (The experience was ultimately costly and therefore valuable.) The Town Hall extravaganza sickened me in retrospect: it was not even effective revolutionary theatre. What the kids were to initiate the very next day in Washington was to run round the world like St. Anthony's fire. Stories of impromptu prison camps were to cause old wounds to ache as tired Europe watched the hardening of America into the most reactionary power on earth. The holocaust was drawing nearer. I left for the Middle West and the crazy questions, "Are you a Communist—answer yes or no." What was one to do about Mailer's defection? Was it worthwhile to win him back?

I heard that Mailer wanted to continue his debate with me on the Susskind show. I was pleased, for it seemed like the answer to my question. I should have been better pleased to have gone fishing with him and refined our dialogue in an old-fashioned gentlemanly way, but we were both creatures of the media, and our master called. A phone call at midnight in San Francisco changed everything. My dear editor had discovered by diligent inquiry that Mailer had acquired the literary rights of our conversation from David Susskind. So much for his respect for his adversary. The money angle was bad enough, but the editorial angle was even worse. Bit by bit the facts about the Town Hall setup were emerging. Mailer had been the drawing card, according to his agent (although on the night he generously ascribed that role to me), and consequently had certain claims which Shirley Broughton, representing the chief beneficiary, the Theatre for Ideas, was charmed to recognize. The women would be taken care of, some proportion or other would be made over to them, but no trouble had been taken to secure an agreement. The matter passed into the hands of McGraw-Hill's corporation lawyers representing my interests. I realized that I had foolishly assumed that Mailer would treat me as an equal, despite my own clear apprehension of his role among the High Media; I remembered the warnings I had been given, by Abbie Hoffman and Gloria Steinem and others. I quarreled with dear David (not Susskind—the cabdriver) who could not understand why I was so upset. Gall and wormwood.

On the day of the proposed taping Mailer called me. He kept saying that he had been writing for thirty years and asking me if I thought he could perform an act so picayune. Moreover he had given up all the rights to anything and everything. We commiserated over the boredom of editing transcripts and the difficulty of satisfying everyone. He pretended to be mad at me for allowing my big corporation lawyers to intervene and all I could think of was that if they had not intervened I never would have known what was going on. I kept saying mechanically that when the lawyers were satisfied I would be satisfied too. The lawyers were never satisfied, as it happened.

That night we met at Marion Javits' house for dinner. I was hectic and miserable and Mailer twitted me for being less good-looking than at our former meeting. In truth I felt awful, watching the Filipino houseboy appearing and disappearing to the tune of the bell under the hostess' chair, eating the paella prepared by a lady who had not sat down to table with us. And yet all the time I was struggling like a neglected and ugly daughter for my father's esteem. I was waiting for him to say he was sorry, to confess to a wounding and careless gamble, but he never did. He rallied me with minor unkindnesses until I recklessly spoke loving words to him like I might have to my own indifferent father, who only ever praised me to other people. "I love you," I kept saying, with the unsaid corollary, "so why do you treat me this way?"—the classic question of revolting women! He was bewildered, mistrustful. Going downtown in a cab I announced my intention of visiting a friend, and was left alone at once. Mailer went to drink in a tough black bar on the Hudson, and I to walk a shaggy dog in Union Square, with my brothers, David and Jimmy, the Hell's Angel. They sensed my misery and bore me company all three, through the short night in my shabby suite before I was to leave for the *Today Show* and The National Press Club luncheon in Washington, where I was to be guest of honor. Even there the phantom of Mailer pursued me. "If you, Norman Mailer and Edward Kennedy were the last three left on earth, whom would you choose?" My answer surprised me by its bitterness. "It would be better that the human race should perish than that either of these men should be its father." What visions of Mailer's beloved primitive were set adrift by the speculation! Kennedy and Mailer setting each other tests and initiations, quarreling over the woman as the spoil, hitting upon the fine idea of clitoridectomy and infibulation as the best safeguard for the breeding female, and forever fighting, fighting each other, their sons and me.

When at last I fled from New York to my fastness in the Tuscan hills, one more attempt was being made to rescue the love affair of the century from total collapse. Mailer had rung the Cavett show and suggested that as a sequel to appearing on adjacent nights, we should appear together. But I was tired of keeping his stage fire alight, tired of contemplating the cruel mysticism which drives him through so many mythical bioscapes where the sperm battle for the consummate egg, like Argonauts in search of the Golden Fleece. And bored, bored with the foolish assumption that the ovum is the subconsciously absorbing artifact of the woman while the man's four hundred million sperm, already equipped with memory, will and understanding, are produced at no psychic cost to himself. What was Mailer after all but a typical patriarch, friend of the fetus and oppressor of the child? All that remains of his title fight with the women is a hundred and twenty quarto pages of transcript and a few reels of film which no one has any right to use. And there let it rest. "When the revolution comes it will not be on television. It will be live." Mailer won't be there, and no one will miss him.

JOYCE CAROL OATES

Male Chauvinist?

*. . . a day had to come when women shattered the pearl of their love
for pristine and feminine will and found the man, yes that man
in the million who could become the point of the seed which would
give an egg back to nature, and let the woman return with a
babe who came from the root of God's desire. . . .*

—*The Prisoner of Sex*

It is appropriate that Norman Mailer
has become the central target of the fiercest and cruelest of Women's
Liberation attacks, not because Mailer is prejudiced against women, or
bullying about them, not even because he claims to know much about
them, but because he is so dangerous a visionary, a poet, a mystic—he is
shameless in his passion for women, and one is led to believe anything he
says because he says it so well. He is so puritanical, so easily and deeply
shocked, like any hero, that his arguments, which approach the fluidity
and senselessness of music, have the effect of making the dehumanized
aspects of womanhood appear attractive.

Here is Mailer: ". . . Why not begin to think of the ovum as a
specialized production, as even an artistic creation?" And: "Yes, through
history, there must have been every variation of the power to conceive or
not to conceive—it was finally an expression of the character of the
woman, perhaps the deepest expression of her character—" What, are
artistic creation and the expression of character, for women, not detach-

able from their bodies? From the mechanism of their bodies? It is terrible to be told, in 1971, that we belong to something called a species, and that we had, throughout centuries, a mystical "power to conceive or not to conceive." Why didn't we know about this power?

No matter if we protest that sexual identity is the least significant aspect of our lives. No matter if we hope, not absurdly in this era, that technology might make our lives less physical and more spiritual. None of this matters for, to Norman Mailer, "the prime responsibility of a woman is probably to be on earth long enough to find the best mate possible for herself, and conceive children who will improve the species."

But we don't know what the *species* is. A post-Darwinist name for "God"? A scientific concept? A mystical concept? A word? An identity? An essence? Do we locate ourselves in it, or does it push through us, blindly, with the affection of a stampeding crowd? And how long is "long enough"? Should we remain on earth for twenty years, or forty, or dare we hope for an extravagant eighty years, though our last several decades will be unproductive and therefore unjustified? The machine of the female body is thought by some to be a sacred vessel, designed to bring other sacred vessels into the world, for the glory of God; but it is also thought to be rather foul, as in Lear's words:

> But to the girdle do the gods inherit,
> Beneath is all the fiend's.
> There's hell, there's darkness, there's the sulphurous pit; burning,
>   scalding, stench, consumption. . . .

It is also considered a means of improving the species, that is, a machine designed to improve the quality of other machines; and the proper artistic creation of a woman is not a novel, a symphony, not a political theory, certainly, but the cultivation of her womb. The "power to conceive or not to conceive" is, after all, the "deepest expression of [a woman's] character. . . ." Not one kind of expression, not even the most pragmatic expression, but the deepest expression! One sees why the mystic is the most dangerous of human beings.

There is a famous remark of Freud's that ends with the question, "What does a woman want?" A good question. And a woman is inclined to ask, with the same exasperation, "What does a man want?" Indeed, a woman must ask, "What does a *woman* want?" The question is a good one, but it is fraudulent. It suggests that there is a single answer—a single "want"—for a multitude of human personalities that happen to be female. Many women are angry today because they are only women; that is, they possess the bodies of women, the mechanisms for reproducing the species, and they are therefore defined simply as "women." But there is no reality to the class of "women," just as there is no emotional reality to the "species." There are only individuals. The individual may be compartmentalized into any number of compartments, the absurd boxes of the poll-taker (the "Irish Catholic," the "suburbanite, affluent," the "35-year-old divorcée," etc.), but he exists in none of these compartments, and his personality will reject them. The only reality is personality. Not sex. Not sexual identity. No categories can contain or define us, and that is why we draw back from the female chauvinists who claim a biological sisterhood with us, just as we draw back from the male chauvinists who have attempted to define us in the past.

"If we are going to be liberated," says Dana Densmore, in a pamphlet called "Sex Roles and Female Oppression," which is quoted in the Mailer article, "we must reject the false image that makes men love us, and this will make men cease to love us." But this viewpoint is not acceptable. It assumes that men demand a false image, that all men demand false images.It does not distinguish between one man and another man. And it assumes that women do not demand, from men, images that are occasionally false. Can an "image" be anything but false? The perfect mate of the toiling, distraught housewife is not a free, marauding male, but a husband stuck to a job that is probably as demeaning as housework, but more grating on the nerves because it is played out in a field of competition. If the woman has become trapped in a biological machine, the man has become trapped in an economic machine that pits him against other men, and for mysterious and shabby rewards. Man's fate may be to languish in imaginary roles, wearing the distorted masks of ideal images, but he can at least improve the quality of these roles by using his intelligence and imagination. But only by breaking the machine. Only by abandoning and climbing out of the machine, the traps of "maleness" and "femaleness."

Freud has been attacked from all sides as a representative of typical male prejudice, but his views on the subject are always worthwhile. In that wise, complex essay *Civilization and its Discontents*, he speaks of sex as a "biological fact which, although it is of extraordinary importance in mental life, is hard to grasp psychologically . . . though anatomy, it is true, can point out the characteristics of maleness and femaleness, psychology cannot. For psychology the contrast between the sexes fades away into one between activity and passivity, in which we far too readily identify activity with maleness and passivity with femaleness." Obviously, the distinctions are not simple.

For if the female finds herself locked in a physical machine marked "passive," the male is as tragically locked in a machine marked "active." As Sylvia Plath says, ironically, " Every woman loves a fascist." What is left, then, but for the man to play the role of a brute? What is masculinity in any popular sense, except the playing of this stupid, dead-end role? In our culture men do not dare cry, they do not dare to be less than "men"—whatever that means.

The mechanical fact of possessing a certain body must no longer determine the role of the spirit, the personality. If Women's Liberation accomplishes no more than this it will have accomplished nearly everything.

But there are further problems, further areas of masculine uneasiness. Mailer criticizes Kate Millett for believing in "the liberal use of technology for any solution to human pain." Yes, that sounds like heretical belief so long as human pain is valued as sacred, or important as an expression of personality, or helpful for salvation . . . or even conversation. But it isn't. It is nothing, it is a waste, a handicap, a mistake. What good is human pain? We are all going to experience it soon enough, regardless of technology's miracles, so there is no point in our ignoring it or romanticizing it. Human pain—the acceptance of a bodily machine without any rebellion—is a way of making us human, yes, but the rewards are chancy and might be as well accomplished by an act of the imagination. Why shouldn't we ask of technology the release from as much pain as possible? Why not? Why not the disturbing Utopian dream/nightmares of the "extra-uterine conception and incubation"—if they are a means of diminishing pain? Mailer, like all heroic spirits, places a primitive value on suffering. And one feels that he would not shy away from suffering, even the suffering of childbirth, if that were a possibility for him. Yes, to suffer, to feel, to be changed—it is a way of realizing that we live. But it is also a way of becoming dehumanized, mechanized. In fact, a way of dying.

To be mechanically operated, to have one's body moving along in a process that the spirit cannot control, to have the spirit trapped in an unchosen physical predicament—this is a kind of death. It is life for the species, perhaps, but death for the individual. Throughout human history women have been machines for the production of babies. It was not possible for them to live imaginative, intellectual, fully human lives at all, if indeed they survived for very long. They lived long enough to find a mate, to have a number of children, many of whom would not survive . . . but it was the process that mattered, the blind, anonymous reproductive process that gave these women their identities.

In a little-known story by Herman Melville, "The Tartarus of Maids," young girls working in a paper factory are seen by a sympathetic narrator: "At rows of blank-looking counters sat rows of blank-looking girls, with blank, white folders in their blank hands, all blankly folding blank paper." They are the pulp that is turned into blank paper out of a certain "white, wet, woolly-looking stuff . . . like the albuminous part of an egg," in a room stifling with a "strange, bloodlike, abdominal heat." The process takes only nine minutes, is presided over by a jovial young man named Cupid, and what terrifies is its relentlessness: it is an absolute process, a godly machine that cannot be stopped. "The pulp can't help going," the narrator is told smugly. And he thinks: "What made the thing I saw so specially terrible to me was the metallic necessity, the unbudging fatality which governed it." Melville, who seemed to have no interest at all in the relationship between men and women, and who created no memorable woman character in all his fiction, has given us the best metaphor for the existential predicament of most of the world's women.

No wonder that the feminists look to technology for deliverance! As they climb out of their machines they must find other, substitute machines to do the work of women. A body is no more than a machine, if it is not guided by a personality—so why not a surrogate machine, an actual machine, why not the escape from as much impersonal pain as possible?

Once we are delivered from the machine of our bodies, perhaps we will become truly spiritual.

Perhaps.

At the start of *The Prisoner of Sex*, Mailer speaks of having taken care of his large family for several weeks during the summer, cooking, cleaning, turning into a kind of housewife, so exhausted with domestic chores that he had no time to write, to think, to contemplate his ego. *No time to contemplate his ego!* After a while, in such a frenzy, one loses his ego altogether . . . one misplaces his personality, and sinks into the routine frenzy of work that adds up to nothing, that comes to no conclusion, no climax. Is this a human life? Can one call an uncontemplated life really a "life" at all? Or is it merely brute existence? One has the time to contemplate his ego—to achieve a personality—only when he or she is liberated from the tyranny of physical burdens, whether they are external in the form of housework to be done eternally, or a commuting distance to be traveled, or whether they are internal, the processes of a body unaltered by technology and human choice. And what grief, what anger and dismay, for the women who—to "liberate" themselves and their men from the possibility of pregnancy—began taking the Pill on absolute faith, only to discover that the Pill carried with it mysterious disappointments and possible catastrophes of its own!—for Technology is probably male, in its most secret essence male.

The problem is: do we control nature, or will we be controlled by nature? A difficult question. A Faustian question. To accept technology and to create surrogate machines that will bear our chidren—this sounds like madness, perversity. Yet, to deny human choice in the matter of reproduction, as we would never do in the matter of, say, ordinary medicine or dentistry, seems an empty sentimentality.

But after all this, after all these considerations, we are still left with the rage of Women's Liberation. How to explain this anger? And we understand slowly that what is being liberated is really hatred. *Hatred of men*. Women have always been forbidden hatred. Certainly they have been forbidden the articulation of all base, aggressive desires, in a way that men have not. Aggression has been glorified in men, abhorred in women.

Now, the hatred is emerging. And such hatred! Such crude, vicious jokes at the expense of men! Most women, reading the accusations of certain feminists, will be as shocked and demoralized as Norman Mailer himself. Somehow, in spite of all the exploitation, the oppression, somehow . . . there are things about the private lives of men and women that should not be uttered, or at least we think they should not be uttered, they are so awful. Women have been the subjects of crude jokes for centuries, the objects of healthy male scorn, and now, as the revolution is upon us, men will become the objects of this scorn, this exaggerated disgust and comic sadism.

Nothing will stop the hatred, not the passage of legislation, not the friendliest of men eager to come out in support of Women's Liberation. It has just begun. It is going to get worse.

And yet, it will probably be short-lived. Hatred goes nowhere, has no goal, no energy. It has a certain use, but it has no beauty. There will be a place in our society for Mailer's heroic mysticism, at the point in history at which women can afford the same mysticism. Until then, it is better for us to contemplate the blank-faced horror of Melville's pulp factory, rather than the dreamy illogic of Mailer's "ovum-as-artistic-creation."

RICHARD POIRIER

The Minority Within

Like all his other theories, Mailer's theories about the relations between the sexes reveal his intuitive taste for "war," for the conflict by which one at last delineates the true form of oneself and of others. "War" is only an occasion, however, for his effort to discover the minority element within any person, constituency, or force which might be engaged in a "war." And it is this minority element which has the most beneficially corrosive effect upon form, forcing it to dispense with its merely acquired or protective or decorative attributes. It might be more accurate to say, in dealing with this very slippery subject, that "war" provides the context within which any creative minority pressure can assert itself formatively within society, the self, or a book.

This feature of Mailer is more complicated than one might infer from the sometimes simplified dichotomies in which he indulges. The minority element is not equivalent, that is, to one side in the "war," the dualisms or oppositions found everywhere in his work. The minority is not God or the Devil, Black or white, woman or man. Rather it is that element in each which has somehow been repressed or stifled by conformity to system—including systematic dialectical opposition—or by fear of some power, like death, which is altogether larger than the ostensible, necessarily more manageable opponent apparently assigned by history. The minority element in males or Blacks or God is the result of their inward sense of inferiority which the outward or visible opposition from women or whites or the Devil did not of itself necessarily create. Blacks do not feel inferior to whites so much as to the psychotic brilliance created and, at once, thwarted within themselves by the accident of white oppres-

From *Norman Mailer*. Copyright © 1972 by Richard Poirier. The Viking Press.

sion; whites do not feel superior to Blacks but inwardly terrified at the possibility that in any open sexual competition they would prove inferior. Behind each of his dualisms, Mailer's imagination searches out, sometimes with a harried ingenuity, the minority incentive that in turn gives dialectical energy to the dualism. . . .

Since about 1957 and "The White Negro," Mailer has come to associate creativity and the imagination with the assertion of a minority position, and his contempt for liberals is a consequence of his conviction that they would deprive us of the vicissitudes and oppositions which are the necessary conditions for art and for any full sense of life. In "The Tenth Presidential Paper—Minorities" he claims that

> Minority groups are the artistic nerves of the republic, and like any phenomenon which has to do with art, they are profoundly divided. They are both themselves and the mirror of their culture as it reacts upon them. They are themselves and the negative truth of themselves. No white man, for example, can hate the Negro race with the same passionate hatred that each Negro feels for himself and for his people; no anti-Semite can begin to comprehend the malicious analysis of his soul which every Jew indulges every day.

Still later, in "A Speech at Berkeley on Vietnam Day," he proposes that anyone in America, even the President, is "a member of a minority group if he contains two opposed notions of himself at the same time." He claims that

> What characterizes the sensation of being a member of a minority group is that one's emotions are forever locked in the chains of ambivalence— the expression of an emotion forever releasing its opposite—the ego in perpetual transit from the tower to the dungeon and back again. By this definition nearly everyone in America is a member of a minority group, alienated from the self by a double sense of identity and so at the mercy of a self which demands action and more action to define the most rudimentary borders of identity.

Such passages indicate why Mailer is a more difficult writer in a book like *An American Dream* or in *Why Are We in Vietnam?* than most critics or reviewers are prepared to recognize. Not everyone is qualified for the kind of reading, the reading as much with the ear as with the eye, that his writing calls for; not everyone is capable of caring for the drama of his argument and of his language, as it plays across the page; and very few are prepared for his unique mixtures of the world of daily news, the world we take for granted, with the world of nightmare and psychotic imagining. He is now quite unlike any other writer of his generation. He is more like

Pynchon than, say, like Burroughs (or Borges), with whom he has similarities enough to make the differences instructive. Burroughs is interested in showing how the world of the underground is a metaphor for the world we all live in, while Mailer insists on the fact that the world we live in *is* the underground. And Borges, for all his marvelous facility and wit, becomes, after any tended reading, tedious and emasculating. He is forever demonstrating the fictive nature of reality, forever calling us away from the dangers of contemporary facts, Argentinian or otherwise, to the refuge of fable-izing and the titillation of literary bewilderment. Burroughs is a writer of genius comparable to Mailer's and essential to the latter's development, especially in *Why Are We in Vietnam?*, but the currently touted Borges is the kind of writer whose relation to the possibilities of literature is like the relation of a good cookbook to food.

Mailer insists on living *at* the divide, living *on* the divide, between the world of recorded reality and a world of omens, spirits, and powers, only that his presence there may blur the distinction. He seals and obliterates the gap he finds, like a sacrificial warrior or, as he would probably prefer, like a Christ who brings not peace but a sword, not forgiveness for past sins but an example of the pains necessary to secure a future. This fusion in the self of conflicting realms makes him a disturbing, a difficult, and an important writer. I use these terms deliberately, to suggest that his willingness to remain locked into "the chains of ambivalence" is a measure of the dimension and immediacy of his concerns, of his willingness not to foreclose on his material in the interests of merely formal resolutions. There is no satisfactory form for his imagination when it is most alive. There are only exercises for it. Of course any particular exercise can in the long run become equivalent to a form, and when that happens Mailer is least interesting to himself or to us, as in those parts in *Of a Fire on the Moon* that boringly reduce everything to favorite categories, or in some of his extended demonstrations of what a smart boy he can be in his self-interviews.

Why Are We in Vietnam? and *The Armies of the Night*, along with parts of *Advertisements for Myself* and *An American Dream*, make Mailer easily the equal, it seems to me, of Fitzgerald and Hemingway, potentially of Faulkner. His accomplishment deserves comparison with theirs precisely because it is of a different kind and because it takes account of the varieties, evolutions, discontinuities, and accumulations of style since World War II. But he could not be to our time what they were to theirs without being in many important respects radically unlike them in the way he writes. No other American writer of this period has tried so resolutely and so successfully to account for the eclecticisms of contemporary life when it comes to ideas of form, of language, of culture, of political and social structures, and of the self.

The reason why most thoughtful and literate young readers prefer Mailer to, say, Updike or Roth or Malamud is that his timing is synchronized to theirs, while the others move to an older beat. Which is to say something not only about Mailer's taste for certain situations but also about a taste for Mailer, for the pace and movement of his writing. I suspect that an enthusiasm for his work means that one shares his partiality for those moments where more is happening than one can very easily assimilate. By and large, the other contemporary writers I have mentioned will not allow more to happen than can be accounted for in the forms they have settled upon. They work away from rather than into the ultimate inconsistencies, the central incoherence in the way we live now. Mailer, on the other hand, is always looking for the stylistic equivalent for that movement of "the ego in perpetual transit from tower to dungeon and back again."

It is no accident that *An American Dream*, which incidentally seems to move rather frequently between the Waldorf Towers and police headquarters, finds its most appreciative audience among serious young students of literature who have a surer instinct for what it offers than have most of Mailer's critics. The always outmoded criteria of verisimilitude, the accusations that the characterization of Rojack is the occasion merely for a vulgar ego trip by Mailer, the charge that the book is simply dirty and that it fails for not making the hero pay for the crime of murder—these allegations sound primitive enough for hill-country journalism of a bygone era, but they happen to have been sponsored by, among others, Philip Rahv, Elizabeth Hardwick, and Tom Wolfe, who complains of "unreal dialogue" as if there were such a thing as "real" dialogue. Even to evoke criteria of this kind betrays an inability to see what the book is about, and I mention these criticisms only because they represent the persistence of standards—and there are of course many young pseudoneoclassicists coming through the ranks—which continue to keep discussions of Mailer at an irrelevant and demeaning level even when some sympathetic critics set about to defend him.

Oddly enough, it is just because it *does* call for the kind of negative response it has mostly gotten that *An American Dream* is such a brilliant achievement. From the first sentence the novel lays a proprietary claim on the so-called real world, and even Tom Wolfe ought to have found the dialogue of the police or of a Mafia don, like Gannuchi, "real" enough. Within a couple of paragraphs we learn that Rojack went to Harvard (so did Mailer); that Rojack met Kennedy (Mailer did, too, though under quite different circumstances); that Rojack ran for Congress and won (while Mailer's first effort to run for Mayor of New York had already floundered); that Rojack killed his wife (Mailer had recently stabbed his second). Both were for a time held by the police; they are roughly the same age, Rojack, forty-four, and Mailer, at the time of writing, forty-one; Rojack is half and Mailer all Jewish; and both pursue the same topic—as writers and television personalities—namely that "magic, dread, and the perception of death were the roots of motivation."

This mixture of history and fiction, of the author's with the hero's biography, of Melvillean metaphysical rhetoric with social talk as vividly "authentic" as any in Philip Roth or in the best of the detective fiction which Mailer sometimes imitates, the adhesion of interior fantasizing to moments of strenuously cool public etiquette—these are frequent enough in literature to have become nearly the trademark of a special, usually large thematic ambition. What is remarkable in *An American Dream* is the extravagance of Mailer's rendition of each of these modes; there is the clear indication that if he so chose he could write any kind of novel that literature has made available to us.

What he wants to do, however, is something altogether more daring. He wants to show that the world of the demonic, the supernatural, the mad is not simply the reverse side of the world that sets the normal standards by which these other conditions are defined as abnormal. Instead he wants to suggest that these worlds are simultaneous, coextensive. Perhaps he would have escaped the strictures visited upon him had he set the novel in Los Angeles, which most literary critics have long since agreed is a city where anything they know about can become anything they don't know about and certainly everything they disapprove of. He chose instead the difficult locale of New York which, as late as 1965, passed for sane, even for fun city.

Rojack resembles Mailer but is not to be confused with him. The difference essentially is that he is only in the process of achieving that level of integration between madness and sanity at which Mailer had to arrive as the precondition for his writing the book at all. In wanting to escape madness Rojack decides he must position himself at some false divide between the world of merely seeming sanity—the party he attends at the beginning, his encounters with the police, his recollected involvements with historical issues, his talk with various recognizable types in the bars and at the apartment of his father-in-law, Kelly—and the world of nightmare and death with which he flirts. He lives on the divide between two kinds of equally unacceptable power: of demonic social and economic systems and of demonic imaginations of himself as a kind of *Übermensch*.

He thus exists on the borders of identity, suicidally placed at different times in the book on the parapet of a balcony high above Manhattan with the moon and the abyss on one side and, on the other, the realities and blandishments of a deadening academic-literary-intellectual-social commitment. In his verbal as well as in his physical excursions between these two worlds, Rojack moves in obedience to a map already charted in Mailer's earlier works, a diagram of the formative workings of Mailer's imagination.

The polarizations and oppositions by which Mailer apportions his material are what provoke him into further discriminations, into the discovery of a minority impulse which disrupts the equilibrium of either side. Rojack emulates this process both physically and verbally. He forces upon himself that sensation which Mailer had earlier defined as peculiar to members of a minority group: the sensation of "the ego in perpetual transit from the tower to the dungeon and back again." His hyperbolic imagination of himself and of his psychic powers occur in language: his experience and his expression are as one. Through language he would escape entrapments in kinds of power which he himself did not invent, power represented, on one hand, by money, the CIA, and Las Vegas, all somehow epitomized in Barney Kelly and therefore in his daughter, Deborah, whom Rojack has murdered, and, on the other, by death and the process of decreation, associated with the debased sexuality of his marriage and of his anal-vaginal transactions with Deborah's German maid, Ruta, just after the murder.

Rojack raises a most interesting question about Mailer. Even to arrive at that question, consider, first of all, that Rojack's efforts at self-creation in language are analogous to his efforts in action in that both are an attempt to discover the shape of his true self by daring each side of the divide on which he chooses to live. Consider further that his verbal transits between worlds are equivalent to Mailer's own movements up and down between the linked oppositions which hold so much of his work and of his world together. The question, then, is this: What does Rojack's condition, once he has escaped from this "perpetual transit," tell us about the kinds of fulfillment that Mailer wishes to arrive at as a writer? In order to be a writer at all, in order quite literally to write, it is perhaps necessary that he remain the embattled embodiment of the two worlds from which, in the hope of becoming a new man, in the hope of having a second birth, Rojack wants desperately to escape. Rojack wants to escape from the world as it is contrived and structured by conspiracies of power.

What is not sufficiently clarified, even by admirers of *An American Dream*—and I am thinking of two astute critics, Leo Bersani and Tony

Tanner—is that Rojack really hopes to do more than that. He would also like to escape from his own, which is to say from Mailer's counter-conspiracies, his alternative but often insane inventions. Above all, he would be "free of magic," not only the "magic at the top," that cluster of the incorporated social-economic-political power which Kelly seems to offer him as a bribe, but also the magic he evokes in order not to be tempted by the bribe. He wants to be free of the enslavement to system that is implicit in the total absorption of his opposition to system. Stepping out of the dialectical frame so nearly compulsive in Mailer, Rojack is allowed to say that he would like to escape "the tongue of the Devil, the dread of the Lord, I wanted to be some sort of rational man again, nailed tight to details, promiscuous, reasonable, blind to the reach of the seas." His prayer simply is that he be allowed to "love that girl, and become a father, and try to be a good man, and do some decent work." At last, with admiration, almost with relief, the reader can welcome back that modest, nice, young Jewish boy in Mailer who won't ever, quite, let himself be forgotten. If Rojack passes over a terrain already thoroughly explored by his creator, he reveals the otherwise scarcely articulated wish of his creator to arrive back home, where it all began.

Mailer's articulate brilliance depends on his not succeeding as a writer in a way Rojack proposes to succeed as a man. Perhaps for that reason Rojack cannot be allowed any palpable equivalence to his own language of love, to the nearly hippie simplicity with which he would replace his Hip embattlement. Rojack's feeling of possible mutation, as if "I had crossed a chasm of time and was some new breed of man," which occurs fairly early in the book, has only a grotesque realization at the end when, in Las Vegas to gamble for his trip onward alone to Guatemala and Yucatán—striking out like the classic American hero to the territory always beyond—he says, "Nobody knew that the deserts of the West, the arid empty wild blind deserts, were producing again a new breed of man." However "new," this breed is, like the old one, suspended between two worlds: the one a horror of nature, "the bellows of the desert," the other of technology, the air-conditioned hotel where he spends twenty-three of every twenty-four hours as if "in a pleasure chamber of an encampment on the moon."

The movement from the desert of this book to the icy North range of *Why Are We in Vietnam?* and then to the magnificently described craters of the moon in *Of a Fire on the Moon* may be Mailer's way of suggesting that because we have denuded and corrupted nature in those parts of our world where it might be hospitable, we are perforce engaging ourselves, by an urgency of the will akin to Sergeant Croft's in his assault on Mount

Anaka, with those sanctuaries of nature which are least hospitable. And there we absorb the savagery and the urge to kill which is part of nature, while at the same time we accept the protections afforded by a wholly technological atmosphere unnatural to the environment in which it has been placed. Mailer thus proposes an insoluble paradox: that human savagery increases in direct proportion to our monumental achievements in those realms of technology which now imperially reach into the very last recesses of the natural world.

Mailer has come to posit situations in which the imaginable alternatives seem to be suicide or "a slow death by conformity, with every creative and rebellious instinct stifled." For a man to operate on the "edge" of such a divide, facing two unacceptable invitations, is less humanly fulfilling, even, than for him to choose, say, to knock another man out in the ring. So that while Mailer concedes that boxing may not be a civilized activity, he can insist, rightly, I think, and even after witnessing the killing of Benny Peret, that "it belonged to the tradition of the humanist; it was a human activity, it showed part of what a man was like, it belonged to his ability to create art and artful movement on the edge of death or pain or danger or attack, and it had much to say about the subtleties of human style."

The question being asked in all of his books from An American Dream to the present is, for him, steadfastly grim: Am I, Norman Mailer, at last an expendable human type, and is the "ability to create art" (which, again, ought not to be confused with the ability to absorb it or revere it as Culture) finally not simply irrelevant but perhaps actually a quixotic imposition that further exhausts the spirit of the writer and reader alike? Hints of exhaustion are evident, I fear, in Of a Fire on the Moon and The Prisoner of Sex. In these, more simply than in any other of his recent work, Mailer seems, in a crotchety and sentimental, an aggressively petulant and self-pitying way, to encamp himself as a Defender of the Imagination in an Age of Technology. Perhaps this explains, again, why some of the best parts of both books are about other artists and writers, other "defenders" of the faith, as in the exquisite discussions of Cézanne and Magritte in the moon book.

Where he has faced the question of creative impotence less explicitly, where he seems rather to get entangled with it against his will, he reveals something even more profitable to his writing than are his admirations for other artists, however much they reassure him that it is still possible, in Empson's phrase, to learn a style from a despair. I am referring to the passionate energy with which he displays his mastery, perhaps unequaled since the parodic brilliance of Joyce in Ulysses, of those expressive modes which threaten to obliterate his own expression, those contemporary styles that provide us too abundantly with images of what we possibly are in our public and in our private selves. He can do this while simultaneously demonstrating the greater inventiveness, inclusiveness, plasticity, and range of his own modes. Nowhere is this more impressively evident than in the most dazzling and the most incomprehensibly slighted of his novels, *Why Are We in Vietnam?*

The novel's answer to the question raised in its title fits none of the schemes of cause and effect that dominate nearly all "responsible" social and political thinking. And "responsible" it has proved to be—for the war. Vietnam is mentioned once, and then only in the last sentence. Instead Mailer is attempting, with a vitality akin to the Circe episode in *Ulysses*, to register the fevered mentality of which this atrocity is not so much a consequence as a part—so naturally a part that no one in the book needs consciously to be aware of the existence of Vietnam as in any way unique. It is not especially worth mentioning. We are in Vietnam because we are as we corporately are. We are all of one another. And for that reason Mailer makes the voices that speak to us in the book, in its various Intro Beeps, and Chaps, a matter of serious but comic bewilderment. Perhaps, as it mostly seems, what we get are emissions from the hopped-up mind of D.J., a Dallas late-adolescent son of corporation millionaire Rusty and of his wife, Hallie Lee Jethroe. We can't be sure. In this work D.J. functions as Mailer has done in others: as the theorist of multiple identity. He cautions us that

> we have no material physical site or locus for this record, because I can be in the act of writing it, recording it, slipping it (all unwitting to myself) into the transistorized electronic aisles and microfilm of the electronic Lord (who, if he is located in the asshole, must be Satan) or I can be an expiring consciousness, I can be the unwinding and unravelings of a nervous constellation just now executed, killed, severed or stopped, maybe even stunned, you thunders, Herman Melville go hump Moby and wash his Dick. Or maybe I am like a Spade and writing like a Shade.

The "voice" here is a composite of styles, tones, and allusions transposed to the pace of a disc jockey's taped talk. Throughout the book this voice manages to incorporate nearly every kind of cant one can hear on the airways of America. To a lesser degree Rojack was also an assemblage of parts, some of them disjunctive with others. The often abrupt but deftly managed shifts of his style are one indication of this. (So, too, with Cherry. Watching her sing under the spotlight in a nightclub, Rojack imagines that "she could have been a nest of separate personalities," a nice formula for his own and for Mailer's willing if more warlike gathering of disparate selves.)

Mailer's healthy and at last dogged refusal to put together a self at the cost of stifling any fragment of his personality enters into what can be called his willingness to decharacterize the people he likes. While giving full expression to the social and psychological identities which could be conventionally assigned to such characters, he proposes at the same time that they are impersonal units of energy, connected to powers quite unlike those which can account for a character in his other, more normal existence. This is why Mailer's heroes and heroines, especially in *An American Dream*, are a kind of battleground where external forces which inhabit the soul or the psyche war for possession. While Mailer admires the strength in a person like Rojack or Cherry that allows such a war even to go on, he also shares the terror they necessarily feel. In *An American Dream* and still more in *Why Are We in Vietnam?* is the acknowledgment that perhaps it is impossible to fashion any self that one can call one's own. Perhaps—and here the increasing influence of Burroughs on Mailer is apparent—we are no more than interchangeable, tooled parts of one another. D.J. is all he says he is and more, while American literature in the person of Herman Melville offers, at one point, a convenient scenario for the hunt in Alaska and, at another, the occasion only for a smart-ass joke.

D.J. is a character some of the time—a wild, brilliant, witty, savage, eager, and not unappealing boy; but he is much more than a character. He is the place, the context, the locus for an American mixture which is finally committed to the kill, and Melville is but one ingredient in the whipped-up, heated, soured mixture. The war already existed in that complex of pressures which shaped D. J. and the character of the nation and thus its fate, the "subtle oppression," as he describes it in *The Armies of the Night*, "which had come to America out of the very air of the century (this evil twentieth century with its curse on the species, its oppressive Faustian lusts, its technological excrement all over the conduits of nature, its entrapment of the innocence of the best)." Vietnam, that is, did not induce this novel, but was itself induced by what the novel manages to gather up and redefine from everything Mailer had been saying for fifteen years or more about his country. And, as we are seeing, what he has to say about America is more than usually dependent upon what American literature has been saying for some one hundred and fifty years.

At a pace that is likely to overwhelm many readers, Mailer demonstrates his stylistic capacity to match the tempo of historical accelerations toward disaster. But he had already described that movement in the quieter tones of earlier work. It is consistent with what the novel is saying that he should have said much of it before—that it was there to be noted—in other, less compelling forms. As early as 1959 he offered a kind of prediction of the novel in "From Surplus Value to Mass Media," an essay which he calls "one of the most important short pieces" appearing in *Advertisements for Myself.* He proposed that if any new revolutionary vision of society is to be "captured by any of us in work or works," the necessary exploration will go

> not nearly so far into that jungle of political economy which Marx charted and so opened to rapid development, but rather will engage the empty words, dead themes, and sentimental voids of that mass media whose internal contradictions twist and quarter us between the lust of the economy (which radiates a greed to consume into us, with sex as the invisible salesman) and the guilt of the economy which must chill us with authority, charities for cancer, and all reminder that the mass consumer is only on drunken furlough from the ordering disciplines of church, F.B.I., and war.

This passage proves particularly apt to *Why Are We in Vietnam?* The style of the novel is mimetic of the arts of the absurd he finds so chilling in a prefatory note to *Cannibals and Christians,* "Our Argument Fully Resumed." He there contrasts the art of self-expression (for which he offers the quite peculiarly inappropriate examples of Joyce and Picasso) which came out of the nineteenth century of iron frustration, with the arts which evolved after World War II, when children "grew up not on frustration but interruption." This later art is designed to shatter the nerves with "style, with wit, each explosion a guide to building a new nervous system." Dealing with "categories and hierarchies of discontinuity and the style of their breaks," it goes out to "hustle fifty themes in an hour." It is an art which mass produces the wastes of art, though he doesn't quite get around to being that explicit about it. As usual, he is not anxious to appear a defender of high culture even when his own logic directs him that way.

Why Are We in Vietnam? is a medley of "empty words" and "dead themes," and Mailer would appear to suggest that these are really the inventions of the mass media. In fact, they represent what the mass media has made out of high culture, of psychoanalysis, of literary criticism, of myth, and of Mailer's own favorite theological evocations, such as "dread." What lays waste to the human mind is a central subject of this novel. But that is to put the matter rather too simply. Still more important in understanding its rapid shifts of style is Mailer's preoccupation with the processes by which the mind is encouraged to turn its own contents, turn itself even, into waste.

This is of course a complicated process. It is dramatized in this novel by a remarkable combination of quick changes and constant repetitions. We find ourselves transported with almost maddening speed from one context to another, while we are forced to absorb along the way an insistent recurrence of phrases, names, allusions, actions, tones of voice. In other words, the constant interruptions which create such a variety of contexts and moods in the book make its structure analogous to the structure, as Mailer has defined it, of contemporary daily life. Whether digested or not, one momentary accumulation of meaning has to be flushed out to make room for the rapid infusion of the next. No word, no name, no allusion, no idea can rest for even a moment in the mood which it is supposed to secure, and so the book proliferates in interruptions which involve the splitting even of titles, like "Moby" and "Dick," and in puns that mock the very authority which licenses them: "But rest for the inst," D.J. tells the reader. The phrase creates a paradox by calling for a rest in a contraction so hurried as to suggest there can be none, and then continues—"Return to civ, which is to say syphilization and fuck James Joyce."

There is no consciousness in the book wherein the reader is allowed to find any security, which is again a reminder of Joyce's *Ulysses* and of the disturbance felt by critics whenever they are confronted with this kind of phenomenon. Their tendency is then to invent now one now another schematization in which to garage their minds. Efforts to locate some source of authority in Mailer's novels reveal only that there is none. This is as it must be, since his intent is to refer us to determinants in American life that are mysterious and unlocatable, and the more powerful for being so. The question addressed by the book is no longer the Marxist one of the exploitation of working time or even of the human sense of time by the profit motive. Rather, the question is the domination of pleasure and of inner time. Remember that in "From Surplus Value to Mass Media," Mailer takes the Marcusean view, without the Marcusean heaviness, that we are "only on drunken furlough from the ordering disciplines of church, F.B.I. and war." The appropriateness of these terms to the novel is evident: the two boys are, in effect, on furlough from the war, the book being a record of what presumably is passing through the head of D.J. as he and Tex sit at their farewell dinner in Dallas. More than that, no one in the novel is ever seen at work, except possibly Hallie's psychoanalyst, Leonard Levin Ficthe Rothenberg, alternately called Linnit Live 'n Fixit Rottenbug or Dr. Fink Lenin Rodzianko. It can be said that the book is given wholly to interruptions and distractions, though there is no telling from what, unless it be the urge to kill or hump.

This is true even for that part of the hunt in Alaska which is called a "purification ceremony" for the boys.

In a book so pointedly evasive about assigning responsibility for its voices, its shifts and modulations, it is all the more curious that the section in which this "rite" occurs gives evidence of a more total engage- ment of Mailer's genius than can be found in any other of his works except for *The Armies of the Night*, written in the next year. The section, from Chapter 8 to the end, making up nearly half the book, covers some of the Alaska safari organized by Rusty Jethroe for the Medium Assholes, as D.J. calls them, of his corporation—Rusty himself being a High Asshole—D.J., Tex, and the guide, Big Luke Fellinka, and it includes all the episodes in which the boys separate themselves from the other hunt- ers, leave their weapons behind, and head north into the icy peaks of the Brooks Range. Their quite conscious ambition to "get the fear, shit, disgust and mixed shit tapeworm out of fucked up guts and overcharged nerves" and to cleanse themselves of the "specific mix of mixed old shit" represented by the talk and the tactics of their companions. These latter, though overarmed and assisted by a helicopter in their search for bear, still have to lie about their credit for the kill, as does D.J.'s father at the expense of his son. They are, as Tony Tanner points out in *The City of Words*, which includes one of the best essays written about Mailer, going "as far into the northern snow as they can, not to kill but to open themselves up to the mystery and dread of this geographical extreme." Tanner connects this not only to Rojack's position on the parapet but to Mailer's position as a writer who tries "to keep an equilibrium on the 'dangerous edge of things' through the resources of his own style."

This is of course a position not unfamiliar to American writers, and especially to Melville. There are Melvillean touches from the begin- ning of his work, as in the notation that Lieutenant Hearn in *The Naked and the Dead* wrote a college honors thesis on "A Study of The Cosmic Urge of Herman Melville"; he is an appropriately felt presence throughout Mailer's accounts of the voyage to the moon, and the character of Rojack has interesting similarities to Ahab. Both men are convinced of the presence of what Ahab calls "malicious agencies," both have been muti- lated by them, both are demonic and opposed to demons, both make use of the mechanisms of capitalistic culture in an effort to reach a reality which that culture has not yet been able to assimilate, both are at once charismatic and repellent, both share a peculiar, manic belief in their powers to exhale influences on others—Rojack by shooting his psychic pellets at obnoxious people in a New York bar, and Ahab in his claims, at one point, that "Something shot from my dilated nostrils, he has inhaled it in his lungs. Starbuck now is mine"—and both have a longing for the ordinary life which is denied them by the very nature of their heroic exertions. Above all, neither imagines that if nature is some alternative to society it is necessarily a benign one. Rojack does not assume that the craters of the moon are hospitable, and Mailer, gazing at moon rock, feels an affection that is also spooky. In Mailer's work, as far back as his first novel, man in nature is what Lawrence said Deerslayer truly proved to be: "isolate and a killer." In *Why Are We in Vietnam?* what is finally bequeathed by the presiding spirit of the North is the order to go forth and kill.

The important issue is not the identification, not even the uses made of other writers in a book like this, be they Melville or Faulkner or Lawrence. What should concern us, rather, is the necessity to bother with literature at all, within a complex of competing, equally urgent, or equally innocuous references. This novel tends to remind us of literature, to remind us that it is literature we are reading. But the literature which gets to us in this book has passed through other media which rend and shred it. Appropriately we are made to think of the diminishing claims of literature, its problematic existence in a book where all forms of expression and of consciousness are made problematic. The references to Melville and the "Dick" of "Moby" are on the same page as other equally possible and proposed models for the narrative voice: movie-cutie George Hamilton, or a choice proposed in saying that "I'm coming on like Holden Caulfield when I'm really Dr. Jekyll with balls."

What I mean to suggest is that the trip by the boys alone into the wilderness, their trip to the "edge," is not quite in the same category as Rojack's imaginary and real extensions of his own power into equally perilous circumstances. Mailer's account of the trip reveals, more than does anything in his other books, a willingness to gamble imaginatively up to the limits of his *own* resources. The trip by the boys is made into an existential experience. But who could doubt that it would be? What is more interesting is that it is also, and emphatically, a literary one, with admixtures of film idols, fashionable intellectual guides like Marshall McLuhan, crossings of Shakespeare with Batman, of Katherine Anne Porter with Clare Boothe Luce. I don't mean that such a cheery and utilitarian treatment of literature is designed merely to characterize the boys and elicit our sad and amused contempt. Actually, the boys are made as bright as any potential reader, certainly as bright as most literary-academic ones. (After all, D.J. has ready access to his "Literary Handbook Metaphor Manual"). Their literary self-consciousness, combined with their intellectual savvy, is what enriches the episode of their excursion beyond anything like it in American literature since *The Adventures of Huckleberry Finn*, an earlier book "written" by an adolescent who, though he tried to avoid the "style" of his times as energetically as D.J. tries to imitate his, was nonetheless also its victim.

While D.J. and Tex can be compared respectively to Huck and Tom, they are both more like Tom to the degree that they eagerly subscribe to system, to doing things "by the book," though now "the book" encompasses film, TV, and disc jockeys. So much so that in important respects they do not exist as characters at all but as expressive filaments of some computerized mind. This is made especially important, for any understanding of what Mailer is up to, by the sudden attention given in Chap 10 to the phrase "purification ceremony."

> They have not cleaned the pipes, not yet. They are still full of toilet plunger holes seen in caribou, and shattered guts and strewn-out souls of slaughtered game meats all over the Alaska air and Tex feels like he's never going to hunt again which is not unhorrendous for him since he's natural hunter, but then with one lightning leap from the button on his genius belt to the base of his brain-pan he gets the purification ceremony straight in his head, and announces to D.J. that they gonna wrap their weapons and lash them in a tree. . . .

Clearly, the "ceremony" is something out of the "Literary Handbook Metaphor Manual," electronically banked and awaiting the proper signal. Just as obviously, the phrase is meant to trigger in the reader's mind some recollection of the "relinquishment" scene of Isaac McCaslin in Faulkner's "The Bear." The difference is that in Mailer's book the "ceremony" is as much a literary-critical exercise as it is an existential act, at least insofar as D.J. chooses to recollect it. If "the purification ceremony" exists as something one can get "straight in his head," then this alone is symptomatic of how even the effort to free oneself of waste is construed in this book as an act that partakes of that waste, that belongs, like so much else, to cultural and literary cliché.

Nor are these corrosive implications extemporized for this specific occasion only. From nearly the beginning, the trek North by the boys has been treated as something predigested. Included in the report of the experience is the kind of literary interpretation usually left to the ingenuity of academic close reading. The zest for the adventure is equaled, probably excelled, by D.J.'s zest for the literary analysis of it, along with instructions on how, when, and where to pay the needed kind of attention:

. . . what they see is a range of mountains ahead with real peaks, and they are going to go on up into them. (Ice needle peaks are crystals to capture the messages of the world.)

There! You all posed y'all ready for the next adventure in the heartland of the North, well hold your piss, Sis, we're about to embark with Tex Hyde who is, insist upon it, a most peculiar blendaroon of humanity and evil, technological know-how, pure savagery, sweet aching secret American youth, and sheer downright meanness as well as genius instincts for occult power (he's just the type to whip asses at the Black Masses) as well as being crack athlete. Such consummate bundle of high contradictions talks naturally in a flat mean ass little voice. Better hear it.

Some measure of the brilliance of Mailer's achievement in *Why Are We in Vietnam?* is that he makes us almost regret that it is such a funny book, among the comic masterpieces of American literature. It is a book that makes us yearn for what it disposes of in its jokes. It induces the wish that it were possible still to restore sincerity to the noble effort of a line of heroes stretching back from Faulkner to Emerson and Cooper: the trek to the "edge" of civilization, there to be cleansed of its contaminations.

In its honesty, however, the novel is even more pessimistic about such a gesture than is the interestingly related example of *St. Mawr.* Lawrence's landscape in that work is as savage and nonhuman in its beauty as is Mailer's. But while the literary pretension implicit in trying to take some encouragement from this landscape is sufficiently noted, the illusion that one can find there a clue to human transformation is nonetheless treated with an at least grim elation. Lawrence is able to elude the ironies of the situation much more directly than Mailer can: he rather bluntly asserts that however ludicrous the form of self-cleansing may be in this particular instance, it can still represent some more general and laudable possibilities of reawakening and renewal. "Man has to rouse himself afresh," he editorializes, "to cleanse the new accumulations of refuse. To win from the crude wild nature the victory and the power to make another start, and to cleanse behind him the century-deep deposits of layer upon layer of refuse."

Lawrence is not at all reticent about using Lou Witt's naïveté as sufficient cause for a large exhortation about "man"; Mailer refuses to arrange any comparable license for himself. D.J. has been allowed effectively to claim that he is the spokesman (which also means victim) of the electrified "mind" that takes us to Vietnam. He represents the oversoul as Univac. Since Mailer's purpose is to lend authority to the claim that D.J.

has incorporated the "mind" of a historical moment, he cannot for that very reason promote an alternative voice capable of redemptive flourishes. He has already sacrificed to D.J.'s satirization the large rhetoric which Lawrence keeps as a privilege. All he can do is try to locate in D.J. some faint, some submerged minority life left behind, as it were, from the washed-out wastes of the humanistic tradition.

Mailer pushes his luck in this novel about as far as a writer can. He creates a consciousness which is disarmingly bright, funny, weirdly attractive, if one thinks of it in terms of "character," while simultaneously making it a kind of computer bank in which is stored the fragmented consciousness of everyone else in the book. In this role D.J. is not so much a character as the medium through which passes the hundreds of identifiable voices that circulate in the nation (and in our literature) and whose final message, ending the book, is "Vietnam, hot damn."

Except for one crucial talent, as we shall see, Mailer surrenders nearly everything to the consciousness identified as D.J. He allows it to desiccate his sense of continuity with the literature of the past. He puts his own sincerities up for parody, as in D.J.'s reference to "the Awe-Dread Bombardment from Mr. Sender" and his marvelous contrast between "love" (which is "dialectic, man, back and forth, hate and sweet, leer-love, spit-tickle, bite-lick") and "corporation" (which is "DC, direct current, diehard charge, no dialectic man, just one-way street, they don't call it Washington, D.C., for nothing"). And he allows parody of himself, familiar enough in his self-interviews, to be joined to the parody of older literature, as when he refers to "shit," "Awe," and "Dread," as "that troika—that Cannibal Emperor of Nature's Psyche (this is D.J. being pontiferous, for we are contemplating emotion recollected in tranquillity back at the Dallas ass manse, RTPY—Remembrance Things Past, Yeah, you remember?"

This passage points to perhaps the most significant way in which D.J. usurps the place Mailer usually reserves for himself. D.J. is allowed to operate narratively in Mailer's own most effective mode, the one which tells us most about his peculiar relationship to the passage of time. Everything in the Chaps is reported from memory, no matter how much it seems of the present, except for the occasional notice given to the dinner party at which all the material issues from the mind of D.J. The Intro Beeps continually alert us to this: "Repeat, all you deficient heads out there and nascent electronic gropers, memory is the seed of narrative, yeah, and D.J. grassed out at a formal dinner in his momma daddy's Dallas house with Tex in white smoking jacket across the table has brought back gobs of Alaska hunt memory two years before." Or, in another example, which includes an allusion to the very pertinent "Le bateau ivre" of Rimbaud and suggests also that D.J. has laid claim even to some of Mailer's Jewish heritage, he tells us that "form is more narrative, memory being always more narrative than the tohu-bohu of the present, which is Old Testament Hebrew, cock-sucker, for chaos and void." Memory, it might be recalled, from "The Political Economy of Time," is the "mind's embodiment of form; therefore, memory, like the mind, is invariably more pure than the event. An event consists not only of forces which are opposed to one another but also forces which have no relation to the event. Whereas memory has a tendency to retain only the oppositions and the context."

D.J.'s account, then, should not be taken as either full or accurate—assuming that an account possibly could be—any more than are the writings after the event in *The Armies of the Night* or *Miami and the Siege of Chicago* or Mailer's various collections of pieces. The importance of this fact to the book is that we are to mistrust the interpretation as much as the reporting of events. The parodistic phrase "purification ceremony"—a product of Tex's mind, if we are to believe D.J., after they have spontaneously set out on the trip—should not limit or even direct our reading of their motives for the trip or their activities on it. Since we cannot even be sure that the phrase occurred to Tex, we can't be sure that the boys were, at the time, actually aware of the literary analogues to their conduct. In other words, Mailer has so contrived things—notably by the speculations in nearly all of the Intro Beeps about the falsification implicit in all narrative—that the mocking lit-crit media-packaged form given to everything in D.J.'s accelerated recollections must itself be mocked. The status even of the parody is brought into question.

For Mailer, probably for any writer of the first rank, questions about literary form are simultaneously questions about the shape of human consciousness. That is why D.J.'s teasing and the joking about the authenticity of the form of his narrative also imply that he is lying about the past or, at the very least, that he is unable to tell the truth, especially about his own feelings at certain moments. At one point it even seems as if D.J. is temporarily dismissed as the narrator:

> Fuck this voice, why is D.J. hovering on the edge of a stall? Make your point! But D.J. is hung because the events now to be recounted in his private tape being made for the private ear of the Lord (such is the hypothesis now forging ahead) are hung up on a moment of the profoundest personal disclosure, in fact, dig, little punsters out in fun land, D.J. cannot go on because he has to talk about what Tex and him were presented with there all alone up above the Arctic Circle.

Even here we can't really believe what we're being told: the style in which we're informed that D.J. "cannot go on," like the style thereafter, is identifiably D.J.'s. The one exception, a long passage at the end of Chap 10, occurs over twenty pages later: the magnificent description of the scene around the pup tent just before the two boys go to sleep, alone in the Arctic wilderness. The feelings summoned to life in this passage might well have belonged to D.J., and might in some diluted form still circulate in him, but the implication is that in telling the story two years later in Dallas he hasn't the nerve or the style or, assuming he ever had it, a full consciousness of those feelings. It is really only here, and nowhere else in the book, that he is apparently silenced—effectively enough, at least, so that the Chap which immediately follows, Chap 11, is the only one in the book without one of D.J.'s Intro Beeps. And this is the Chap in which the boys come close to a sexual joining. The surge of feeling that builds up in the passage at the end of Chap 10 and carries into Chap 11 is noticeably free of the various cants and mixed-media gags that otherwise lace every phrase in the book, even while carrying, as it must if it is to hint at existent if nearly inaccessible elements in D.J.'s consciousness, just the faintest touch of his recognizable style:

> . . . and D.J. full of iron and fire and faith was nonetheless afraid of sleep, afraid of wolves, full of beauty, afraid of sleep, full of beauty, yeah, he unashamed, for across the fire and to their side the sun was setting to the west of the pond as they looked north, setting late in the evening in remembering echo of the endless summer evening in these woods in June when darkness never came for the light never left, but it was going now, September light not fading, no, ebbing, it went in steps and starts, like going down a stair from the light to the dark, sun golden red in its purple and purple red in the black of the trees, the water was dark green and gold, a sigh came out of the night as it came on, and D.J. could have wept for a secret was near, some mystery in the secret of things—why does the odor die last and by another route?—and he knew then the meaning of trees and forest all in dominion to one another and messages across the continent on the wave of their branches up to the sorrow of the North, and great sorrow up here brought by leaves and wind some speechless electric gathering of woe, no peace in the North, not on top of the rim, and as the dark came down, a bull moose, that King Moose with antlers near to eight feet wide across all glory of spades and points, last moose of the North, came with his dewlap and his knobby knees and dumb red little eyes across the snow to lick at salt on the other side of the pond, and sunlight in the blood of its dying caught him, lit him, left him gilded red on one side as he chomped at mud and salt, clodding and wads dumping from his mouth to plop back in water, like a camel foraging in a trough, deep in content, the full new moon now up before

the sun was final and down silvering the other side of this King Moose up
to the moon silhouettes of platinum on his antlers and hide. And the
water was black, and moose dug from it and ate, and ate some more until
the sun was gone and only the moon for light and the fire of the boys
and he looked up and studied the fire some several hundred of feet away
and gave a deep caw pulling in by some resonance of this grunt a herd of
memories of animals at work and on the march and something gruff in
the sharp wounded heart of things bleeding somewhere in the night, a
sound somewhere in that voice in the North which spoke beneath all
else to Ranald Jethroe Jellicoe Jethroe and his friend Gottfried (Son of
Gutsy) "Texas" Hyde. They were alone like that with the moose still
staring at them. And then the moose turned and crossed the bowl the
other way and plodded through the moonlight along the ridges of snow,
moonlight in his antlers, gloom on his steps. And the boys slept.

A cadence that is to become more and more familiar in Mailer is
beautifully at work here. It is to be found throughout *Of a Fire on the
Moon*, with its constant telescoping of dimensions, and even more effectively in *The Armies of the Night*, in the passage about helicopters in "A
Half-Mile to Virginia," and in the fanciful flights in "Grandma with
Orange Hair," where he suggests that the poison of small-town life has
been released into the national bloodstream because "technology had
driven insanity out of the wind and out of the attic, and out of all the lost
primitive places," only to concentrate it in Vegas, pro-football, suburban
orgies, and, at last, Vietnam. The great achievement of the sentences in
these instances, and in the passage from the novel, is that they allow the
most supple possible movement back and forth between minutely observed
"journalistic" details and a panorama that includes the forces that impinge
upon and transform those details, perhaps to inconsequentiality. Thus the
moose can be seen to have "knobby knees and dumb red little eyes," even
while the "sunlight in the blood of its dying caught him, lit him, left him
gilded red . . ."

The cinematic effect of this kind of writing—which can be seen
sometimes in Hemingway, as in "Hills Like White Elephants," and even
more frequently in Faulkner—is especially right for Mailer. Before he
managed to work such sentences with the power displayed here, his need
for them was already implicit in his desire to bring various styles into the
closest syntactical and grammatical conjunction, especially when he wants
to mix obscenities with abstractions of theory. Even more, he needed
some stylistic movement that would let him find in any particular item, like
Negro jazz, manifestations of a confluence of forces. In "The White
Negro" the need was notably apparent as a defect in those places where he
was forced to conjure up reasoned arguments—as in his claim for the

possible heroism of three young hoodlums who have killed an old grocery storekeeper—where if the notion is to be promoted at all it would have to be by the power of style working to overturn rational conventions of cause and effect. And his discussion of context in the same essay, however confused, offers direct testimony that he wished consciously to blur the usual separations between an event, a participant in the event, and the context.

Each, as he sees it, is a creation of the other. The context in which a man finds himself at any given moment derives in part from the failure or success he experienced in a previous and somehow related moment. So that the context for Mailer as writer of *The Armies of the Night* was importantly affected, as we have seen, by the context of Mailer as actor, his inability as a participant in the Washington march to speak as often or as well as he would have liked. He writes as he does because he could not speak as he wanted to. Sentences of the kind being considered indicate in their very structure, that is, a writer who might have been predicted to choose, after *Why Are We in Vietnam?*, to write extraordinary spectacles. That is perhaps as good a term as any to describe *The Armies of the Night, Miami and the Siege of Chicago*, and *Of a Fire on the Moon*. We are invited to see him in these books within intricately related fields of force, and then to watch him act simultaneously as a participant, witness, and writer, who evokes in the clashes of his style a "war" among the various elements that constitute the life of the country and of the self. Interestingly enough, the situation of D.J. and Tex when they camp down for the night is very similar to Mailer's: they are at a place where messages are gathered from the whole continent, we are told, and where there is, at the same time, "no peace."

In these instances Mailer's style, very much in Faulknerian mode, keeps everything in motion; everything contends with, joins, is infused with everything else. Looking back at the passage just quoted, it might be said that Mailer's fondness for participles—"going," "fading," "settling," "silvering"—expresses his taste for actions that go on simultaneously, for a kind of bombardment of impressions, registered also in his repetitions of phrase, the echoings of sound, and the use of negatives which caution against fixing the picture in any familiar frame ("September light not fading, no, ebbing"). These habits, again as in Faulkner, are consistent with a tendency to collapse the rational insistence on distinctions between time and place, so that most get measured by the seasons, and between the presumably assigned functions of the senses, so that by a synesthesia of light and sound it can be suggested that the landscape sends out and receives signals. Nature, it would seem, has its own communications system without any need for technological assistance: it also has a memory that appears to work as well as a computer, made visible in the setting sun and audible in an animal grunt of the moose; it even expresses itself dialectically, as in the contending lights of the sun and moon on the two sides of the moose.

And yet if this landscape carries a message that the boys might possibly read, if its self-sufficiency frees it from human "shit" or from any kind of human genius in the form of technology, its beauty is wholly inhospitable to human love or tenderness or trust. No one could "relinquish" to it, as in Faulkner, and though the boys left their weapons behind, they wisely corrected a first impulse to leave everything and took along their bedroll, pup tent, food, matches, and binoculars. They are going into a landscape antithetical to human life, and Mailer chose to imagine it that way, rather than as anything even momentarily hospitable, like the forest in which Isaac McCaslin learned to give up his more easily disposable inheritance of "shit." In the scene that follows, the landscape induces in them a need for love, for joining together. But this need cannot ever be separated from the accompanying and equally induced desire for power and domination. Each wants to enter the other; each knows he would be killed somehow if he ever succeeded. So as they lie together, tensed in desire and fear, there was

> . . . murder between them under all friendship, for God was a beast, not a man, and God said, "Go out and kill—fulfill my will, go and kill," and they hung there each of them on the knife of the divide in all conflict of lust to own the other yet in fear of being killed by the other and as the hour went by and the lights shifted, something in the radiance of the North went into them, and owned their fear, some communion of telepathies and new powers, and they were twins, never to be near as lovers again, but killer brothers, owned by something, prince of darkness, lord of light, they did not know.

Their love for each other is a minority element already sickened by a homoerotic lust for masculine power. Such, in general, is Mailer's view of the possibilities of homosexual love, as in his writing about Genet in *The Prisoner of Sex*, where he proposes that the irony of homosexual practices is that the seemingly passive partner is really trying to take on the masculine resources of the man who enters him, and often succeeds in doing so. Homosexuality is doomed, in his view, by a contest between the partners for sexual identity which each could achieve only with a woman; they compete for what each of them has surrendered, and the sexual act ceases to have any life-giving dialectical energy.

There is scarcely any point in arguing, as some have, that the boys might have been saved for humanity if they had been able to make love. I doubt that the question is a real one here or in any of the other American novels where one finds similar male pairings. The imagination of possible destinies for friends and neighbors is a legitimate and sometimes irresistible pastime, but it is a wholly inappropriate concern when it comes to characters in a book. D.J. and Tex, Huck and Jim, for that matter, exist not to enact a life but to help realize a form; they exist in and for a structure of meaning wherein character is merely one contributory item. Mailer's maneuver at the end of the novel in fact demonstrates how the form of the book cannot be wholly surrendered to the form even of the governing consciousness within it. D.J. cannot himself express that possible saving remnant of human feeling within him which was apparently deadened at Brooks Range by the "crystallization" of his and Tex's mind. It is this same "crystallization" which in turn gives form to the narrative. We are at least allowed to wonder if D.J. and Tex possibly did have in them some thread of tangled humanity, and the pessimism of Mailer's view is most evident in the fact that when this humanity does come near to expressing itself, its only possible form is buggery—which Tex indulges in now and then anyway, just for the hell of it.

The Tenth of *The Presidential Papers*, entitled "Minorities," is given to a review of Genet's *The Blacks* which anticipates and helps explain the complex significance to *Why Are We in Vietnam?*—and also to Mailer's posture in it as a creator—of sexually perverse tensions, tensions of the kind found in Tex and D.J., in Rojack of *An American Dream*, and in Mailer himself. Buggery between two men is the equivalent in sexual conduct of D.J.'s literary conduct in the whole book. I am speaking, again, of D.J. not merely as a character, a Texas adolescent, but as a unit of energy, a composite mind, a medium for the way things are. In effect this whole book is about buggery. D.J. is merely unable to accept the clearest evidence of this in his lust for Tex, while Tex, being a sometime bugger anyway, brings this propensity into the "electrified mind" which is sealed as their common property. Recognizing this is important to an understanding of D.J.'s style, with its incessant jokes about buggery and the allusions to the North Pole as the hole of Satan. Another pair of travelers in Dante's Inferno, it might be remembered, also encounter the asshole of Satan: in the blooded arctic ices of the pit reserved for traitors. Mailer would know this, but his allusiveness in this case, interestingly enough, is never submitted to the destructive literary parody of D.J.

The book is about buggery because it is about the destruction of meaning, about that process of decreation which here, in its imagined sexual exercise, does not even alternate with acts of possible creation, as in the sexual exchanges between Rojack and Ruta in *An American Dream*. The now actively functioning connection in Mailer's imagination between sexuality, creativity—meaning writing—and the state of culture is what makes *Why Are We in Vietnam?* perhaps his most brilliant and certainly one of his central texts. It realizes in a style of fantastic comic energy a position he had articulated in *The Presidential Papers*:

> As cultures die, they are stricken with the mute implacable rage of that humanity strangled within them. So long as it grows, a civilization depends upon the elaboration of meaning, its health maintained by an awareness of its state; as it dies, a civilization opens itself to the fury of those betrayed by its meaning, precisely because that meaning was finally not sufficiently true to offer a life adequately large. The aesthetic act shifts from the creation of meaning to the destruction of it.
>
> So, one could argue, functions the therapy of the surrealist artist, of Dada, of Beat. Jaded, deadened, severed from our roots, dulled in leaden rage, inhabiting the center of the illness of the age, it becomes more excruciating each year for us to perform the civilized act of contributing to a collective meaning. The impulse to destroy moves like new air into a vacuum, and the art of the best hovers, stilled, all but paralyzed between the tension to create and the urge which is its opposite. How well Genet personifies the dilemma. Out of the tension of his flesh, he makes the pirouette of his art, offering meaning in order to adulterate it, until at the end we are in danger of being left with not much more than the narcissism of his style. How great a writer, how hideous a cage. As a civilization dies, it loses its biology. The homosexual, aliented from the biological chain, becomes its center.

D.J.'s mind is an instrument for the destruction of meaning, as in the inveterate punning on names and identities, and the adulteration of the literary, philosophical, psychological authorities to which the book alludes. Indeed, the implication is that the form of the book, which is also the form of D.J.'s memory, expresses the instinctive fury of a mind which feels itself betrayed by a civilization no longer able to sustain or elaborate in its language any meanings which provide a life adequately humane or large. The very effort to escape that civilization, to ventilate and cleanse the mind of its "mixed-up shit," is betrayed both by the inhospitable landscape to which the act, by this point in the twentieth century, has of necessity been restricted, and by the implicit mockery of the act in the way literary analogues to it are suggested. D.J.'s memory is doomed to scatology, and, though he dare not bugger his mate, his mind is obsessed with jokes and images of buggery, of sexual entrances that lead not to the centers of creations but to the center of waste.

The book, like Mailer's comments on Genet, proposes a connec-

tion between creativity in art and in sex that takes us to the nerve of
Mailer's sense of himself as a man and writer. "The art of the best hovers,
stilled, all but paralyzed between the tension to create and the urge which
is its opposite." It is at just such a point of near paralysis in *Why Are We in
Vietnam?* that Mailer momentarily takes over the narrative from D.J. What
then happens is an infusion of creative vitality into an imaginative
landscape dominated by frigidities of environment and of feeling. The
boys are doomed to the kind of masculinity which has none of the
dialectical vitalities so profitably at work in Mailer: of being female as
well as male, of feeling a space within where the gestations of imagination
take place, and a keen sense of the space without, which calls forth the
will and lust for public power. He had already written in his long debate
about scatology, "The Metaphysics of the Belly," that "if we wish to be
more masculine we must first satisfy something feminine in ourselves."
The homosexual urges of D.J. and Tex promise the reverse of this satisfaction. All they will produce is a competitive effort which will affirm the
mastery of an unmodified masculinity, a narcissism of masculinity which
becomes eroticized by the desire to engross the masculinity of an equally
obsessed man. They are Mailerian boxers *manqué*.

For Mailer, a masculine nature that denies the minority claims
within it of feminine feeling—which is how he might account for a
masculinized sensibility like Kate Millett's—stiffens the imagination, prevents it from encompassing even such admission of feminine inclination,
or the need of masculine support, as D.J. might have had to make in order
to recall his desires for Tex. That is why Mailer, at the appropriate point,
has to imagine these desires for him, and for the book, even if, as a result,
the book doesn't become "crystallized." Mailer's commitment to dialectics
means that he includes materials which threaten the symmetry of any
possible form. His is the art of not arriving. In this case and throughout
his work, dialectics is equivalent to imagination, and imagination evolves
from his acceptance in himself of a feminine nature. It is probable that he
associates being a writer with being a woman, and his remark in *The
Prisoner of Sex* about Henry Miller and Kate Millett, even to the feminiza-
tion of the males he alludes to ("dances," "curves") is a telling instance:
"His work dances on the line of his dialectic. But Millett hates every
evidence of the dialectic. She has a mind like a flatiron, which is to say a
totally masculine mind. A hard-hat has more curves in his head." If
writing, creativity, a personal style distinct from an imposed one, could
all be associated with femininity, then, Mailer's selection of subjects, like
war, boxing, politics, moonshots, and his own brawling activities, about

which he writes with a boyishly self-approving apology, can be taken as counter-balancing attempts to affirm his masculinity.

In some such way it is possible to understand a central contradiction in him: there is on one hand the marvelously fastidious stylist, a writer almost precious in his care for phrasing and cadence, and, on the other and seemingly at odds, the boisterous, the vulgar actor. More often than not his style will sound like Faulkner or James, like Proust or Lawrence, even while he is pushing Papa Hemingway as a model and precursor. As recently as *Cannibals and Christians* he misreads Lawrence out of what I would guess is an anxiety to appear tougher than he really is, which means that Lawrence must be made less so. Lawrence, he there claims, is so sentimental about lovers that he misses their desire to "destroy one another; lovers change one another; lovers resist the change that each gives to the other."

This is of course not what Lawrence misses. It is what he insists on. Not Lawrence but Mailer is deficient in imagining such relationships between a man and a woman. When the sexes meet in Mailer's novels it is either for frantic sexual experiences or for conferences about manners and role-playing that never significantly modify either one. When he tries to get beyond this, as in *An American Dream*, he surrounds the relationship with portents and circumstances that prevent it from ever becoming more than an alliance for some mutual escape to an imagined ordinariness never to be achieved. Perhaps the reason for this is that the conflicts that might bring about a change in the relationships between men and women actually take place only *within* the nature of all the men in his works, within his own nature. Mailer is finally the most androgynous of writers. Perhaps that is why, of what are now nineteen books, only five are novels, a form where some developed relationship between the sexes is generally called for, and the rest (except for a quite good volume of poems entitled *Deaths for the Ladies (and Other Disasters)* and the scripts for his play *The Deer Park* and his film *Maidstone*) is a species of self-reporting.

Yet for all the self-reporting what do we know about him? Very little. Next to nothing about his childhood, his schooling; very little about his love affairs, not much more about his friends or his wives. Though there are bits of incidental intelligence about drinking and drugs in *Advertisements for Myself* and about his fourth marriage in *The Armies of the Night* and *Of a Fire on the Moon*, and though we learn in *The Prisoner of Sex* that for part of one summer he kept house for six children before an old love, who was to become the mother of a seventh, arrived to rescue him, most of what we get from this presumably self-centered, egotistic, and self-revealing writer are anecdotes about his public performances.

Even these prove to be not confessions so much as self-creations after the event, presentations of a self he makes up for his own as much as for the reader's inspection.

This is not said critically but rather to suggest that Mailer's genius is excited by those very elements in him and in the nation which prevent the solidification of either one. Solidification, or what D.J. calls "crystallization," is not the function of Mailer's art and is instead ascribed to those forces in contemporary civilization to which his art opposes itself. With what seems at times obtuseness, he chooses to put his stress of appreciation on those aspects of a subject which anyone working in the rationalist, humanist, liberal tradition would generally choose to ignore or condemn. He is, therefore, necessarily committed to the democratic principle that all parts of any subject are at least initially equal. Like Glenn Gould playing Bach or Beethoven, Mailer decides that what everyone else treats as a subordinate sound can be treated as a major one. This significantly complicates the responses called forth by some of the characters in his later work. Thus, while D.J. and Tex are agents of some horrid, proliferating power that propels America into Vietnam, they are also in another sense "good." They are emphatically and unapologetically what they are; they do what they do well, and it is possible in Mailer to do anything well, to perform well even in the act of murder.

For that reason the obscenity in *Why Are We in Vietnam?* is not a symptom of what is the matter with D.J. Instead, it is a clue to what might possibly be "good" about him. In "An Evening with Jackie Kennedy, or, the Wild West of the East," Mailer proposed to tell her "that the obscene had a right to exist in the novel," a desire typical of his wish to bring apparently uncongenial ideas into situations designed to exclude them. As "queen of the arts" she would understand, he likes to think, that it was "the purpose of culture finally to enrich all the psyche, not just part of us" because "Art in all its manifestations . . . including the rude, the obscene, and the unsayable . . . was as essential to the nation as technology." Elsewhere he makes the point that an artist who does not bring into art those qualities which might disrupt formal coherence is guilty of doing to art, and to culture, what Eisenhower did to politics during what were for Mailer the worst years of his time in America: "He did not divide the nation as a hero might (with a dramatic dialogue as a result); he merely excluded one part of the nation from the other. The result was an alienation of the best minds and bravest impulses from the faltering history which was made."

Mailer will exclude nothing in the interests of formal arrangements. This has led to the most consistent misunderstanding of his work:

the failure to grasp why he is given to obscenity and violence. In "An Impolite Interview" with Paul Krassner of *The Realist*, he makes his position on these matters clear enough, but in such a way as perhaps only further to confuse his detractors. Alluding to an Italian bombardier who reported that the bombs bursting over an Ethiopian village were beautiful, he writes that while he does not necessarily disapprove of violence in a man or a woman, "what I still disapprove of is *inhuman* violence," which is of course the kind infused into D.J. and Tex at Brooks Range.

> I disapprove of bombing a city. I disapprove of the kind of man who will derive aesthetic satisfaction from the fact that an Ethiopian village looks like a red rose at the moment the bombs are exploding. I won't disapprove of the act of perception which witnesses that: I think that act of perception is—I'm going to use the word again—noble.
>
> What I'm getting at is: a native village is bombed, and the bombs happen to be beautiful when they land; in fact it would be odd if all that sudden destruction did not liberate some beauty. The form a bomb takes in its explosion may be in part a picture of the potentialities it destroyed. So let us accept the idea that the bomb is beautiful.
>
> If so, any liberal who decries the act of bombing is totalitarian if he doesn't admit as well that the bombs were indeed beautiful.
>
> Because the moment we tell something that's untrue, it does not matter how pure our motives may be—the moment we start mothering mankind and decide that one truth is good for them to hear and another is not so good, because while we can understand, those poor ignorant unfortunates cannot—then what are we doing, we're depriving the minds of others of knowledge which may be essential.
>
> Think of a young pilot who comes along later, some young pilot who goes out on a mission and isn't prepared for the fact that a bombing might be beautiful; he could conceivably be an idealist, there were some in the war against Fascism. If the pilot is totally unprepared he might never get over the fact that he was particularly thrilled by the beauty of that bomb.
>
> But if our culture had been large enough to say that Ciano's son-in-law not only found that bomb beautiful, but that indeed this act of perception was *not* what was wrong; the evil was to think that this beauty was worth the lot of living helpless people who were wiped out broadside. Obviously whenever there's destruction, there's going to be beauty implicit in it.

Truth for Mailer is equivalent to the acceptance, with respect to any subject, of such a range of diverse feelings that some seem to cancel or mutilate the others, and there are times when his commitment to truth cannot escape a perverse exaltation of the submerged at the expense of the humanly self-evident. While he is clearly aware of this danger, he will not allow the presumed exigencies of the humanly self-evident, much less the exigencies of literary form or of logic, to dictate what he puts in or leaves out. This is what distinguishes him from his contemporaries in fiction. However different, they all find it necessary at some point to suppress what I have called the minority within: those feelings, expressions, possibilities in the material that are perhaps incommensurate with the effect being striven for. Mailer's honesty in this is rather more strenuous and altogether more expensive than theirs.

RANDALL H. WALDRON

The Naked, the Dead, and the Machine

In 1914 T. E. Hulme predicted with accuracy that now seems akin to prophecy that twentieth-century art was moving toward the creation of forms "associated in our minds with the idea of machinery"; toward the time when a sculptor would prefer to organic, natural forms "the hard clean surface of a piston rod." Fifteen years later Hart Crane, who dubbed himself "the Pindar of the Machine Age," and whose poem *The Bridge* has been termed "the most extraordinary example of the psychological impact of mechanization of modern poetry," called for the poet to embrace the world of the machine, "for unless poetry can absorb the machine, i.e., acclimatize it as naturally and casually as trees, cattle, galleons, castles, and all other associations of the past, then poetry has failed of its full contemporary function." And Crane's friend and editor Waldo Frank, also writing in 1929, echoes the poet's call for the "acclimatization" of the machine, attributing its growing capacity to pervade and dominate human experience to "a negative reflex of man's incapacity as yet to create a Whole in modern terms and to assimilate the machine as a means and a symbol within it."

But in spite of such admonitions to absorb mechanization and to recognize its rightful and defining place in life and literature; even in spite of the degree to which Hulme's prediction about the influence of machine forms on art has been realized, American writers have for the most part resisted the overtures of the machine. The Dynamo and the Virgin

From *PMLA* 1, vol. 87 (January 1972). Copyright © 1972 by The Modern Language Association of America.

continues as a central and informing metaphor for the "tragic doubleness" in modern history, and the dominant tone of the century's literary treatments of the machine remains one of tension. This tension is particularly evident in the novel.

Norris' Magnus, associated with the life force as symbolized by the wheat, battles the machine in the form of the railroads. Nearly all of Dreiser's major characters, from Carrie to Clyde—and especially Cooperwood, victimized by his inordinate hunger for big business—are studies of the individual and his natural, biological drives in contest with the oppressive forces of industrial, financially and materially oriented society. Sherwood Anderson's Hugh McVey, though esthetically in tune with the machines he invents, is helplessly caught up in the shifting values of the new industrial Midwest. Steinbeck's Joad family, driven from their land by a tractor owned by big financial interests, are relentlessly harassed by the machine brutally symbolized in the broken-down automobiles that are the hallmark of their pathetic migration. Robert Jordan and his band of Spanish guerrillas battle planes and armored vehicles with horses, handguns, and homemade bombs. Ike McCaslin lives to see his beloved wilderness transformed into a land of flashing neon, speeding automobiles, sheet iron, and hooting locomotives. In all of these the basic conflict between man and machine is presented as a central dilemma of modern life.

From the earliest times, Lewis Mumford points out, "war has been perhaps the chief propagator of the machine." It is in war that mechanization—and its associate forces of industrialism and statism—reach their most dramatic ascendancy and make themselves felt most immediately. Thus it is in war novels that the man-machine conflict finds its most intense and direct expression. In *World War I and the American Novel* Stanley Cooperman gives considerable attention to the conflict as it manifests itself in the novels of the first war. He relates the books of Cummings, Dos Passos, Hemingway, Faulkner, and others to the "impact" of machine warfare on a generation that, having been comfortably and naïvely optimistic about the humanizing and liberating miracles of technology, was profoundly shocked to discover what a horrible monster the machine could be. In the closing pages of his study Cooperman distinguishes between the novels he has examined and those written during and after the second war. By the time of World War II, he contends, the machine had been thoroughly assimilated into our culture. As opposed to the shock effect of mechanized warfare as he describes it in relation to the violently antiwar, antimachine novels of the twenties, the generation of the forties was so reconciled to machine civilization that such shock was no longer possible. What had been a "*dance-macabre* absurdity" at the Marne and Verdun had become a "universal situation" in which the writer's focus was not on the machine itself but on the "drama of human values" just as it might be examined in "the drawing room or office, industrial plant or courtroom."

But a close examination reveals in many American World War II novels a very definite focus on the machine and a violent protest against it. Underlying the lighthearted story of John Hersey's *A Bell for Adano* (1944), the tension between mechanism and humanism is symbolized by the conflict between General Marvin's armored cars, tanks, and guns and the painted wooden carts of the Italian villagers. In Frederic Prokosch's *Age of Thunder* (1945) the essentially quiet, leisurely movement of a group of people in a rural landscape is regularly interrupted by sudden, screaming air attacks that emphasize the overwhelming noise, violence, and destructiveness of the most horrible of war machines. A theme similar to Hersey's in *A Bell for Adano* helps to unify the series of sketches that make up John Horn Burns's *The Gallery* (1947), as the time-honored dignity of European culture is contrasted to the ugliness and vulgarity of machine-oriented Americans—"automatons from the world's greatest factory." In James Jones's *From Here to Eternity* (1951) the army is a metaphor for the bureaucratic, impersonal systems of twentieth-century industrial and political institutions, as those systems conflict with the efforts of the three major characters to maintain their individual integrity. The central conflict in Hersey's *The War Lover* (1959) is between the humanist Boman and a twisted hero of the machine, pilot Buzz Marrow, who confuses strength, masculinity, even sexual potency with flying his airplane. The bizarre world of Joseph Heller's *Catch-22* (1961), in spite of its hilarious absurdity, is a brutal exposé of machine society carried to its most frightening extreme—an Orwellian nightmare peopled by totally amoral creatures, in which absolute power is vested in the state through military, financial, and industrial control. The crucial point of Jones's second war novel, *The Thin Red Line* (1962), is precisely that the individual has been swallowed up by the machine in the form of the only main "character," the ominously personified "C-for-Charlie Company."

Each of these writers envisions a world in which not only life and dignity, but human moral, spiritual, and rational processes are opposed by unreasoning forces of anonymous brute mechanism. And they each attempt to come to grips in their art with the problems posed by such a world. They draw on the substance and language of the machine world itself for themes, characters, structures, rhythms, imagery, and symbolism from which to forge a new set of forms and metaphors capable of defining the condition of man threatened by what Frederick Hoffman has called "the extravagant and irrational demonstrations of pure force."

This informing influence of the machine can nowhere be studied with greater interest or reward than in Norman Mailer's *The Naked and the Dead*. To reread *The Naked and the Dead* in these terms is important on two counts. First, it views the book in a light that has not been trained on it before, and that illuminates and enriches our understanding of it as a novel. Second, it underlines and clarifies the function of the machine as a controlling metaphor in World War II novels by demonstrating the organic importance of that metaphor in the first really significant, probably the best, and certainly the most imitated of those novels.

II

The Naked and the Dead has been interpreted in a number of ways. Mailer himself has maintained that it is an ultimately hopeful "parable about the movement of man through history." Admitting that it sees man as corrupt and confused to the point of helplessness, he insists that it also finds that "there are limits beyond which he cannot be pushed, and it finds that even in his corruption and sickness there are yearnings for a better world." Most readers have denied these positive elements, making the book a pessimistic, bleak, and hopeless account of men defeated before they start by all sorts of deterministic forces. Some see it as a roughly existential document in which the horror and absurdity of war are presented as normal in the context of the human condition at large, which is itself essentially absurd. Still others—perhaps taking Mailer at his word—put it in the class of novels in which war is horrible enough, but still an educational, broadening experience in which the soul is tested and purged by adversity, and positive values triumph. Each of these interpretations is defensible; the book is by no means clear in its thematic conclusions.

The central conflict in *The Naked and the Dead* is between the mechanistic forces of "the system" and the will to individual integrity. Commanding General Cummings, brilliant and ruthless evangel of fascist power and control, and iron-handed, hard-nosed Sergeant Croft personify the machine. Opposing them in the attempt to maintain personal dignity and identity are Cummings' confused young aide, Lieutenant Hearn, and Private Valsen, rebellious member of Croft's platoon. Mailer fails to bring this conflict to any satisfying resolution: at the novel's end Hearn is dead and Valsen's stubborn pride defeated, but likewise Croft is beaten and humiliated and Cummings' personal ambitions thwarted. But while the resolution of the conflict may be ambiguous, the nature of it is not. The principal burden of the novel is to explore the condition of man struggling against the depersonalizing forces of modern society: the forces of "the machine." Structure, character, imagery, and symbolism all contribute to the formation of a sustained and pervasive metaphor in which war, army, and battle stand as a complex of figures for the machine age.

The main structural device of alternation between sections dealing with action on the island and the "Time Machine" flashbacks into the past lives of the characters places them in the context of the twentieth century: pressured, driven, molded by forces associated in general with modern industrialism and often specifically mechanistic. Cummings, apotheosizer of the machine, is the son of a prototype American financier-industrialist "(named [Cyrus] after the older McCormick)" and a direct product of the heartland of American industrialism, the Midwest just after the turn of the century. His father teaches him a "dog-eat-dog" business and industrial ethic based on hate and fear, which he later incorporates with his military ambition to form the fascistic ideology he expounds to Hearn on the island. Hearn, also the scion of a factory man, escapes from the crude materialism of his father and the family business into the confused humanism that makes him the foil for Cummings in the island sections. Aboard ship on his way to the Pacific, he agonizes over the seemingly futile condition of the young in mechanized America:

> Somewhere in America now were the cities, and the refuse sitting on the steps, the electric lights and the obeisance to them.
>   (All the frenetic schemings, the cigar smoke, the coke smoke, the passion for movement like an ant nest suddenly jarred. How do you conceive your own death in all the marble vaults, the brick ridges and the furnaces that lead to the market place?)

> And all the bright young people of his youth had butted their heads, smashed against things until they got weaker and the things still stood.
>   A bunch of dispossessed . . . from the raucous stricken bosom of America.
>   (This and all subsequent references to The Naked and the Dead are to the Rinehart Edition, New York and Toronto, 1948, 352–53.)

The choleric Boston tough guy Gallegher is trapped in civilian life between the drab, boiled potato routine of a city worker's stereotyped existence and a pathetically romantic idealism in which he dreams of heroism:

> What's in it in for a guy?
>   Work tomorrow.

(He would defend the lady in the lavender dress with his sword.)
He fell asleep in the chair, and in the morning he had a cold.
(p. 279)

Goldstein is caught in the facile and mediocre conformity of the material-ist lower middle class. On his twenty-five-dollar welder's salary, he and his wife settle down in their three-room flat, full of cheap furniture, calendar pictures, and tacky bric-a-brac, their infrequent marital storms "buried in the avalanche of pleasant and monotonous trivia that makes up their life" (p. 489). Brown is the typical industrial salesman, wooing customers on the golf course, in nightclubs, and in brothels, hating the system that forces him to "produce 'cause that's what you gotta pay off on" (p. 559). Red Valsen takes to the hobo's road to escape the very real and present threat of the machine, which, with smothering Dantesque horror, traps him in a mechanistic inferno:

> By the time he is fourteen he is able to use a drill. Good money for a kid, but down in the shafts, at the extreme end of the tunnel there isn't room to stand. Even a kid works in a crouch, his feet stumbling in the refuse of the ore that has been left from filling the last car. It's hot, of course, and damp, and the lights from their helmets are lost quickly in the black corridors. The drill is extremely heavy and a boy has to hold the butt against his chest and clutch the handles with all his strength as the bit vibrates into the rock. . . . Red has ten hours a day, six days a week. In the wintertime he can see the sky on Sundays.
>   Puberty in the coal dust.
> (pp. 222–23)

By abruptly shifting again and again from the "raucous stricken bosom of America" back to the island, and the army which is only more intensely mechanistic, the structural pattern keeps the machine metaphor con-stantly to the fore. The novel is not simply about men in mechanized war, but men in mechanized society, the epitome of which is war.

In addition to basic structure, the novel's two primary symbols, the mountain and the army, emphasize the tensions of the man-machine dichotomy by providing a broader, more fundamental, intimately related conflict against which those tensions are projected. That is, the efforts of Hearn and Valsen to preserve their human integrity by resisting the mechanistic intimidations of Cummings and Croft are paralleled by the broader resistance of nature to the threat of violation by the machine. It is important that the Japanese play a very insignificant role as the enemy in the Anopopei campaign. The real objective of the battle—prosecuted mainly by Cummings and Croft—is to utilize the men and machines they command in order to conquer the island. The mountain, towering with "new purple robes at its feet" above the dense jungle, symbolizes the regal force and natural formidability of the uncorrupted organic world. The army machine is pitted against the mountain and its jungle in a conflict that is both literal and symbolic. Cummings' attempts to penetrate the jungle are resisted by the most elemental forces of nature, the machine's primal opponent: rain that batters down the bivouacs and washes away the roads, and the hyper-organic barrier of the jungle itself, "damp and rife and hot," and alive with "the rapt absorbed sounds of vegetation growing." "No army," Mailer adds to secure the point, "could live or move in it" (p. 45). Croft's sadistic drive to cross the mountain with his patrol is equally thwarted by opposing forces of nature: the numbing, bruising river; the impenetrable jungle; then the mountain itself, huge and treacherous; and finally, with brutal comic irony, the swarm of hornets that turn the machine's grim assault on Mt. Anaka into Mack Sennett farce.

Thus the primary structural and symbolic quality of *The Naked and the Dead* is informed by the conflict between man (and the natural forces with which he is associated) and the machine. Within this broad and pervasive metaphorical environment the conflict comes most vividly to life in the persons of the four major characters. Much of the dramatic and ironic power of the novel comes from its double view of the battle for Anopopei island. We see the campaign from afar as it is directed by General Cummings, and, with the ironic shock of abstraction converted to immediate reality, how it is carried out in the field. This double view also reveals that another battle—the one between man and machine—is raging both in Cummings' tent and in Sergeant Croft's platoon.

This conflict as it functions on the officer level between Cummings and Hearn is complicated by ambiguities and complexities in each of them. The General's latently homosexual attitude toward Hearn is at once cruel and tender, and Hearn discovers in himself some of the same lust for power and control that he hates in his ruthless superior. Apart from these provocative ambiguities, however, the tension between Cummings as a character representing the machine system and Hearn as a man acting in desperate opposition to it is abundantly clear. As I have already pointed out, while Cummings is the perfected product of an industrial-materialist background, Hearn is a frustrated *escapee* from just such a heritage, bewildered and confused by the plight of his generation, lost in the machine context. As an aide to Cummings, Hearn is thrown into contention with the General that marks him as the book's chief representative of the anti-machine. He counters Cummings' repeated insistence on the necessity of individual subservience to the machine with arguments in defense of "the continual occurrence and re-forming of certain great ethical ideas" (p. 177). That these arguments are weak and stammering in comparison with Cummings' brutally rigorous theories helps to sustain the consistent theme of the individual smothered by overwhelming forces of the system. In the tense climax of their conflict, Hearn leaves a cigarette on the General's tent floor in an act of wildly courageous defiance of that system. But the result is that Cummings, not satisfied with forcing the mutineer to his knees by an exercise of power vested in hate and fear, cannot tolerate the threat to that power that Hearn now represents for him. Hearn is ordered to the patrol and to his death.

Cummings himself is in many ways like a machine. Coldly efficient and physically inexhaustible, he works for hours directing the opening of the campaign "without taking a halt, indeed without referring once to a map, or pausing for a decision. . . . It had been a remarkable performance. His concentration had been almost fantastic" (p. 77). Studying a host of subjects as a young officer, "he absorbs it all with the fantastic powers of memory and assimilation he can exhibit at times, absorbs it and immediately transmutes it into something else" (p. 420). Such mental powers, so reminiscent of a computer, clearly point to Cummings' function as a machine-like, other-than-human character. The suggestion takes on more weight in a passage describing his quarters: "Wherever he was . . . he never seemed to live in a place. The tent was so austere. The cot looked unslept in, the desk was bare again, and the third and unoccupied chair rested at perfect right angles to the larger of the two foot lockers. The tent floor was bare and clean, unmarred by mud. The light of the Coleman lantern threw long diagonals of light and shadow across all the rectangular objects of the tent, so that it looked like an abstract painting" (p. 172). Cummings is different from other men, who get things dirty and rumple the blankets and bring mud in on their feet; he leaves no human tracks.

In this barren, sterile, angular tent, Cummings reveals the broader, more abstract manifestations of his machine mentality in the lectures on social, political, and military philosophy that he delivers to Hearn. It is a philosophy based on manipulation of the masses through power maintained, as he maintains his over the division, by hate and fear: "The Army," which he considers as a model for future society, "functions best when you're frightened of the man above you, and contemptuous of your subordinates" (p. 176). And it is specifically a philosophy for the mechanized world: "The machine techniques of this century demand consolidation, and with that you've got to have fear, because the majority of men must be subservient to the machine, and it's not a business they instinctively enjoy" (p. 177).

Cummings' role as a product of and symbol for the machine becomes most explicit and effective in a moment when he comes into intimate contact with the actual machines of his division. Firing one of the big guns himself, he experiences a kind of mechanistic orgasm, from anticipation, to climax, to detumescence:

> He realized the tenseness with which he had been waiting for the shell to land by the weak absorptive relief that washed through his body. All his senses felt gratified, exhausted. The war, or rather, *war*, was odd . . . and yet there was a naked quivering heart to it which involved you deeply when you were thrust into it. All the deep dark urges of man, the sacrifices on the hilltop, and the churning lusts of the night and sleep, weren't all of them contained in the shattering screaming burst of a shell, the man-made thunder and light? . . . In the night, at that moment, he felt such power that it was beyond joy; he was calm and sober.
>
> (pp. 566–67)

Moved and inspired by this orgasmic encounter with the guns, the General makes entries in his journal that continue the equation of the sexual with the mechanical: "The phallus-shell that rides through a shining vagina of steel, soars through the sky, and then ignites into the earth. The earth as the poet's image of womb-mother, I suppose" (p. 568). He goes on to liken other machines to animals—the tank and truck are like "buck and rhinoceri"—but most significantly, he sees men as machines: "And for the obverse, in battle, men are closer to machines than humans. A plausible acceptable thesis. Battle is an organization of thousands of man-machines who dart with governing habits across a field, sweat like a radiator in the sun, shiver and become stiff like a piece of metal in the rain. We are not so discrete from the machine any longer, I detect it in my thinking." Then with pointed dramatic irony: "The nations whose leaders strive for Godhead apotheosize the machine. I wonder if this applies to me" (p. 569).

Cummings is a man so imbued with the machine, its language, its power, its value, that he not only defends it as the instrument of military and political control, but has allowed it to penetrate to the very depths of his being. It is his aphrodisiac; the object of his lust and passion. He confounds its forces with those of life and regeneration, its objects with human beings. Thus Cummings' function as symbolic character has crucial implications for the central theme of the novel: that the machine is capable of extending its domination to the most fundamental levels of man's existence; of becoming a threat to his very nature and to his humanity.

The conflict between man and machine is joined on the enlisted level in the running battle of wills between Sergeant Croft and Red Valsen. In physical appearance and temperament each personifies the force he represents. Never smiling, "made of iron," and reputed to have no nerves, Croft is almost like a robot man: "His narrow triangular face was utterly without expression . . . and there seemed nothing wasted in his hard small jaw, gaunt firm cheeks and straight short nose. His thin black hair had indigo glints in it" (p. 10). Whereas Croft is thus cold, machine-like, the color of gun-metal, Valsen, whose stubborn resistance to the Sergeant's dehumanizing tactics is symbolically like the jungle's resistance to the machine, is markedly sanguine, alive, organic. Red-haired, florid, and freckled, he has "a large blob of a nose and a long low-slung jaw," and he laughs readily, "his rough voice braying out with a contemptuous inviolate mirth" (p. 12). As this physical and temperamental contrast reflects, the two are natural enemies, Croft brutally demanding meek obedience and Valsen constitutionally opposed to being controlled.

The contention between them, which begins very early in the book when they quarrel over a minor point of discipline and ends in their dramatic encounter on the mountain when Red is finally broken, parallels the contention between Cummings and Hearn. Valsen, who like Hearn is an escapee from the machine, also like him finds in that escape a fragmented, unsettled, and lonely life. On the island he pits the only thing that life has left him—his jealously guarded individuality—against Croft's authority in an opposition that mirrors Hearn's challenge of Cummings. The likenesses between Croft and Cummings that mark them as co-machine characters are many and sometimes subtle. While Cummings learns a mechanistic, industrialist philosophy from his father, Croft learns from his to love the guns that he uses, like the General, with strange masculine excitement. While Cummings confounds power and violence with his sexual virility and "fights out battles" on his wife's body, Croft, making love to his wife, boasts "Ah'm jus' an old fuggin machine. (Crack . . . that . . . whip! Crack . . . that . . . WHIP!)" (p. 162). While Cummings, at the moment when he discovers Hearn's revolt against his power, feels that "if he had been holding an animal in his hands at that instant he would have strangled it" (p. 318), Croft, at the peak of his wild demonstration of power on the mountain, crushes a bird in his hand. While Cummings formulates theories about making men subservient to the machine, Croft, running the platoon by hate and fear, translates those theories into everyday practice.

Croft's function as representative of machine forces and counterpart to Cummings is consummated in the novel's final section when he becomes a surrogate for the General by assuming the role of enemy to

Hearn. Cummings had assigned the Lieutenant to the patrol because he threatened the power of the machine; now Croft deliberately leads him to his death because his humane approach to leadership again threatens that power. The quickened dramatic intensity of this final section is primarily the intensity of Croft's mad drive to conquer the mountain. His compulsion to force the platoon to his will as the instruments of this mania is parallel to Cummings' desire to make the division the instrument of his own larger conquest. The movement up the mountain is accompanied by the progressive submergence of Croft's humanity, which deserts him completely when he crushes the bird in his fist, prefiguring his virtual murder of Hearn the next day. Thus the rifle that he levels at Valsen in their final climactic standoff is no better symbol for the destructive power of the machine than he; it is a confrontation between the machine incarnate and the individual man in a last abortive act of rebellion against it. As Hearn, in stooping to pick up the cigarette from the General's floor, had submitted to the combined pressures of Cummings' will and the threat of military punishment, Red surrenders to the force of Croft's will and the threat of his rifle.

But as Cummings' obsessive lust for personal victory is frustrated by the almost accidental winning of the campaign while he is absent, now Croft's last short climb to the peak is thwarted in a most unexpected form, the swarm of hornets.

Again, the conclusion of *The Naked and the Dead* and its total meaning are unclear. The failure of Cummings' and Croft's designs would seem to indicate the failure of the machine to work its will upon man and nature, and to justify reading the novel as a "parable" of man's refusal to be dehumanized by the forces of mechanized society. Yet Hearn's death and Valsen's shattering humiliation clearly dramatize the defeat of man by the machine. And the final scenes leave the definite impression of man lost, helpless, passive in the grip of the anonymity and meaninglessness of modern life. In the boat returning to camp the men discover that the campaign has been easily won while they were gone, that all their suffering has been for nothing, and that they are going back to the same old deadening routine. In this context the song they feebly sing to cheer themselves takes on a bitterly ironic significance: "Roll me over / In the clover. / Roll me over, / Lay me down / And do it again" (p. 707). The final thoughts of Red Valsen, beaten representative of the anti-machine, seem best to capture the concluding mood: "You carried it alone as long as you could, and then you weren't strong enough to take it any longer. You kept fighting everything, and everything broke you down, until in the end you were just a little goddam bolt holding on and squealing when the machine went too fast" (pp. 703–04). And they also sound a last clear note in evidence for the informing nature of the man-machine metaphor in the most influential American novel of World War II.

ROBERT MERRILL

"The Armies of the Night"

Critical discussions of Norman Mailer have a way of avoiding the questions we usually ask of a serious writer. Almost invariably there is much talk about Mailer the public personality and Mailer the would-be philosopher, but very little on the aesthetic value of his individual works. This is true even when the work in question is judged to be successful. Witness the reception of *The Armies of the Night* (1968), Mailer's account of the 1967 March on the Pentagon. Even Mailer's most hostile critics were willing to acknowledge that *Armies* was a work of great importance, his one book that would almost surely last. But Mailer's friends and foes alike were reluctant to examine the work itself to explain his achievement. There was praise for Mailer's ironic self-portrait and speculation on the emerging form of the "nonfiction novel," but no one was very eager to characterize the actual structure of *Armies*. I don't think the problem is academic. Here we have a book which comes to us in two radically different parts, one disguised as a "novel," the other as a "history." What is the relationship between the two parts? If *Armies* is a work of real distinction—if it is more than a "report" on Mailer's role in a peace demonstration—then surely something must be made of its unusual narrative structure.

I am suggesting that we should begin to look at Mailer's books with the close attention we reserve for such contemporaries as Saul Bellow and Bernard Malamud. Unless we do so, we will never do justice to Mailer's *artistic* achievement. Because *Armies* is so central to that achievement, we

From *Illinois Quarterly* 1, vol. 37 (September 1974). Copyright © 1974 by Illinois State University.

might well begin by trying to answer the questions about its structure which I have raised.

As I have suggested, the structure of *Armies* is unique. Mailer divides his book into two sections, the first devoted to an account of his own actions during the March on the Pentagon, the second to a general history of the event. Analysis of *Armies* must begin with the question of how Books One and Two are related. Ultimately, I hope to show that Book One is an elaborate preparation for Book Two, Mailer's presentation of the true *raison d'etre* of *Armies*: his "discovery of what the March on the Pentagon had finally meant" (Norman Mailer, *The Armies of the Night*. New York: The New American Library, 1968, p. 216. Future references to *Armies* will be incorporated into the text). First, however, we must see how Mailer came to this "discovery." This is rendered for us in Book One, where Mailer introduces his "comic hero" (p. 53). He will refer to him later as "a simple of a hero" (p. 215). Readers who come to Mailer's book by way of his legend as a self-advertising egomaniac must be puzzled to learn that Mailer is here laughing at Norman Mailer.

Mailer's decision to write about himself in the third person is oddly reminiscent of *The Education of Henry Adams*. While a full-scale comparison. of *Armies* and *Education* would be absurd, the similarities are interesting. D. W. Brogan has summarized *Education* in this fashion: "It is indeed, on the surface, the story of one who failed because, trained to be at home in Franklin's world, he had to live in a world transformed by the new science and the new technology." Mailer's readers will recall his obsession with the evils of technology, his increasing conservatism as he confronts the modern technocracy. In much of his writing (*Cannibals and Christians*, for example), Mailer rivals Adams as a pessimistic analyst of the machine age. In *Armies*, Mailer's Pentagon is as much a symbol for this age as the dynamo was for Adams. I don't want to push this comparison too far—Henry Adams and Norman Mailer will not seem every reader's idea of soul brothers—but the likeness does suggest Mailer's increasingly conservative image of himself, rendered most fully in *Armies*. It also suggests the seeming objectivity of this image, achieved partly by use of the distancing third person, partly by an exceedingly scrupulous—and Adams-like—inquiry into the author's personality.

Mailer's baroque personality is the figure in the carpet so far as *Armies* is concerned. And this personality is baroque—as baroque as Mailer's description of it:

> Now Mailer was often brusque himself, famous for that, but the architec-
> ture of his personality bore resemblance to some provincial cathedral
> which warring orders of the church might have designed separately over

several centuries, the particular cathedral falling into the hands of one architect, then his enemy. (Mailer had not been married four times for nothing.)

(p. 17)

Indeed, Mailer is fairly merciless in pointing up his own mistakes and unworthy feelings. He tries always to view himself as others do, no matter how unflattering the result. He can admit that he is "much too vain" to wear eyeglasses before professional photographers (p. 106); he can acknowledge the "hot anger" he feels because Robert Lowell is loved and he is not (p. 45); he can note his desire for a hasty arrest at the Pentagon in order to return to New York for a dinner party (p. 118–19); he can characterize some of his actions in jail as those of a "mountebank" (p. 173).

Yet our comic hero is not so much unlikable as he is contradictory. He is a "notable," a famous writer worthy of being petitioned to lend his name to the antiwar demonstrations; yet he is capable of beliefs like the following: "He had the idea—it was undeniably over-simple—that if you spent too much time on the phone in the evening you destroyed some kind of creativity for the dawn" (p. 4). He is "a snob of the worst sort" (p. 14) and captive to a "wild man" in himself, referred to rather tolerantly as "The Beast" (p. 30); yet he is a loving, even sentimental, husband and father (pp. 166–70); he is even a patriot of the first rank (pp. 47, 113). Once dedicated to revolutionary socialism, he is at heart a *grand conservateur* (p. 18). Mailer's many contradictions are best illustrated by his current political position: he is a Left Conservative (p. 124). During his mayoral campaign of 1969, Mailer was fond of saying that he was running further to the Left and further to the Right than any of the other candidates. In *Armies*, too, Mailer can be seen running in many directions at once.

But in Book One Mailer does not expose randomly the many fine and ugly features of his character. Book One traces an extremely important moment in the history of this complex personality, as Mailer's divided self achieves at least temporary wholeness during the March on the Pentagon. Later, we will see that this account is crucial to Mailer's interpretation of the March. For the moment, it is enough to remark that the structure of Book One corresponds to the stages of Mailer's spiritual experience.

Mailer's less endearing features are naturally emphasized early in Book One, for here we encounter that side of his personality which will be transcended in the course of the March. Here we are introduced to Mailer's theory of evening telephone calls, his "virtual" conservatism on the subject of drugs (p. 5) and his "neo-Victorianism" on the subject of sex (p. 24). Here we observe his very reluctant acceptance of Mitchell Goodman's invitation to attend the antiwar demonstrations in Washington. Our hero is not very heroic in his first appearance. He is shown as more concerned about editing his latest movie and attending his Saturday night dinner engagement than with actively protesting the war in Vietnam. For Mailer, such protests are "idiot mass manifestations" (p. 18). Mailer's portrait of himself as a touchy and incongruous "revolutionary-for-a-weekend" is confirmed by his distaste for the "innocent" young girls and liberal academics who surround him at the buffet he attends his first night in Washington (pp. 13–16). His masterless performance as Master of Ceremonies at the ensuing rally climaxes the portrayal of our much-flawed hero on the eve of the demonstrations (pp. 28–52).

But if Mailer begins *Armies* by revealing the more comical aspects of his character, he does so in full confidence that Book One as a whole will place them in an artful and not unappealing perspective. In fact, the rest of Book One records Mailer's conversion to the cause he has ostensibly come to Washington to support. Part II of Book One depicts his shift from apathy to involvement, as Mailer is variously impressed by a number of demonstrators who don't conform to his stereotype of the ineffectual "liberal academic": by the students representing different chapters of Resist (pp. 61–63); by William Sloane Coffin, Jr., Chaplain at Yale (pp. 66–67); by Robert Lowell as the poet addresses the demonstrators at the Department of Justice. Lowell has figured in the events of Part I, where Mailer offers a cool account of Lowell's motives and general character. Now Mailer concedes that "all flaws considered, Lowell was still a fine, good, and honorable man, and Norman Mailer was happy to be linked in a cause with him" (p. 74). Unmistakably, as this first day of protest nears its end, Mailer has begun to join the "cause" himself. He even speaks to the demonstrators, advising that perhaps the time had come "when Americans, many Americans, would have to face the possibility of going to jail for their ideas" (p. 79). It is after this speech, after this day of antiwar activities, that Mailer first commits himself to staying for the March on the Pentagon.

As Saturday arrives (Part III), it is clear that Mailer has assimilated Friday's lessons. No longer does he think of the protest as "idiot mass manifestations." Now as later he believes that the March is "that first major battle of a war which may go on for twenty years"; he even entertains the idea "that in fifty years the day may loom in our history as large as the ghosts of the Union dead" (p. 88). Mailer is all but liberated by the prospect of leading his newly-discovered "troops," the hippies and other young people who are a majority of the demonstrators (he is to be their general, of course). Assured that he is engaged in a noble work and capable of performing his part without fear (p. 113), subsequently "lifted" into a sense of "comradeship" by the tribalistic music of the Fugs (p. 125), Mailer gives himself up to the spirit of the protest by "transgressing" a police line and getting arrested (pp. 129–31). The act is not obviously heroic—in Mailer's words, it is a "picayune arrest" (p. 138); yet it is an act issuing from Mailer's new sense of commitment and comradeship, the growth of which he has traced throughout Book One. Therefore he can describe this act—with saving humor—as "his Rubicon" (p. 138).

During Part III Mailer has not portrayed his hero as altogether transfigured. The great Mailer ego is still on display, as when he remarks that he cannot see across Arlington Memorial Bridge because he will not wear glasses, or when he decides on a quick arrest in order to obtain a quick release ("Such men are either monumental fools or excruciatingly practical"—p. 119). References to one's Rubicon don't signal absolute humility. But these reminders of Mailer's none too flawless personality only emphasize by contrast the remarkable conversion he undergoes. They take the curse off his account of how he got religion in the country of the young and the liberal academic.

It is hardly a metaphor to say that Mailer "gets religion" during the March. For Mailer, the experience is nothing less than a rite of purification. At Lincoln Memorial, he decides to observe a fast until the March is over (p. 106). This hint of a purification ritual is reinforced once he is arrested. Mailer notes that "he felt as if he were being confirmed" by his arrest (p. 138); later, he says that "he felt shriven" (p. 158). He breaks his fast only when assured that he has passed his "test": "He had felt, despite every petty motive, or low calculation on how to get back to New York for the party, a mild exaltation on which he had traveled through the day, a sense of cohering in himself which was he supposed the opposite of those more familiar states of alienation he could always describe so well" (pp. 162–63). When released on Sunday morning, Mailer is sure that his experience has been liberating: ". . . he felt one suspicion of a whole man closer to that freedom from dread which occupied the inner drama of his years, yes, one image closer than when he had come to Washington four days ago" (pp. 212–13).

Book One dramatizes this change in Mailer. It describes an experience almost religious in nature. This conviction lies behind Mailer's otherwise curious remarks upon leaving the makeshift courtroom at Occoquan, Virginia. Here Mailer says that protests like the March may have to become more militant because " 'we are burning the body and blood of Christ in Vietnam. Yes, we are burning him there, and as we do, we destroy the foundation of this Republic, which is its love and trust in Christ' " (p. 214). Behind his statement rests Mailer's conception of America as a Christian country. For Mailer, Christianity is marked by its belief in mysteries, the greatest of which is "the bleeding heart of Christ." Vietnam reveals that America has lost its soul to "a worship of technology," for Vietnam is the technological war (p. 188). Mystery ("the bleeding heart of Christ") has been replaced by the procedures of technology; therefore, by implication, we are burning the body and blood of Christ in Vietnam.

Mailer's statement issues from the dramatic context not only of his release from prison but also the completion of a liberating, quasi-religious experience begun in apathy but ended in "mild exaltation." It derives from a mind spiritually refreshed and inclined toward the solemnity of things religious. We will encounter this mind again, at the end of Book Two, where Mailer will speak not of his own experience but the general experience of the demonstrators. In tracing his own belated conversion, Mailer therefore prepares for the more general rite of passage which is to be celebrated in Book Two. What appears to be an egotistical emphasis on his own actions is really Mailer's attempt to persuade us that his reactions are representative. We see as he sees; we share his initial indifference to this "radical" act of civil disobedience; then, if we are in fact persuaded, we undergo with him the transforming event the March ultimately became. And having passed through this experience with Mailer, we are prepared for his retrospective analysis of the March which follows in Book Two.

That is one answer, of course, to the question of how Mailer's personal story is relevant to the materials of Book Two. At the beginning of Book Two, Mailer takes up this question himself. Here he tells us that Book One is to be "a tower fully equipped with telescopes to study—at the greatest advantage—our own horizon" (p. 219). He makes it clear that Armies should not be read as a novel, for the "novel" of Book One is a means toward an end. Book One—our metaphorical tower—is to provide the perspective we need on the massive and somewhat chaotic particulars of the March itself. It does so in at least three ways: it offers intimate portraits of the various political factions—Left, Right and Center—involved in the March; it establishes Mailer's right to speak of the March in the impersonal, authoritative tone of Book Two, for it bears witness to his profound involvement in the event ("I suffered, I was there"); and it provides, in Mailer's transformation from comic hero to mildly-exalted initiate, a model for the experience of the demonstrators, who will be shown undergoing an analogous experience from the initial, humorous negotiations for the March to the final, transfiguring events of Saturday night at the Pentagon.

Book Two returns to the beginning to trace the genesis and execution of the March. "Obedient to a general style of historical writing" (p. 255), Book Two is a history of the March which focuses on its major figures, the antiwar leaders and their counterpart in the government, the students and soldiers who confront each other at the Pentagon. In 1963 Mailer could write,

> The play of political ideas is flaccid here in America because opposing armies never meet. The Right, the Center, and what there is of the Left have set up encampments on separate hills. . . . No Man's Land predominates. It is a situation which calls for guerilla raiders.

Book Two documents the emergence of such guerrillas. It is a history of opposing armies very much in conflict.

Of course, Mailer has depicted these "armies" throughout Book One. His portraits there both illustrate and occasion his analysis of America—always the final end in Mailer's fiction-like nonfiction. Chapter 2 of Part IV offers, in the Marshal and the Nazi, prototypes of that Cannibalistic Right Wing described so well by Mailer in his account of the 1964 Republican Convention, "In The Red Light." Latter-day versions of the Wasp, these men speak to Mailer of the bigotry his own army must transform if it is to alter America. Other figures of the Right described in *Armies* are more sympathetic but no less alienated from the demonstrators who have come to Washington in protest of the war. In the eyes of a turnkey, for example, Mailer discovers "narrowness, propriety, good-will, and that infernal American innocence which could not question one's leaders, for madness and the boils of a frustrated life resided beneath" (p. 169). Mailer is equally saddened by those "clean American kids" who stare at the demonstrators, for they bring home the fact that Marshals and turnkeys have children who will never gather in Washington to protest American wars (p. 156).

Mailer's attention in *Armies* is more often devoted to figures of the Left. As his book makes clear, the Center and the Left of American politics are somewhat inharmoniously united in the peace movement. The Center for Mailer is liberalism, represented by those liberal academics whose bourbon Mailer drinks at the pre-Ambassador buffet. Mailer feels little sympathy for these people. If they oppose the war in Vietnam, they do not oppose the technological machine behind the war—their opposition to the Johnson administration is "no more than a quarrel among engineers" (p. 15). Mailer is temperamentally opposed to the pacifism and rationality of the liberals; they are not the guerrilla raiders he has dreamed of commanding. But then neither are the Old Left, the first and least impressive radical force in the March. For Mailer, the Old Left are but a step removed from the liberal technologues. Their penchant for speeches ("The Great Left Pall") is more impressive than their disposition to act (p. 98); their programs detail "the sound-as-brickwork logic of the next step" (p. 85); like the liberals, they are "the first real champions of technology land" (p. 96). Much more interesting are the New Left. Among the young girls and hippies and SDS provocateurs, Mailer discovers a true if ignorant army to engage America's Marshals and technologues.

Mailer is not entirely charmed by his troops of the New Left, however. They are too much like the young girls he meets at the buffet, "innocent, decent-spirited, merry, red-cheeked, idealistic, and utterly lobotomized away from the sense of sin" (p. 14). Mailer's sense of sin is such that he has come full circle from his search for the apocalyptic orgasm ("The White Negro") to his present "neo-Victorianism." Not for nothing is he a Left *Conservative*. He can describe his troops as "middle-class cancer-pushers and drug-gutted flower children" (p. 35); he can suggest that they are "bombed by the use of LSD as outrageously as the atoll of Eniwetok, Hiroshima, Nagasaki, and the scorched foliage of Vietnam" (p. 93). Yet they are his troops still. Mailer is immensely impressed by the young people he meets during the March. He doesn't have Charles Reich's faith in the children of flowers, but neither does he feel an alien in the country of the young. And he is very much taken with the political tactics of the New Left. For Mailer, the New Left is truly a new political phenomenon.

Mailer finds that the young radicals make an almost absolute contrast with their older comrades:

> A generation of the American young had come along different from five previous generations of the middle class. The new generation believed in technology more than any before it, but the generation also believed in LSD, in witches, in tribal knowledge, in orgy, and revolution. It had no respect whatsoever for the unassailable logic of the next step: belief was reserved for the revelatory mystery of the happening where you did not know what was going to happen next; *that was what was good about it.*
>
> (p. 86; my emphasis)

We recall Mailer's words at the Ambassador, where he advised those assembled that they were up against "an existential situation," the outcome of which was uncertain (p. 38). Mailer's admiration for those who embrace such a situation is obvious. Here he goes on to say that

. . . the New Left was drawing its political aesthetic from Cuba. The
revolutionary idea which the followers of Castro had induced from their
experience in the hills was that you created the revolution first and
learned from it, learned of what your revolution might consist and where
it might go out of the intimate truth of the way it presented itself to your
experience.

(p. 87)

Mailer sees such an aesthetic at work in the March on the Pentagon. It is
for this reason that he finally endorses the March. He has always sponsored such "existential" acts, for they betray static political and social
situations and force the powers involved to reveal their true natures. Thus
he once wrote that

an existential political act, the drive by Southern Negroes, led by Martin
Luther King, to end segregation in restaurants in Birmingham, an act
which is existential precisely because its end is unknown, has succeeded
en route in discovering more of the American reality to us.

Thus he applauds the guerrilla tactics of the New Left, for they too reveal
something of the American reality.

Unhappily, what they reveal is that "the center of America might
be insane." The March on the Pentagon confirms Mailer's most pessimistic analysis of the American scene: "The country had been living with a
controlled, even fiercely controlled, schizophrenia which had been
deepening with the years. Perhaps the point had now been passed"
(p. 188). Mailer defines this schizophrenia as our irreconcilable allegiance
both to Christianity ("Mystery") and to technology ("the love of no
Mystery whatsoever"). Because they have witnessed the effects of this
condition on their elders, the young have arisen in protest (p. 188). Our
plight is therefore what it seemed to Mailer as early as 1962: a tragic
impasse in which "we diverge as countrymen further and further away
from one another, like a space ship broken apart in flight which now drifts
mournfully in isolated orbits, satellites to each other, planets none,
communication faint." The March on the Pentagon is a "symbolic battle"
in which no one is killed (p. 199), but what it symbolizes is so agonizing
that it constantly reminds Mailer of the Civil War (pp. 88, 89, 91, 93,
113, 126, 263).

Mailer's purpose in *Armies* is to discover the meaning of one
episode in this second Civil War. Though he is drawn to the demonstrators, his title implies that he must deal with armies equally ignorant. (The
title comes, of course, from Arnold's "Dover Beach": "And we are here as
on a darkling plain / Swept with confused alarms of struggle and flight,/

Where ignorant armies clash by night.") In a sense, both armies should be seen as "villains" (p. 93). Indeed, Mailer fears that "nihilism might be the only answer to totalitarianism" (p. 176). Thus we see that Mailer's ignorant armies—Nihilism and Totalitarianism, respectively—embody very unattractive alternatives. Mailer adds that his "final allegiance" was with the villains who were hippies (p. 93), but his reading of the embattled armies inspires no enthusiasm for his choice. If the March on the Pentagon were nothing more than a symbolic battle between unappealing forces, it would not seem to issue in anything resembling catharsis.

Yet the March does produce a catharsis. It has this effect on Mailer himself, as we have seen. And it has this effect on the "best" of the demonstrators. What Mailer charts in Book Two is the conversion of nihilism into purposeful rebellion. He refers to this conversion as a rite of passage (pp. 278–80). Fittingly, it is enacted at the very end of *Armies*, where it climaxes not only the demonstration but Mailer's narrative as well.

When he comes to describe the confrontation between the sons of the middle class (the demonstrators) and the sons of the working class (the soldiers), Mailer's history of the March undergoes a definite shift in tone. The first half of Book Two is full of the humor of embattled armies which negotiate when and where they will confront each other, what routes the demonstrators may take and what territory they may occupy. This section of Book Two is therefore analogous to the first part of Book One, where Mailer's misadventures are recorded with a similar eye for the ridiculous. But just as Mailer's experience intensifies and with it the tone of the book, so the humor of Book Two dissolves once Mailer turns to the events of Saturday night after the masses have departed and the most dedicated demonstrators are left alone with the soldiers. Mailer gives 20 pages to these events, and they are among the most impressive pages he has ever written. Here we listen to the voice not of the bourbon-inspired Master of Ceremonies but of the much-humbled veteran of the March who cautions that we are burning the body and blood of Christ in Vietnam.

What emerges is Mailer's interpretation of the March. In Mailer's view, the demonstrators are visited with grace as they sit face-to-face with the soldiers: ". . . some hint of a glorious future may have hung in the air, some refrain from all the great American rites of passage when men and women manacled themselves to a lost and painful principle and survived a day, a night, a week, a month, a year" (p. 280). These "tender drug-vitiated jargon-mired children" (p. 280) endure a night which begins in "joy" but includes the terror of military attack (The Wedge). Those who remain to the end are subtly transformed: ". . . they were forever different in the morning than they had been before the night, which is the meaning of a rite of passage, one has voyaged through a channel of shipwreck and temptation . . . some part of the man has been born again, and is better" (pp. 280–81). Where Mailer has come through his experience "one suspicion of a whole man closer to that freedom from dread which occupied the inner drama of his years," these flower children and fledgling revolutionaries are "forever different in the morning than they had been before the night." The particular experience of Book One is generalized in Book Two. The knot of nihilism is untied, if not "forever" at least for the moment. This is the "mystery" Mailer discovers in the March on the Pentagon, first in his own experience, then in the collective experience of the demonstrators. Transcending the count of bodies, the tactical success or failure of the demonstration, there is the spiritual renewal attested to by the now impersonal narrative voice of *Armies*.

Perhaps the most important contribution of Book One is that it makes this voice possible as the achieved result of the experience recorded there. Therefore Norman Mailer—dwarf alter ego of Lyndon Johnson himself (p. 49)—can plausibly conclude his book with the moving image of "naked Quakers on a cold floor of a dark isolation cell in D.C. jail," and a question almost worthy of Jeremiah, the prophet Mailer once said he hoped to emulate:

> Did they pray, these Quakers, for forgiveness of the nation? Did they pray with tears in their eyes in those blind cells with visions of a long column of Vietnamese dead, Vietnamese walking a column of fire, eyes on fire, nose on fire, mouth speaking flame."
>
> (p. 287)

Finally, Mailer can leave us with nothing less than his own prayer for America: "Deliver us from our curse. For we must end on the road to that mystery where courage, death, and the dream of love give promise of sleep" (p. 288). Mailer's narrative has left us on that road, for having presented a vivid and brilliantly annotated account of our condition as a people, Mailer leaves us with the images of young demonstrators undergoing their rite of passage and Quakers praying for the forgiveness of sins: images bearing witness to courage and the dream of love in the face of our death as God's chosen country.

JOHN GARVEY

"The Executioner's Song"

In the opening line of Norman Mailer's
An American Dream there is a casual link between John F. Kennedy and F.
Scott Fitzgerald. It's a great throwaway beginning which sets a tone, like
"Call me Ishmael." That linkage of history and fiction shows up in the
rest of the novel, and in Mailer's later journalism. He is obsessed with
power and prestige and good and evil, and with making choices that
matter morally—morality here having to do with specific rightness, being
true to the moment, a working out of Mailer's unique version of "existen-
tialism." His journalism is full of this concern: he sees himself doing
things, cleverly and stupidly, sneaking cleverly (for example) into the
Republican convention disguised as a guard, and stupidly approaching
Sonny Liston with good advice on boxing. Mailer's journalism, and much
of his fiction, was full of Mailer or Mailer substitutes.

It was good stuff, because Mailer simply does see things which
nobody else notices. But about some things his most recent approach
wouldn't work, the way he has taken on of describing his own reactions in
third person form, with some fancy name like "Aquarius" standing in for
Mailer: "Seabiscuit could sense his own failure here, charged with the
tang of ammonia which follows sudden unexpected exertion, or the
glue-factory smell of a losing race-horse led away . . ."—people began to
parody it. The third-person device was a means of keeping in shape for
novels, maybe, and it made for some fine journalism. But it wouldn't work
close to some subjects, and when I saw that *Playboy* was excerpting
something from a book by Mailer on the execution of Gary Gilmore I

From *Commonweal* 5, vol. 107 (March 14, 1980). Copyright © 1980 by Commonweal
Publishing Co.

imagined a third-person Mailer under another name trying to figure out how he felt about a person getting shot. It promised to be a tasteless thing, brilliant and low.

A friend sent me a copy of *The Executioner's Song*. I began to read it before going to work one morning, and by the middle of the day I resented the work and family obligations which kept me from it. As most reviewers have pointed out, there is a remarkable self-effacement here: Mailer vanishes, to let the book appear. It isn't that Mailer's own concerns don't surface in *The Executioner's Song*—what other modern American writer could write, "Gilmore had also felt compelled to take a chance with his life. Gilmore had been keeping in touch with something it was indispensable to be in touch with." Certainly Gilmore fascinates Mailer for reasons that are as personal as they could be. But comparisons of Mailer with previous Mailer can distract us from seeing how faithful this book is to the way people really talk. If future readers want to know how Americans sounded in the 1970s they can come to this book. In some recorded interviews with Mailer you can hear his accent change, from clipped careful Mailer to Southern to east-coast Irish American, as if he can't help tailoring his emotions to the rhythms which he thinks will handle the feeling best. His ear for the way Americans talk is clean, and what can seem flat for pages, the plain speech you hear in the midwest and west, can rise suddenly to wonderful moments. There is not too much apparent self-consciousness in this handling of the American language; it seems nearly effortless, but it is the most impressive thing about the book.

The Executioner's Song is also a remarkably compassionate work. Mailer got to know a lot of the people and families he writes about, and they appear here as full people. The Mormon families whose lives were torn open by Gilmore's murders are decent people whose hopes were modest and good, and Mailer is able to write about them without condescension. What I mean by that is the tendency of some writers who deal with criminality to see in the victims a naiveté or smugness of stuffy respectability which draws violence, almost justifiably. What Mailer shows us is the horror which occurs when decent people happen on a man like Gilmore at the wrong moment. But Mailer is also fair to Gilmore and Nicole, Gilmore's lover, and this romance—exploitative, manipulative, also complicated and true—is the center of the book.

Despite the dark subject, or maybe because of it, there are funny moments. When Larry Schiller (who had the "rights" to Gilmore's story and in fact got Mailer involved in writing the book) wanted to reproduce Gilmore's prison letters to Nicole, full of sex and art education, he worried about the sort of machine he might find to do the job most efficiently, and phoned from Provo to Denver's Xerox headquarters to locate one, "when damn if they didn't tell him that right in Provo, the Press Publishing Company had just a machine. Right in fucking Provo. A Christmas card company. Schiller shook his head. Sometimes these things happen.

"Obviously he was not going to tell a Christmas card company that Gary Gilmore was what he intended to use their machine for . . ."

Mailer has been criticized for not being more specific within the pages of this book about his relationship with Schiller. He has pointed out, rightly I think, that his relationship with Schiller and his work on the book began after Gilmore's execution. And Schiller certainly doesn't come off as well as some of Mailer's critics have implied. When Mailer has Schiller thinking of Gilmore's letters to Nicole, "must be tons of meat and potatoes in those envelopes," we know Mailer isn't writing about Francis of Assisi.

I do have a couple of problems with the book. It is about existing people— not imagined people, like Raskolnikov; the people in *The Executioner's Song* aren't inventions. As real as a novelist's characters are, they are the author's work and are his sole responsibility, an act of imagination. But Nicole, whose sadness and lovemaking and suicide attempts are all described here, is a person who was around before this book and will be forced one way or another to deal with it, as will the relatives, victims' families, friends, lawyers, etc., who are made part of this book. I believe that Mailer has been compassionate and probably fair—but how will they feel about seeing themselves revealed this way?

This is, of course, not an artistic question, but it leads to one. How much of what people understand about Gary Gilmore will be filtered through Mailer's reworking of Gilmore's letters and his fascination with Gilmore's obvious intelligence? This problem of reworking, deletion, and selection is as true of any reporting as it is of "true life novels" (the book's subtitle), but it is still a problem, especially when the mind at work is allowed to rewrite Gilmore to the novelist's satisfaction. People doing straight reporting, not a hybrid of fiction and reporting, are forced to worry about this, and the worry is not unimportant. Gilmore didn't want to be represented as insane, and Mailer is fair to him here: he shows him as a man who was not crazy, whose life was limited, driven, and terrible, but not insane. (Insanity can be a consoling word for the rest of us.) He killed the decent men he killed because the alternative that day would have been to kill Nicole. In *The Stranger* Camus tried to handle the same sort of incident without reducing it to comfortable, manageable dimensions. By making the letters a little better than they were, Mailer may be backing away from Gilmore's reality; the impression is that he must be made to look more interesting than the con he was. I can see the novelist's reasons for wanting the prison letters to be better, but whoever Gary Gilmore was begins to blur with the alteration.

Still, it doesn't matter to me if what I encounter here is Mailer's Gilmore and not history's. This is the best thing Mailer has done in years, and considering the good books he has given us that's saying a lot.

ALVIN B. KERNAN

The Taking of the Moon

At the center of the institution of
literature there is . . . a world-view or myth which informs the various
activities of the institution and is in turn objectified by them. To speak of
the myth of literature, as Frye does, is probably a mistake since no two
minds seem to conceive literature in exactly the same way, and since the
dialectic interaction of world and mind results in constant change in the
myth. Nevertheless, the great central statements about the nature of
literature during a given period tend to hang together well enough to
permit us to speak of a governing world-view or myth of literature of that
particular time. Within the romantic period with which we are concerned,
from Wordsworth's *Prelude* to Shade's "Pale Fire" the major works of
literature, for all their individual differences, join with the major works of
criticism such as Arnold's *Culture and Anarchy* or Frye's *Anatomy of
Criticism*, to create a romantic myth of a vast and mysterious universe,
filled with the magic of the unexpected, which is therefore a perpetual
source of wonder and joy, never quite to be explained. Its world is a
plenum of many things endlessly different from one another, individuals,
each with its own special quality and beauty. But in this infinity of variety
all the parts are ultimately linked with all other parts in organic ways
which can only be apprehended by intuition, imagination, or powerful
sensory excitement—not by reason and logic. Only by paying careful
attention to the unique being of each person or thing, only by responding
to its "thou" of being with the "thou" of its own deep being, can
imagination hear the music of the spheres. In this romantic cosmology,

From *The Imaginary Library: An Essay on Literature and Society.* Copyright © 1982 by
Princeton University Press.

the world is not static as in the Great Chain of Being, or circular, as in a Myth of Eternal Return, but is in movement, through struggle, towards some only dimly perceived but surely glorious future. Its plot is a titanic struggle of opposites, God and the Devil, thesis and antithesis, Apollo and Dionysus, Id and Ego, poet and society. The great enemy is passivity, stasis, the lack of energy, entropy. In this struggle mighty Promethean heroes emerge, charged with divine or daemonic energy, to carry the fire through great apocalyptic battles with the forces of darkness.

Despite the various forms of the myth of literature, it provides, however differently it may be conceived in different minds, the enabling charter of the remainder of literature. So long as it is believed in, thought of as a true picture of the world, so long the texts, the poets, the word craft, the criticism and all the other many activities which compose the institution of literature are valid and worth the labor expended on them. Attacks on the myth questioning its usefulness or its truth come therefore very close to the heart of literature. Such attacks, usually centered on the fictional aspect of literature, have been fairly constant from Plato to the present, and have been met in the usual way of institutions by assimilation, as Aristotle adjusted poetry to meet Plato's objections, or at times by a radical change in the myth to accommodate itself to changed social conditions, as the romantics redefined poetry in the face of the new society brought about by the democratic and industrial revolutions. Recently . . . that romantic myth of poetry, as modified over the two centuries since its construction in the late eighteenth century, has been coming under increasingly heavy attack from Marxists who see it as merely an instrumentation of class interests, from philosophical critics who are deconstructing the logic of its assumptions, and from radical changes in the beliefs of the society which deny the basic literary principles. In *Of a Fire on the Moon*, a description of the landing of two Americans on the moon in 1969, Norman Mailer dramatizes these attacks on literature in a conflict of two great myths, science and poetry, for the control of reality.

In identifying the basic threat to the believability of poetry's myth as another myth, that of science, Mailer is following a long line of distinguished romantic predecessors—Blake, Carlyle, Arnold, and Ransom, to name only a few—who well understood that the social world is always an arena of competing systems of belief or myths and that literature's great competitor for belief has been, at least since the late eighteenth century, science. From Aristotle through Pope, poetry was usually defined by its difference from philosophy on one hand and history on the other as more specific than the first, more general than the second. But in the eighteenth century, at about the same time that the more universal term "literature" began to replace the older "poetry," a new social paradigm of the arts began to develop. The crucial first step, described by Paul Kristeller in a remarkable article, "The Modern System of the Arts," was the full statement of a long-developing concept of Art as consisting of five fine arts—poetry, architecture, sculpture, painting, and music—distinguished from other activities by a shared purpose, the creation of pleasure through beauty, and by their total lack of any workaday function such as imitation or instruction. . . .

Kristeller goes on to show that this conception of the identity of the arts under the concept of Art was spread through the *Encyclopédie*, and a philosophical and psychological basis for the special status of the arts was provided by Kant, in whose *Critique of Judgment* "Aesthetics, as the philosophical theory of beauty and the arts, acquires equal standing with the theory of truth (metaphysics or epistemology) and the theory of goodness (ethics)."

If poetry, and later literature, has been defined by its similarity to the other arts, within the broad category of art, or, as Raymond Williams would have it, culture, it also has found its opposite, as we have seen, in a utilitarian industrial society, and chiefly in its principal philosophy, science. In good structuralist fashion, then, literature has been known, and has known itself, by those things it is like, the other arts, and by what it is unlike, science. The warfare between science and poetry, or C. P. Snow's two cultures, has from this structuralist point of view been long and fruitful in that it has enabled literature to define itself in the great system of social institutions by contrasting its subjectivity to science's objectivity, imagination to reason, connotative language to mathematics, and its sense of the mysterious uniqueness of events and things to the scientific assumption of the uniform behavior of particles of charged matter. But the opposition of science and poetry remains functional only so long as the poets can maintain in the face of science at least the possibility that their myth can describe or create a reality as true and believable as the scientific myth. In fact, of course, the poets have been far more nervously aware of science than the scientists of poetry, and the poetic myth telling of a world organized in conformity with human desire has long been on the defensive because the opposing scientific myth has proved so extraordinarily powerful in the control it gives over nature that it has by its achievements increasingly discredited the poetic myth. *Of a Fire on the Moon* dramatizes what it conceives of as the last battle in this long war, for in the late 1960's, Mailer feels, the scientific conception of the world has all but triumphed, and the landing on the moon will demonstrate conclusively the enormous power of science, validate its myth, and complete its dominion over the minds of men. The world will now become what science makes it, a world of objects moving in relationship to one another in accordance with immutable laws, coming from nowhere and going nowhere, lost in an infinity in which being is only relative. Literature and its humanistic conception of a world corresponding to human desire, organically related and metaphysically purposive, will disappear. As if to make clear its final assault on literature, science has now appropriated the myths of poetry: the mission is named Apollo 11, claiming for a rocket the name of the god of poetry and art, and it will land on and seize the traditional symbol of the poetic imagination, the moon, transforming it into a dead object, another scientific fact, "alien terrain where no life breathed and beneath the ground no bodies were dead." The uncannily accurate prophecy of the poet Keats at the beginning of the nineteenth century will at last be fully realized:

> Do not all charms fly
> At the mere touch of cold philosophy?
> There was an awful rainbow once in heaven:
> We know her woof, her texture; she is given
> In the dull catalogue of common things.
> Philosophy will clip an Angel's wings,
> Conquer all mysteries by rule and line,
> Empty the haunted air, and gnomed mine—
> (Lamia, II, 229–36)

Against this scientific imperialism, this desacralization of the myths of a weaker culture by a stronger one, stands the poet Aquarius, Norman Mailer's persona, commissioned by a magazine to write a factual description of the moon-shot, but using the occasion to fight what he sees as the last battle between science and poetry, the Armageddon of art. But before we turn to a consideration of Aquarius and the myth he tries to make work once more, let us look at the beliefs of science as Mailer defines them in a typically romantic fashion, making them the exact opposite of poetic beliefs.

NASA-land, "the very center of technological reality (which is to say that world where every question must have answers and procedures, or technique itself cannot progress)" is almost overwhelming in its power, its complexity, its effectiveness. Its machines are made of millions of parts, all of which are perfectly designed to interact smoothly with each other in flawless perfection and perform the most complex tasks without fail. Its buildings are taller than cathedrals, and its booster rockets as large as destroyers. The rocket fuel is maintained at fantastically low temperatures, where gases change to liquids, and when the fuel burns at thousands of gallons per second it produces fires with such enormous thrust power as to overcome the earth's gravity. The capsules sent into the vastness of space are navigated with pinpoint precision from the earth to the moon and back again. Every detail of the flight is monitored, every variation corrected with exactitude, by thousands of men working together with the same emotionless efficiency as their machines. Voices and images are transmitted clearly over thousands of miles of space, emergencies are handled with ease, and no contingency among millions of possible variables is not foreseen and procedures for dealing with it worked out beforehand. No one, not even the poet Aquarius, can remain unimpressed when the great rocket leaves its launching pad to journey into space:

> two horns of orange fire burst like genies from the base of the rocket. Aquarius never had to worry again about whether the experience would be appropriate to his measure. Because of the distance, no one at the Press Site was to hear the sound of the motors until fifteen seconds after they had started. Although the rocket was restrained on its pad for nine seconds in order for the motors to multiply up to full thrusts, the result was still that the rocket began to rise a full six seconds before its motors could be heard. Therefore the lift-off itself seemed to partake more of a miracle than a mechanical phenomenon, as if all of huge Saturn itself had begun silently to levitate, and was then pursued by flames.
>
> No, it was more dramatic than that. For the flames were enormous. . . . Two mighty torches of flame like the wings of a yellow bird of fire flew over a field, covered a field with brilliant yellow bloomings of flame, and in the midst of it, white as a ghost, white as the white of Melville's Moby Dick, white as the shrine of the Madonna in half the churches of the world, this slim angelic mysterious ship of stages rose without sound out of its incarnation of flame and began to ascend slowly into the sky. . . .

There is a good deal of the poet as well as the rocket in this lyric passage, particulary in its imagery, which tries to keep the humanistic world in play with the rocket, but the event in itself is powerful enough to be impressive in its own right.

But elsewhere, though he is always respectful of the power of the event he is witness to, Aquarius is more often repelled by than attracted to the marvels of science and its technological creation, NASA-land. Like the America out of which it comes, NASA-land is "An empty country filled with wonders." For all of its intricacy and efficiency, it presents a smooth, emotionless face to the observer, gives off no smells—a particularly important sense for Aquarius—no signs of mystery or vitality. Its buildings are bleak and windowless, usually placed in some barren setting, its atmosphere air-conditioned, its procedures developed from abstract rules rather than from human needs.

Aquarius first sees the astronauts at a press conference behind a screen of glass—to protect them from germs—and they never appear close up and in the flesh, but always as some distant, removed image, seen from far away as they move in their plastic helmets to the launch, are projected on television, and, finally, are glimpsed in a quarantine box on the carrier *Hornet* after they have landed. The personalities of these "shining knights of technology" are as removed and alien as their distant images. "What we can't understand, we fear," says the wife of one of them, and their internalization of scientific understanding relieves them of fear, of excitement, of pleasure, even of competitiveness. Like interchangeable parts of the machines they design and operate, one astronaut seems much like the other, and each could in fact exchange roles with the others and function effectively. The third astronaut, Collins, who does not land on the moon but remains in the command ship circling the moon while Armstrong and Aldrin land, could equally well have been chosen to walk on the moon, and he insists that his failure to be chosen doesn't bother him at all since he is merely part of the team, and it is the mission, the group, not the individual which counts.

This emphasis on the group, on the project, on the field, as it were, rather than the individual is close to the center of the scientific myth which empowers NASA. Behind Apollo 11 lies a vast bureaucracy, a host of contractors, an army of scientists and engineers, all working together like one of their machines with a minimum of friction and a predictable outcome. Individuality, the unique or unpredictable, is frowned on, and the men who make up NASA are, according to Aquarius, all cut from the same cloth of middle America, short-sleeved shirts of synthetic material with several pencils in the pocket, crew-cut hair, muscular and trim, humorless, WASP, intent, rational, the statistical norm. The astronauts themselves are the farthest extensions of this human machine, and any hint of the unusual about them, physically or mentally, would disqualify them for the mission. Neil Armstrong, the leader, is particularly without any irregularities or psychic bumps. He comes from a small town in Ohio, worked hard as an errand boy to earn the money to learn to fly, waited long to marry a school teacher, served as a Navy pilot in Korea and then as a test pilot. Although he has known difficulties and tragedy in the death of a young child, he is still the American Dream personified, small-town poor beginnings, hard work and determination, courage in the face of danger, intelligence and hard training, and now the biggest of all pay-offs, the first man to walk on the moon. Perfectly programmed for this mission, following their learned routines exactly and almost never called on for individual decisions, linked at all times to Mission Control in Houston, with even their heartbeats monitored, watching their thousands of instruments, locked into and entirely dependent for their lives on the complicated machinery of which they have become parts, the astronauts in their plastic helmets and protective space suits are the perfect image of scientific man when they step clumsily and uncertainly out onto the surface of the moon, unable to live or move except within the vast support system that extends back to earth. And though they are the principal figures in the trip to the moon, they can never become heroes, to the intense frustration of the millions who watched them, because systems emphasize teamwork, and heroes are romantic individuals. And they know this, are perfectly programmed to this pattern, so that every remark they make plays down their own importance and emphasizes that success is the result of joint effort, just as their smooth quiet exteriors and calm voices efface all traces of personality. . . .

Language is, we now believe, the central structure of meaning and values in a culture, and it is the NASA language which generates its scientific myth and its social manifestation, the impersonal world of technology. When the reporters in an interview press the astronauts for "disclosure of emotion, admission of unruly fear—the astronauts looked to give replies as proper and well-insulated as the plate glass which separated them." Their words never yield much—"Our concern has been directed mainly to doing the job"—and the famous phrase uttered by Armstrong as he first stepped on the moon, "That's one small step for a man, one giant leap for mankind," is so neat, so flatly delivered, so patently manufactured on Madison Avenue for the event that it reverberated with not even the slightest heartfelt spontaneous delight of a man doing something truly extraordinary. The language of the astronauts and of the NASA adminis-trators, always carefully controlled to eliminate or conceal emotion, is further insulated by the jargon Aquarius calls "computerese."

> The use of "we" was discouraged. "A joint exercise has demonstrated" became the substitution. "Other choices" became "peripheral secondary objectives." "Doing our best" was "obtaining maximum advantage possi-ble." "Confidence" became "very high confidence level." "Ability to move" was a "mobility study." "Turn off" was "disable"; "turn on" became "enable."

Computerese tends toward abstraction and the stripping away of emotional content, subjective responses, and the historical accretions words have gathered over the centuries as a result of their involvement in the lives of men. Much of the vocabulary of computerese is made up of acronyms, EVA for "extra-vehicular activity," i.e., walking on the moon; PTC equals "passive thermal control." VAB, the acronym for the Vehicle Assembly Building where the great rockets are readied for flight could be, Aquarius remarks,

> the name of a drink or a deodorant, or it could be suds for the washer. But it was not a name for this warehouse of the gods. The great churches of a religious age had names: the Alhambra, Santa Sophia, Mont-Saint-Michel, Chartres, Westminster Abbey, Notre Dame. Now: VAB. Nothing fit anything any longer. The art of communication had become the mechanical function, and the machine was the work of art. What a fall for the ego of the artist. What a climb to capture the language again!

But the dull language of fact, the acronyms, the jargon, the scientific cant, the plain but still somehow pompous statements of the astronauts and their spokesmen, these are only the various *paroles* of a *langue* whose alphabet is ultimately number, numbers which because they are "abstracted from the senses . . . made you ignore the taste of the apple for the amount in the box, . . . shrunk the protective envelope of human atmosphere. . . ." The paradigm underlying computerese is finally that simplest and most reductive of all mathematical forms, the binary system in which all things are ultimately plus or minus, one or zero, yes or no, go and no go, a flash of energy or its absence. Computers are built upon this *langue*, and computers are the very heart of Apollo 11, plotting its orbits and vectors, tracking its progress, monitoring the heartbeats of the astronauts and the consumption of fuel, and doing all these in an infinitesimal fraction of the time it would take human beings to work out the problems. Without computers there would have been no moon walk, but the price paid for their service is that every question "fed" to them, every problem they solve, every pattern they work out has to be reduced to "bits." As a result this particular reductive structure of "thought" informs all the activities of NASA, the language of men as well as its technical procedures. And so NASA and the astronauts think of things as yes or not yes, presence or absence, fear or no fear, go or no go, success or no success, true or not true. Computerese does not work in terms of the old romantic dualisms such as good *and* evil, or true *and* false, where the second term has an existence in its own right, but in terms of one *or* zero, the presence of a thing or its not presence, like Orwell's "Newspeak" in 1984, or like the orthodox but little-believed Christian theology which tried to eliminate evil by making it merely the absence of good. For Aquarius this radical monism of the computer makes it "some species of higher tapeworm . . . quietly ingesting the vitals of God." As it is applied to more and more situations "to simulate what had hitherto been out of the range of simulation," it solves "problems whose outer margins would be lost as the center was sucked into the binary system."

The binary language of the computer is at the heart of NASA and by its simplification of everything to presence or absence makes finally possible the achievement of the ultimate "world-vaulting . . . assumption that sooner or later everything would be understood—'I paid a trip to death, and death is a pleasant place and ready for us to come in and renovate it.' " Computerese eliminates misunderstanding and mystery to create a universe that is "no majestic mansion of architectonics out there between evil and nobility, or strife on a darkling plain, but rather an ultimately benign field of investigation. . . ." Beauty in this world is merely "system perfection," and truth only the possession and structuring of clear, uncontroversial data.

But as the contradictions disappear, so does what Aquarius calls "firm sense of magnitudes," by which he means the architectonics of the romantic world, the existence of many things in relationship to other things by virtue of their firmly established uniqueness. It is just this firm sense of magnitudes that the country as a whole lacks—"the American disease: Focus on one problem to the exclusion of every other"—and which is personified by the astronauts who "like narcissists, like children, like old people, . . . all exhibited a single-minded emphasis on each detail which arrived before them, large or small." In the empty space in which they journey, all orders of human magnitude disappear, and on the moon as the astronauts see it through the eyes of technology there is no sense of scale, and therefore no differences, for a crater may be as large as New York or as small as a house. Everything blurs into a sameness which, according to Aquarius, Cézanne, followed by Picasso and Cubism, prefigured when he abandoned the traditional emphasis on particular surfaces, "the sheen and texture, the hairs, the dust, the flickering motes of light on the surface of a drape," for a vision in which "the similarities between surfaces [are] now more profound than the differences."

An organization so internally consistent and coherent as NASA has no teleology and needs none. It is in a condition of homeostasis, runs in order to run, is entirely self-sufficient; therefore so long as it continues to function—and who will raise troublesome questions about it internally?—it really needs no purpose outside itself. To go to the moon, yes, but why? Collins, the most perceptive of the astronauts, realizes that something is lacking, "It's been one of the failings of the Space Program . . . that we have been unable to delineate clearly all the reasons why we should go to

the moon." But Armstrong when pressed with the question of why all this
expense and effort can only come up with the flat, canned cliché used a
thousand times to explain activities that have no purpose outside themselves: "I think we're going to the moon because it's in the nature of the
human being to face challenges." And to other questions outside the
system defined by computerese—"What will you do if you find the moon
inhabited?" or "Will landing on the moon create any psychic disturbances
on earth?"—NASA can only respond with a polite shrug of incompre-
hension.

Aquarius perceives that there is something pointless, tautological,
about the entire venture, "a meaningless journey to a dead arena in order
that men could engage in the irrational activity of designing machines
which would give birth to other machines which would travel to meaningless places. . . ." Perhaps the best image of this monolithic quality, this
enclosed system which reduces the world to itself and then blankly ignores
whatever remains outside, giving off no odors of vitality, no hints of
meaning, is a painting by Magritte, which Aquarius sees in a house in
Houston, "a startling image of a room with an immense rock situated in
the center of the floor. . . . it was as if Magritte had listened to the
ending of one world with its comfortable chairs in the parlor, and heard
the intrusion of a new world, silent as the windowless stone which grew in
the room, and knowing not quite what he had painted, had painted his
warning nonetheless." Solidly there, immensely powerful, impervious,
self-contained, the rock gives visible form to what Aquarius had earlier
felt. "The horror of the Twentieth Century was the size of each new
event, and the paucity of its reverberation." As more and more happens
and events get bigger and bigger, wars, mass murders, famines, GNP, speed,
they come somehow to mean less and less, to simply be, like the trip to
the moon of Apollo 11.

Of a Fire on the Moon quite obviously presents science in the
images of NASA and Apollo 11 in a hostile fashion, but the undeniable
power of technology, its perfect confidence, the ability of its system to
manage events and bring them to the desired end give it a solid and
impressive reality. It is there, it is real, and somehow the literary artist
like Mailer must deal with it, not the other way round. His commission
from Esquire magazine is simply to write a lively but factual description of
the moon landing, and Mailer fulfills his contract, managing at the same
time to criticize the venture very sharply for its banality and lack of what
he as a good romantic would call meaning. Werner von Braun, the genius
of the rockets that powered the space program, may describe the landing
of two men on the moon on July 20th, 1969, as "equal in importance to

that moment in evolution when aquatic life came crawling up on the land," but for Norman Mailer writing about and trying to comprehend the event, "something was lacking, some joy, some outrageous sense of adventure."

> Strong men did not weep in the streets nor ladies copulate with strangers. . . . It was as if on the largest stage ever created, before an audience of half the earth, a man of modest appearance would walk to the center, smile tentatively at the footlights, and read a page from a data card. The audience would groan and Beckett and Warhol give their sweet smiles.

But Mailer is not content with merely analyzing the reasons why the moon shot was so disappointing to him and to millions of viewers of the event on TV. Instead, and this is what makes his book so remarkably interesting, he attempts to make literature out of the fact of science, to impose the romantic literary myth on the very "reality" which denies its efficacy and truth. The center of *Fire on the Moon* is a confrontation of the poet with science in a titanic struggle to restore "magic, psyche, and the spirits of the underworld to the spookiest venture in history, a landing on the moon, an event whose technologese had been so complete that the word 'spook' probably did not appear in twenty million words of NASA prose." In the most obvious terms, Mailer's immediate problem is to lift the book "like a boulder out of the mud of the mind," by making the moon shot, as we would say, "interesting," in the face of its resolutely mechanical quality, its lack of mystery, its elmination of danger, its determination not to allow personality to intrude, in short, its objectivity. This difficult problem is approached by facing it squarely and making the real plot of the book the struggle of the poet to humanize, and thereby make interesting, the stone of the fact itself, to sieve "the transcript for lunar gold." The task is, however, a Herculean one, for events had, Mailer realizes, developed "a style and structure which made them almost impossible to write about."

In the pursuit of his task, Mailer is, it is important to note, severely handicapped from the beginning by his inability to transform the fact of the moon shot into the fiction of literature. Fictionality has long been the most prominent, perhaps the defining, characteristic of literature—"the poet nothing affirmeth and therefore never lieth," as Sidney puts it—and the poets have paradoxically maintained that though their fictions mirror the world obliquely, they reveal it more truly than do other more literal modes of description. The defenses of fiction range all the way from Aristotle's preference for poetry's probable over history's actual, or Boccaccio's explanation that fictions are necessary covers of sacred truths which prevent them from becoming known to the vulgar, to the modern view, dramatized most effectively by writers like Borges and Nabokov, that *all* views of the world are fictional orderings of events which in themselves have no absolute meaning or form, and that therefore the creation of fictions in literature openly reveals the essential process by which men make the world. However its truth has been justified—and the ways are many—fiction has remained not only the primary method of the artist but the expression of his belief that the poetic imagination can create a truer world than that of muddy fact. But where less troubled romantic writers, like Jules Verne and later writers of science fiction, simply imagine voyages to the moon, filling the bleakness of space with color and animating it with humanoids, Mailer's imaginative vision is blocked by the unavoidable fact of NASA, which prevents him from making up his own fictional world and denies the validity of his other literary techniques. "The world," he realizes, "*had* changed, even as he had thought to be pushing and shoving on it with *his* mighty ego. And it had changed in ways he did not recognize, had never anticipated, and could possibly not comprehend now. The change was mightier than he had counted on." This overwhelming factuality saps the confidence of the poet who faces the encounter with NASA, the Armageddon of poetry. He is aware of and frankly talks about both the tremendous power of his antagonist and of his own consequent disorientation and lack of secure belief in his heartfelt artistic values: "he no longer had the remotest idea of what he knew. . . . He was adrift." His mind is "a pit of wrenched habits and questions which slid like snakes," and with uncertainty and confusion comes a frequent loss of confidence in the ability to write—"It was a terror to write if one wished to speak of important matters and did not know if one was qualified." Old, fat, tired, depressed, at times he accepts the final triumph of science over poetry, "the heroes of the times were technologists, not poets, and the art was obliged to be in the exceptional engineering, while human communication had become the routine function." This artistic weakness in the face of fact had already been evident in Mailer's earlier work, where his artist-heroes regularly fail, and his own writing had already yielded to the "real" world in that he had abandoned fiction—that mark of confidence in the writer's ability to create reality out of his own imagination—and turned to the writing of "novels of fact" in which the events are supplied by the objective world but interpreted, i.e., given meaning, by the methods and subjectivity of the artist.

This invasion of the "real" into art continues in *Fire on the Moon*, where Mailer is prevented by the overwhelming scientific facts from writing fiction, and his narrative is swallowed up entirely by fact in numerous places where he simply gives in and reprints PR handouts and verbatim transcripts of long radio conversations between the astronauts and their Houston base. But elsewhere in *Fire on the Moon*, though denied the freedom of fiction by a reality grown too real to permit it, Mailer tries to transform scientific fact into literature by imposing upon it the romantic myth, using the rhetorical strategies which instrument and embody the values of the myth.

He begins, in good romantic fashion, by putting an artist into the scene, himself in the persona of the writer Aquarius—a name with the associations of astrological magic and life-giving wetness in a dry land. *Of a Fire on the Moon* begins with a lament for the suicide of Hemingway, "the greatest living romantic," who while he was alive had made it still possible to believe that fear could be kept at bay by courage and style. But Aquarius-Mailer's romantic affinities extend far beyond Hemingway, for the poetic persona Mailer creates to dramatize himself and his views in the confrontation with science derives primarily from the entire radical wing of romanticism, the energetic, tough, revolutionary line that leads from Blake and Byron, for all their differences, through such poets as Rimbaud to Sartre and Genet. Like an existentialist hero, he has without motive stabbed his wife at a party. He is a strutting, swaggering macho lover, a brawler and a drinker. He admires blacks, ethnicity, athletes, charismatic figures, the poor, but has no interest in rich and powerful but dull people, the managers, the bureaucrats, the pious, the middle-class. His politics are leftish—he has run for mayor of New York and lost badly—but although his instincts take him in this direction they do so not so much because he has any theoretical political-philosophic leanings as because it is on the left that he finds those romantic values he prizes above all else, energy, generosity, strong emotions, action, a desire for change, a sense of deeply felt engagement with the world, some suffering at its hands, and the consequent awe of its unpredictable powers.

Aquarius is a very old-fashioned, very standard romantic poet: "his philosophical world" is a place ultimately of mystery and uncertainty, built "on the firm conviction that nothing was finally knowable." Although trained as an engineer, he is intensely suspicious of reason and science as ways of dealing with his enigmatic universe, and his distrust of machinery and scientific ways of knowing descends directly from such writers as Carlyle and Arnold. "He has little to do with the immediate spirit of the time," and trusts instead, in a Keatsian manner, to his senses, particularly to his sense of smell, to put him in communcation with the real and vital nature of things, to tell him where life is present and where it is not. In characteristic romantic fashion, the senses in turn lead him to feeling the identity of things and their ultimate relationship in some great unified whole. But despite his close association with the poets of the romantic tradition, Aquarius is at the end of that heroic line of great imaginers, and his own reality, actually the reality of Norman Mailer, weighs as heavily upon him as the reality of science presses down upon his imagination. Forty-six years old, overweight, with his fourth marriage breaking up, subject to fits of deep depression, uncertain of his own powers, witty, vulgar, self-conscious enough to be able to laugh at his own egocentricism, baffled by his world but still feeling it deeply, envious that *he* is not the center of the moon adventure, he is partly Childe Harold and partly Sancho Panza. His sweaty clumsy appearance in the same scenes with the cool, effortless efficiency of the astronauts and engineers immediately enlarges the world of NASA enormously and complicates it with the presence of something familiarly human, with an individual "I," to oppose the collective "we" of NASA. With his appearance on the scene all the complexities and the poetic beliefs he embodies become real, and what was monolithically one immediately becomes differentially two. A rudimentary plot that can confer poetic meaning on events then becomes possible: a struggle between Aquarius and NASA, poetry and science, good and evil.

As the book proceeds, the human context is constantly expanded as the poet's art populates the NASA world with the ghosts of the old Indians who once walked the land where the rockets are now launched, with the memory of older adventurers—Odysseus, Columbus, Magellan— with the faces of poor blacks representing all mankind deeply etched by life:

> the faces of saints and ogres, of emaciated angels and black demons, martyrs, philosophers, mummies and misers, children with the eyes of old vaudeville stars, children with faces like midgets and witches, children with eyes which held the suffering of the lamb. But they were all faces which had gone through some rite of passage, some purification of their good, some definition of their remaining evil.

No scene in *Fire on the Moon* is more powerful, more deeply rooted in the human stuff of life, than the description of the people who gather to watch the great Saturn rocket of Apollo 11 fired at Cape Canaveral. The cars they drive, the cheap whisky they drink, the fears of losing their jobs, the despair, the sexual urgencies, the hero worship, the deep antagonisms between husband and wife, the play of the children, all surround the launch with a Breughel-like fullness of life, culminating in the most earthbound of images: "Out a car window projected the sole of a dirty foot. The big toe pointed straight up to Heaven in parallel to Saturn V."

It is not only people who make up the fullness of the poetic world Aquarius creates, but things as well, rendered in all their variety and their specificity, in contrast to the abstractions of science. Aquarius furnishes the void of every NASA scene with careful description of objects, the canteens, the food-serving machines that don't work, the red tiles, the broken-down dusty bus, the plastic webbing of the chairs, the round bed and floor-level bath of the luxury motel, the bleakness of the Venetian blinds, the color and quality of the land, the trees, and the sun rising and setting over the sea. All of this is partly the descriptive realism of a careful craftsman, but it ultimately functions in the book to create the solidity and reality, the sensuous plenum, of a cluttered landscape that gives the feel of the real world as human senses know it.

Aquarius' copious style is a typically romantic response to the monolithic quality of the event. His flood of words, his willingness to follow up every detail and raise every possibility of meaning, his relentless naming of parts and exploration of technological matters, his constant analysis of his own thoughts and feelings, his evocation of a vast world, past and present, around NASA, all are a frantic, at times excessive, verbal effort to give the landing on the moon some meaning, to break its self-contained isolation and pierce its stony sameness. But the copious style also suggests Aquarius' lack of certainty about his ability to deal with NASA—it is as if all the words in the world would somehow never be enough to humanize the technological fact by surrounding it with the variety and plenitude of the world and thus giving it the desired romantic magnitude.

These large-scale attempts to find meaning in, or force meaning on, NASA are backed up by the constant use of a variety of typically romantic rhetorical devices which work on a smaller scale, but at higher frequency, to achieve the same end. "To regard the world once again as poets," says Aquarius, we must "behold it as savages who knew that if the universe was a lock, its key was metaphor rather than measure." Metaphor, the central trope of romantic poetics, is employed steadily and with great skill by Aquarius, who is nothing less than a genius at finding the striking and the telling comparison which brings objects to life in a sudden flash. His metaphors, various and numerous as they are, all tend to perform the same task: to translate the mechanical world of technology into immediately human terms, and to bind the abstract world of science into a larger continuum with the existential world of men. The Saturn rocket at takeoff consumes as much oxygen as half-a-billion people, a sixth of the world's population, drawing breath at once; "physics was love and engineering was marriage"; the procedures of science resemble efforts to bring together a couple compatible except that the husband has a body odor repugnant to the wife; the safety precautions in the space vehicle are designed on a principle like the 613 laws of the Talmud; the astronauts on the moon walk with "about as much coordination as a two-year-old in three sets of diapers."

If metaphor creates or discovers meaning by reassembling those isolated things which belong together in the romantic world view, ultimately building the world into a great whole, then the symbol, that other primary romantic trope, intensifies the power of a chosen object until it radiates the meaning it contains or loses its opacity and focuses a world of meaning lying behind it. The computer, the machine, and the rock are transformed from things into symbols which reveal to Aquarius the nature of NASA; an old car buried at the end of the book—about which more later—manifests the condition of modern industrialism; and the rocket itself reveals the phallic worship of the technological society. Like other romantics, Aquarius assumes that objects "are shaped in a way which offers meaning, not only scientific meaning, but existential meaning," and he follows the painters in believing that "form is a language which seeks to express itself by every means." He looks carefully at every object, like some "medieval alchemist rubbing at a magic stone whose unfelt vibration might yet speak a sweet song to his nerve," hoping that the arrangement of its parts will speak to him of its nature and its history in miraculous language. He speculates that even "the face of the moon might be a self-portrait which looked to delineate the meanings of its experience in that long marriage with the earth and its long uninsulated exposure to the solar system and the stars." There is very little that is not made a symbol by the romantic Aquarius, and his ability to turn objects into symbols by focusing language on them until meaning flares out is one of his major techniques for attempting to enlarge the world of scientific fact.

Working in this fashion, Aquarius surrounds the rock of NASA with an extensive context, verbal, human, cultural, and historical, and by bringing it into opposition with the poet puts it into the movement of a rudimentary plot. But the monolith itself remains as yet intact, and to extend and demonstrate the truth of his romantic view of things, Aquarius must somehow split it, break into its center. To do so he must probe until he finds within NASA the conflicts, paradoxes, ambiguities, and mysteries which the romantic mind considers essential to reality. But these are the same qualities NASA has eliminated; like the machine its parts all work toward the same end and its components are interchangeable; co-operation not conflict is its guiding principle; and it moves toward the achievement of clarity and certainty in the place of mystery and ambiguity. So tight is its organization and so coherent are its theories that it is nearly impenetrable, but Aquarius believes that he can split the monolith if he can find the slightest aperture for his imagination to enter in: "where there is a little magic, there can be mighty magic." He notes that the maiden name of one of the astronauts' mothers was "Moon," hoping that it may indicate some astrological influence; he eagerly seizes on each malfunction of the machinery as an indication of mysterious non-scientific forces at work; he expands on the possibilities of fate manifesting itself in the lightning which strikes an oak in Collin's yard on the night before the launch; he extensively pursues the possibilities of visionary foreknowledge in a dream that Armstrong had when he was young of holding his breath and being able to hover motionless above the earth; he tries to relate the apocalyptic figure Apollyon in *Revelations* to Apollo 11, even though logic tells him that the names are etymologically unrelated. By continuing to probe and lever in a thousand little ways, he keeps opening the cracks wider and wider until he finds contradictory elements within NASA, ghosts in the machines, unconscious forces at work deep in the minds of the astronauts beneath their bland exteriors, apocalyptic tendencies in the emotionless efficiencies of science, and a metaphysical message in the smell of the dry dust of the moon. Using "every effort . . . to find an edge of the sinister in this first expedition to the peculiar soil of the moon," Aquarius ultimately locates a mystery concealed behind all the confidently reductive terms of science: what is electricity finally? or magnetism? or gravity? We know how to make these forces work, but their ultimate nature remains an enigma. Huge answerless questions are thus raised to cast their shadows over NASA's clarity.

The deep powers of the mind posited by romanticism as the source of true knowledge, the imagination, the collective unconscious, the Dionysiac, the id, "the mansions, theaters, and dungeons of the deepest unconscious where knowledge of a more poetic and dread-filled nature may reside," have been a fortress of literature long after science and rationalism conquered the surface of the daylight world. Psychology therefore inevitably becomes one of Aquarius' most powerful methods for opening up the depths of NASA and discovering concealed mysteries and latent conflicts. By investigating their dreams and looking deep into all the peculiarities of their personal lives, he hopes to discover "how much at odds might be the extremes of [the astronauts'] personality. From their conscious mind to their unconscious depth, what a spectrum could be covered!" Aquarius is very much a Freudian, and wherever he locates or creates a psychology, he assumes that it will have unconscious energies which will be individualistic, willful, freedom-seeking, and in conflict with the controls exerted by the reality principle. He tries therefore by means of hints and guesses to endow every person he meets in NASA with a psychology, a mind internally at war, and in one of his most desperate efforts to psychologize the world even tries to demonstrate a psychology of machines, "for if machines have psychology, then technology is not quits with magic." By demonstrating the uncertainties of science about how its apparatus ultimately works, and by showing that even the simplest machines are not always predictable, Aquarius is able to animate the machines and find "some all but undetectable horizon between twilight and evening where [the machine] is free to express itself, free to act in contradiction to its logic and its gears, free to jump out of the track of cause and effect."

Aquarius does not, however, try to impose his desired meaning on the moon shot merely by revealing the possibilities of latent conflicts and mysteries which the scientific myth ignores. To achieve his goal of making literature out of the science which denies its validity, he must put NASA into some great dialectical struggle, some romantic plot which moves it toward an end that will explain the mystery of existence and tie it to the order of the universe. NASA has, of course, its own plot derived from the linear logic of the computer: to go to the moon and return. But the inability of NASA and the astronauts to explain satisfactorily even to themselves just why they are going to the moon suggests the inadequacy of this plot, a lack of meaning felt by Aquarius and most of the people who looked at its climax on TV.

In the failure of the scientific plot, Aquarius finds his opportunity to impose on the event his own larger romantic plot. A sense of history, of the organic relationship of present things to the past and the development of the future from them, has always been central to the romantic consciousness, and Aquarius labors mightily to give the trip to the moon this kind of history. It is a very romantic history he constructs, a *Geistesgeschichte* of titanic forces involving the spirits of peoples and the struggle of mighty powers for the control of the universe. The frontier has at last disappeared in America, and now the people, half afraid and half eager, are ready for new adventures in space. The motive power driving the mission forward is twentieth-century corporate capitalism, and its *deus ex machina*, the German engineer Werner Von Braun, is literally dropped into a meeting on the eve of the launch by a helicopter. After developing the German rockets fired at London in World War II, von Braun brought his crew of rocket experts to America and developed the big boosters which power the exploration of space. Aquarius plays with the idea that there is some meaning in the similarity of NASA and Nazi, but the *geist* that really creates NASA and shapes it in its own image is modern capitalism, "the marriage of huge profit with huge service, of teamwork . . . and of detestation of contradiction." In the Aquarian view of history, corporate capitalism has "run amuck" in the twentieth century, producing a flood of shoddy goods, spending its money on advertising rather than on crafting its products well, and in the process has wasted the earth, gagging "the bounty of nature" with "plastic wastes," polluting the atmosphere, and burdening the people with factory work death-heavy in its pettiness. But the corporations have lost their nerve, their own ideas having gone dead in triviality and in fear of what has been done, and now in the 1960's, a fierce reaction, of which Aquarius is a part, has taken the offensive: "for years, the forces of irrationality had been mounting into a protective war against the ravages of corporate rationality run amuck." The voyage to the moon is a last effort by "corporate rationality" and the political system which mirrors and serves it: "to save itself [corporate capitalism] would commit the grand, stupendous, and irrational act (since no rational reasons of health, security, wisdom, prudence or profit could be given) of sending a ship with three men to the moon."

This earthly history is only a part of a much greater war in heaven between good and evil which Aquarius imposes on the venture. He draws attention to his own Manichean inclinations early in the narrative, and throughout the book he poses the metaphysical question: "was our venture into space noble or insane, was it part of a search for the good, or the agent of diabolisms yet unglimpsed?" "Man," he says, "was voyaging to the planets in order to look for God. Or was it to destroy Him?" Whether God or Satan is at the helm of this new *Pequod* becomes for Aquarius the most crucial issue of his entire attempt to understand Apollo 11, but the question is never answered to his own satisfaction, though in the end, as we shall see, he asserts that in the long run the venture into space is on the side of good, even if those who create it do not know what they are doing and he cannot specify what the good will be.

Aquarius continues to insist throughout his book that this cosmic plot is his chief instrument for transforming "a conceptual city of technologese to one simplicity—was the venture worthwhile or unappeased in its evil?" But the cosmic plot never quite succeeds in actually becoming the plot of *Fire on the Moon*. It remains merely one of Aquarius' many attempts at sympathetic magic, and the actual plot emerges as a conflict between science and poetry, personified in NASA and Aquarius, for control of the book. If NASA wins, the book need not, cannot, be written at all, since the official version of the astronauts' journey to the moon will provide the needed record of the facts, or it can be merely a reprint of PR handouts and transcripts of communications between the astronauts and Houston base. If Aquarius wins, the book will be written and will transform the moon shot into the new Jerusalem of the poetic myth embodied in Blake's prophetic books, Shelley's *Prometheus Unbound*, or, at the least, Byron's *Don Juan*. No such poetic triumph takes place, and instead we get a fragmented, disordered narrative of a poet lacking any firm *a priori* grasp of events, trying confusedly to impose his romantic ways of understanding on events he cannot control. Baffled by NASA, he must use a process of blind and furious association, a seizing of any stray possibilities, "sifting of haystacks of technological fact for the gleam of a needle or a clue." Going back again and again over the details of the flight and his own responses to it, like the detective to whom he frequently compares himself, he hopes that somehow with enough words and enough feeling he can write a book that will eventually animate the trip to the moon and make it shine with a light which sears the senses and satisfies the human desire for meaning to fill the void.

The hero-poet as underdog, the Miltonian single just man isolated from his fellows, doing battle with a fearsome enemy, is a standard romantic plot, *The Prelude* retold in modern terms. But the feelings of the inadequacy and failure of the poetic vision are far deeper in *Fire on the Moon* than in Wordsworth, and there is, as we shall see, a very real question of whether they are finally overcome. Nothing causes Aquarius-Mailer more distress and more doubt about his values than his allies in the great battle against corporate capitalism and its technology. At the end of his time as an observer of events in Houston and at Cape Canaveral, Aquarius returns to Provincetown to try to write his book. His friends, the artists and swingers of that intellectual community, have been drunk or stoned out of their minds all the summer during which NASA has taken the moon. As Aquarius looks at these late inheritors of the romantic tradition, though he loves them still, they disgust and frighten him:

> they had used their years, drinking, deep into grass and all the mind illuminants beyond the grass, princelings on the trail of hip, so avid to deliver the sexual revolution that they had virtually strained on the lips of the great gate. They had roared at the blind imbecility of the Square, and his insulation from life, his furious petulant ignorance of the true tremor of kicks, but now it was as if the moon had flattened all of his people at once, for what was the product of their history but bombed-out brains, bellowings of obscenity like the turmoil of cattle, a vicious ingrowth of informers, police agents, militants, angel hippies, New Left totalists, entropies of vocabulary. . . .

This is the counter-culture, the burnt-out ends of the romantic tradition in the summer of 1969. The poet feels betrayed on all sides by the course it has taken: the hippies, those "outrageously spoiled children who cooked with piss and vomit," Teddy Kennedy at Chappaquiddick, the Manson family, and Woodstock. What disturbs Aquarius most is the utter futility of all this "while the Wasps were quietly moving from command of the world to command of the moon," and his sense of hopelessness is perfectly concentrated in a scene at the end of the summer when some radical-chic friends give a party at which a car is buried. An old wreck used for summer transportation has broken down, and now a hole is dug for it in the sand—the work done by a very technological bulldozer of course—and amid much drinking and laughing the car is pushed in backward so that it rests on its trunk. Sand is pushed around it, but the front end remains pointing upwards above the sand like some sad broken monument of technology. Passages from Vergil and the Song of Songs are intoned, the children animate it by painting ribs and belly on its underside in green luminescent paint, and a sculptor welds pieces of it into odd angles to transform it into a piece of statuary. It is a tribal ceremony, one of the rituals of sympathetic magic about which Aquarius has been reading all summer in The Golden Bough, and it is a recapitulation of what he has been trying to do with the voyage to the moon, the humanization of the machine by means of art expressing romantic values. But Aquarius knows that this is weak magic, which finally has no more effect on the world than an earlier Provincetown ritual with the same import in which the image of a vagina with fluttering lips is superimposed on the TV screen and the image of the face of Richard Nixon, the political manifestation of the technological society and the robot man, as he speaks in the political version of computerese about the journey to the moon. In this attempt to instrument the romantic dream, love, or at least sexuality, replaces politics, the living organ the machine; but in the end it is only an illusion, for the substitution doesn't hold in the real world. Technology has conquered the moon.

Fire on the Moon portrays the possible death of art, romantic art at least, its disappearance into fad and joke, as a result of its failure to control the world, to grasp reality and to shape it in the image of its own desires, to be, to put it most simply, any longer believable. Aquarius suspects that the end has come—"what if radio, technology, and the machine had smashed the most noble means of presenting the Vision [of the Lord] to the universe?"—but he ends the book which has been so difficult to write on a small note of affirmation. He returns to Houston "looking for the smallest sign" and finds there "a true object, a rock from the moon," the last appearance of the monolith he has been trying to breach. Through two layers of glass deep in the "plastic vaults" of NASA he *smells* the rock, "tender as the smell of cleanest hay . . . like the subtle lift of love which comes up from the cradle of the newborn," and this evidence of the senses tells him that some living thing is there, gives him his sign and "certitude enough to know he would write his book and in some part applaud the feat and honor the astronauts because the expedition to the moon was finally a venture which might help to disclose the nature of the Lord and the Lucifer who warred for us. . . ."

On the whole, this final note of affirmation is a noble effort, and characteristic of *A Fire on the Moon* in its hard-working, intense effort to come to grips with issues of fundamental importance, to assert despite doubts that art and the values it carries can still shape the world. But the scene in which the rock is made to give off smell seems contrived, imposed on a book whose only slightly concealed doubts about itself are sounded again in the words "might help to disclose." Throughout the book the large metaphysical schemes and meanings that Aquarius has sought to fasten on the voyage to the moon have not been asserted as fact but smuggled in as subjunctive possibilities or as questions. Events "*suggested* that it was in the nature of structures to address each other." "*Was* the world more polluted" because a great novel had not been written? "The astronauts *could* even be men with a sense of mission so deep it was incommunicable even to themselves." *Did* an ape sent into orbit "sicken and die because of some drear but most recognizable message its animal senses had received from space . . . ?" "*Was* a curse building like the curse of the Pharaohs on the explorers who would open their tomb?" Suspense is built by such means, but when almost every major statement of meaning, metaphysical, moral, psychological, is bracketed as only a possibility, such deep uncertainty is not overcome by the joyous proclamation of the smell of a moon rock, through two layers of glass.

It is not, of course, a question of NASA and the technological world it represents having some absolute claim on reality, of being themselves "real" in some absolute sense, while the poet is only a dreamer of what might be, some heroic wish-fulfiller. Mailer sees science and poetry as alternative world-views, myths, struggling for the human mind and the right to shape the world throughout the nineteenth and twentieth centuries. Science has at last almost triumphed because its machines are capable of delivering such awesome power. What the steam engine and the spinning jenny started, the great rockets and the computers finally achieve, the authority to organize society, to create a new language, and to define the individual as another machine, mechanical or electronic. The conquest of the moon is the supreme achievement of the technological society, and its power in the world reveals that the romantic conception of the world and of meaning, far from being inevitable human ways of thinking, however "natural" they may by now seem, are rather a particular set of values, one way among many of organizing the phenomena of the world into a myth which endows the parts with meaning. Literature, or art in general, is not, *Of a Fire on the Moon* reveals, some unchanging, immutable thing, some eternally privileged way of writing about reality whose authority is located in some perennial psychological power—genius, imagination, sensitivity—or in some especially true way of writing— fiction, plot, hero, character, organic form—or in some special form of language metaphor, symbol. It is rather the expression of a set of values, a humanistic way of looking at and understanding the world, which has selected and stressed, made the essence of poetry, those ways of thinking and writing that, among all the many possibilities available, express its values and satisfy its needs: metaphor which binds diverse things together, fiction which creates new worlds from old, plots which bring the struggle of opposites to meaningful conclusions, heroes who express human individuality, symbols which contain infinity in a grain of sand, the sublime which reveals the mysterious wonder of the world, and organic form in which each thing speaks in its structure and development of its own essential nature. These ways of thinking and writing which constitute the romantic myth of literature exist, *Fire on the Moon* tells us in striking ways, in society where they must compete with other great systems of belief and their institutional organizations for power and continued existence.

JESSICA GERSON

Sex, Creativity and God

Sex is the mirror of how we approach God.
—NORMAN MAILER, *The Prisoner of Sex*

Norman Mailer—whose well-publiciz-
ed sexual attitudes are an idiosyncratic blend of hipsterism, apocalyptic sexuality, machismo and old-guard sexual morality—has become one of
the prime targets of feminist literary critics. Mary Ellmann or Kate Millett,
for example, who approach fiction from the vantage point of the treatment female characters receive at the hands of masculine protagonists or
authors have accused Mailer of being the prototypical male chauvinist.
Mailer, in turn, has responded at length to their charges, in *The Prisoner
of Sex* and elsewhere. Both sides, in waging this war, have fired many
brilliant and witty shots; unfortunately, just as many have been misfired.
Now that the smoke has cleared, it is time to see what the war was about
in the first place.

Millett sees Mailer as a "warrior for male supremacy," a "milita-
rist," an "advocate of genocide" and a latent homosexual who indulges in
"heterosexual posturing." Such misfired shots need not have been discharged at all if Millett had understood that Mailer's attitudes toward sex
and women have their philosophical base in mystical Judaism, not in
repressed homosexuality. Millett is not alone in missing this link; most
critics think of Mailer as a writer whose concern with Jewish themes,
characters and attitudes (unlike Roth, Bellow, Singer and Malamud) is
peripheral. No one, so far, has pinpointed the fact that Mailer's philoso-

From *Mosaic* 2, vol. 15 (June 1982). Copyright © 1982 by *Mosaic*.

phy, as expressed in his novels and non-fiction, is solidly rooted in the traditions of Jewish mysticism. Yet when this mode of perception is recognized, many puzzling facets of Mailer's work move into focus. His sexual attitudes, for instance, can be understood only in the light of his mystical preoccupation with the nature of God and how He manifests Himself.

Mailer first expressed this all-pervasive concern in 1954: "I have some obsession with how God exists. Is He an essential God or an existential God; is He all-powerful or is He, too, an embattled existential creature who may succeed or fail in His vision?" This "obsession" became the cornerstone of his philosophy: "That simple conception of God as an embattled vision . . . every one of his notions had followed from that, for if God were a vision of existence at war with other visions in the universe, and we were the instruments of His endeavor . . . then what now was the condition of God?" Mailer's views on sex and procreation are based on his concept of the role we, as God's "instruments," play in God's struggle. Accordingly, sex is "the mirror of how we approach God."

If Mailer's views are permeated by Jewish mysticism, the latter is characterized by a dualistic view of women which more than equals Mailer's own. The *Kabbala* is a masculine doctrine, pervaded by an inherent tendency to stress the demoniac nature of women. Indeed, the demoniac are offspring of the feminine side of the *sefiroth*. . . . (The *sefiroth* are the rays of light which emanate from the Godhead. They represent polarities which are in a perpetual state of tension, or delicate balance. Only when they are in proper balance can they be fused into the unity of beauty, which is in the middle. Unity is, accordingly, the goal of all action of the *sefiroth*, and of all mystical perceptions.)

There are two sides to the tree structure of the *sefiroth*, which correspond to the masculine and feminine. They reflect a dualism which Jewish mysticism inherited from the gnostic myths and incorporated into the *Kabbala*. The feminine, or left side, is the side of negation.

This feminine side is formed of three qualities: *Binah, Din* and *Hod. Binah*, or intelligence, is the power of rational analysis, which can also be seen as technique, or craft. This is the paired opposite of *Hokhmah*, the intuitive, inspirational quality, which is masculine, and which Mailer and the mystics regard as crucial, seeing the rational faculty as the enemy of inspiration. Thus Mary Ellmann is correct, if sarcastic, when she pinpoints Mailer's equation of the writer's technique with his "Great Bitch," who is "devious" and "full of swilling crafts by which writers can be contaminated. . . . The vision, then, [in art] must be of an achievement beyond craft, something wildly and spontaneously pure." The Kabbalists, like Mailer, dislike systematic analysis, preferring "flashes" of illumination set down without apparent order. As Gershom G. Scholem says, "the more genuinely and characteristically Jewish an idea or doctrine is, the more deliberately unsystematic it is." Thus Mailer's "Great Bitch" can also be seen as *Binah*, or the power of craft and systematization.

The masculine, associated with genius and inspiration, is in consequence creative, restless and striving. This masculine quality of *Hokhmah* is emphasized by Mailer, to whom "man was a spirit of unrest who proceeded to become less masculine whenever he ceased to strive." Masculine inspiration, however, is fragile, always subject to the powers of *Binah* and *Din*, which is the feminine quality of stern judgment, also considered punishment, or law, and often equated with evil or death. No wonder Mailer is "afraid of the power of woman" and protective of man, who is "relatively fragile."

Women also possess demoniac and occult powers. Deborah, the "Devil's daughter," is a "Great Bitch who delivers extermination" and "transmits messages to some distant force." Similarly, Marilyn Monroe gives a "witch's turn to the wheel at Chappaquiddick." They are reminiscent of Lilith, the female demon of Jewish folklore.

But if the Jewish tradition is, as Simone de Beauvoir says, "anti-feminist," it is also intensely dualistic and ambivalent. Woman may be evil, but she has benign qualities as well, and in both her roles is as necessary to man as she is to the workings of the *sefiroth*. Without her, the dialectical interaction of polarities so essential to the creation of the unity which calls forth God's grace to the lower spheres cannot exist. Accordingly, Mailer feels threatened by feminist stress on elimination of sexual differentiation. His "aversion remained to the liberal supposition it was good that men and women become more and more alike; that gave him a species of aesthetic nausea . . . a sense of displacement." His "sense of displacement" is caused by his profoundly felt conviction that life and creativity emerge "from a cauldron of boiling opposites," a restatement of his oft-affirmed belief that the dialectical interplay of opposites is necessary for interaction between the upper and lower worlds. Any erosion of masculine or feminine distinctions is in Mailer's eyes the erosion of a dialectic. Obviously, this kabbalistic viewpoint brings him into virtually irresolvable conflict with that aspect of feminist ideology which tends to regard most sexual differentiation as the product of erroneous social conditioning.

Perhaps the chief reason why women and the feminine principle are so essential to the cosmic scheme is their role in sexual intercourse (which will be discussed later) and, more pertinently for our present purposes, their procreative and creative role. While the masculine principle contains the idea of inspiration, struggle and formation of the seed, both in a sexual and creative sense, the feminine principle is that of a vessel which nurtures the seed that *Hokhmah* has placed within *Binah*. Man is the creator, but woman is the passive, nurturing recipient of this active creative force, without which the created form would never be realized. *Tefireth*, or beauty, is placed *between* the masculine and feminine sides of the *sefiroth*, for beauty (the final created form) is the result of the interaction (Mailer's "dialectics") of the masculine and feminine. Hence Mailer feels that "beauty has its root" in the creation of "any being which is harmonious, imaginative . . . artful, good for life, good for the continuation of life." "Life comes from the meeting of opposites," states Mailer, and "life is gained every time opposites meet each other nicely."

The division of the *sefiroth* into masculine and feminine sides corresponds to a deep-seated dualism in Judaism. Although women are respected for their dialectical necessity in the cosmic scheme, they are also feared by virtue of their power, so closely allied with "the Other Side." Woman is enormously powerful because of her link to Satanic forces and because of her creative capacities. She occupies, according to Mailer, a "position one step closer [than man] to eternity (for in that step were her powers)." For this reason, "men look to destroy every quality in a woman which will give her the powers of a male, for she is in their eyes already armed in the power that she brought them forth." Mailer reminds us of the Hassidic sage, the Koretzer, who sees woman as the God-given Evil Impulse which must be "mastered," before she overwhelms man.

This hostile aspect of sexuality is reflected in "The Time of Her Time," a story which feminist critics often single out for attack, precisely because its protagonist, Sergius, is a chauvinistic sexual athlete whose pride in his masculinity depends on his feminine conquests. His antagonist, Denise, is an independent, dominating, quasi-intellectual. Sergius' attraction to Denise is undoubtedly based on masculine pique and viciousness, and he does employ "anal rape," as Millett says, to bring her to her first orgasm. Millett, however, neglects to point out that Denise is fully as aggressive and vicious as Sergius, although in a verbal, rather than physical sense. These two are evenly matched antagonists, truly engaged, as Sergius says, in "the dialectic of an affair." One might even say that Denise. wins the match, for she walks out on a desolated Sergius who has come to realize, too late, that "she was a hero fit for me." Thus Sergius has won a Pyrrhic victory at best, indicating that Mailer's attitude toward his hero's sexual pretensions is not admiring, as Millett charges, but ironic.

Until *Marilyn* (1973), Mailer did not create any female characters of genuine depth and importance. The women in his novels are subsidiary characters, providing only dialectical interaction with the hero, who is engaged in the major struggle of the novel—to come to terms with his manhood, and his relation to God. Sergius, Rojack, and their predecessor Mikey Lovett, struggle for a new consciousness. They sink in an abyss of despair, disillusionment and non-definition at the beginning of their novels, but emerge from the Slough of Despond into a new awareness of their personal roles at the end. Their ascent toward redemption is achieved, at least in part, through their relationships with women.

There are, roughly speaking, two kinds of women in Mailer's fiction; they correspond to the split which is at the heart of mystical Judaism. One kind mirrors the darker feminine aspect of the *sefiroth*. Denise is such a heroine, and Deborah Kelly, of *An American Dream*, is another, much more full-blown and invested with specifically demoniac abilities. Ruta, Deborah's maid and her corollary in the novel, is similarly allied with Satanic forces. Such female characters are counterbalanced, however, by Mailer's second kind: Elena of *The Deer Park* and Cherry of *An American Dream*, who represent, each in her own way, the possibility of redemptive good to the men they love.

Deborah's sexual attributes signal her demoniac quality. Sex with her is painful, even dangerous: "There was something so sly at the center of her, some snake . . . rare was the instant I could pay my dues without feeling a high pinch of pain as if fangs had sunk into me. . . . I always felt as if I had torn free some promise of my soul and paid it over in ransom." In other words, Rojack has engaged with demoniac forces (symbolized by the snake) and has ransomed himself to the Devil, rather than allying himself with God.

Deborah and Rojack, significantly, have a childless marriage; the child they conceived "came brokenly to birth, in terror, I always thought, of the womb which was shaping it." As we shall see, children are God's reward, or grace, for "good sex"; Deborah did not deserve this reward, nor did Rojack in the context of this marriage, for he had "ransomed his soul."

Rojack had been thus tempted partly because of Deborah's "Great Bitch" qualities—i.e., her ability to confer "wit and style." Mailer (like his persona, Rojack) reveres and hates "the Bitch," for she, like Deborah, can confer these gifts, which he openly cherishes. She does this at her whim, however, just as Deborah does, so that the male is left in the position of supplicant for her favors. It is no wonder that this all-powerful force is hated as much as it is desired.

Interestingly, Deborah's specifically defined connection with Evil ("I'm evil if truth be told," she says) is completely overlooked by Millett, *et al.* Millett sees all Mailerian sexual relationships as victimization, and views Rojack's relations with Deborah in that light. But only if the reader does not perceive that the core of *An American Dream*'s novelistic intent is the emergence of Rojack as saint and hero, a quest for which it is necessary to conquer evil, can he regard Deborah, who is murdered by Rojack, as a victim. Deborah is not murdered, as Millett claims, because her "sodomous adultery" is "the final blow to [Rojack's] vanity, his sense of property, and most material of all, his fancied masculine birthright of superordination." She is killed because she is a manifestation of the evil forces which Rojack must overcome. Deborah had to be slain for the same reason that Saint George had to slay the dragon; to regard her as the victim is to bewail the slaying of dragons.

Unlike Ruta and Deborah, Elena and Cherry, who exemplify Mailer's second type, are benign, redemptive and creative women. They and Marilyn, their successor, are all involved, with varying degrees of success, in the arts. They are performers, people for whom the creation of art is a motivating force. This quality indicates their alliance with the benign aspect of the feminine *sefiroth*. These women also repeatedly offer their men redemptive love which, in Elena's case, is rejected.

The case is different for Cherry in *An American Dream*. Cherry, who is specifically identified as a "sign" from God, offers such love, which Rojack accepts. The Jewish mystics believe that there are some souls which have a special ability to lift those who are on a lower plane, so that they are enabled to begin the return journey to a higher form of existence. Cherry is such a soul, offering Rojack a love which is really grace, for at the moment of orgasm Rojack feels "wings in the room" and forgiveness for his sins: "Had flesh ever promised to forgive me so?" In addition, Cherry offers him her "gift" for winning at the gambling tables, so that he can continue his journey. At the end of the novel, she and Marilyn Monroe, from heaven, send their blessings to Rojack, thus giving him strength to go on to salvation.

Mailer's portrait of Marilyn Monroe, in *Marilyn*, is an extension and enrichment of Lulu, Elena and Cherry. She is Mailer's first fully-developed heroine. Although strikingly similar in physical and psychological characteristics to Elena and Cherry, she is more complex. If she is an "angel," she is also a "killer," rather like Mailer's "Great Bitch." While she offers "redemption" and "deliverance" to her public, in her personal life she is narcissistic and destructive. Two-sided, she combines in herself all the benign and redemptive qualities of Cherry and Elena with some of the killer qualities of Deborah and "the Bitch." This is possible because Monroe did become, in her best roles, as Mailer claims, a true artist; she did achieve wholeness and beauty. Thus she may be said to embody the coupling of the *sefiroth*, which produces art or beauty.

If the Kabbalists' attitude toward women is dualistic, their attitude toward sexuality is not. Heterosexual relations are not only approved, but considered absolutely necessary. The *Zohar* insists upon the "duty of cohabitation," for "this pleasure is a religious one, giving joy also to the Divine Presence." This duty is based on the *Zohar*'s conception of man's spiritual and physical functions as an analog for the divine process. The phrase from Job 19:26—"And I shall behold God out of my flesh"—is used to prove that the body of man can provide understanding of God and His functioning. As Herbert Weiner states: "The *Zohar* sees nothing unspiritual about examining the human body, and particularly the sex act, as a paradigm of the hidden spiritual universe from which all existence draws its life." Grace, life or joy cannot flow from the upper worlds until the proper couplings (called *zivvug*) of the *sefiroth* occur, in the world below. The most important way to effect this "proper coupling" is the sex act. Thus the *Tzaddik* (holy man) says: "The perfection of the upper worlds waits upon the perfection of the lower worlds . . . Adam and Eve must be turned face to face before the upper union is perfected."

Sex, accordingly, becomes a means of transcendence, for in the moment of intense orgasmic pleasure, one transcends oneself in order to come closer to God, providing Him with strength and joy. One reason, then, why Mailer regards sex as "the connection of all things," is that in intercourse one "connects" not only with one's partner, but with God and the cosmos. It is also the concomitant dissolution of the ego and loss of identity which Rojack experiences in his transcendent sex with Cherry: "I had no brain left, no wit, pride, no itch, no smart, it was as if the membrane of my past had collected like a dead skin to be skimmed away." This loss of ego is akin to a purification rite.

As a corollary, the loss of intellect or rationality is always desired by the mystical consciousness, and this emphasis on the holiness of physical desires over and above intellectual striving is reflected in Rojack's first perfect orgasm: it "came up through my body rather than down through my mind . . . bliss and honey." Such ability to rise above rationality is necessary in all creative processes, including love-making. Since our sex lives, at their best, provide us with "comprehension of the mysterious by the same way one went to faith," the hipster's search for the "ultimate orgasm" in "The White Negro" is in its essentials a "mysticism of the flesh" much like the Jewish mystic's.

The orgasm also offers the moment in which one earns redemption, or salvation. Mailer feels that "the physical love of men and women

. . . is the salvation of us all." Redemption is, then, signaled by the "grace" Rojack experiences during his redemptive sex with Cherry, when he achieves a glimpse of "the heavenly city." God has, as the Kabbalist would say, sent grace and joy flowing to the lower worlds as a reward for *zivvug*, or perfect coupling.

A close connection between sex, procreation and creativity exists in the *Kabbala*, as it also does in Mailer's thought processes. The process of *zivvug* results in the creation of a child or a work of beauty (*Tefireth*). This "creation of something out of nothing," according to Scholem, "is only the external aspect of something which takes place in God Himself."

The orgasm, then, is intimately linked with God's purposes. Mailer "preferred to believe that the Lord, Master of Existential Reason, was not thus devoted to the absurd as to put the orgasm in the midst of the act of creation without cause of the profoundest sort, for when a man and woman conceive, would it not be best that they be able to see one another for a transcendent instant, as if the soul of what would then be conceived might live with more light later?" He echoes the words of the *Zohar:* "If his wife should conceive, the heavenly partner bestows upon the child a holy soul: for this convenant is called the covenant of the Holy One." Such a "holy soul" is the fulfillment of God's plans, "something which took place in God Himself."

Hence Mailer's statement that "God's destiny is flesh and blood with ours" bears a close resemblance to the Kabbalist's belief that the union of male and female is the mystical symbol of the union between God and the *Shekhinah* (holy spirit). The embryo which, according to Mailer, is "the fluid consciousness of God" or work of art is the product of this sacred mystery. To Mailer, then, "the social contract" involves the "principles of God, nation, family, marriage . . . and the distinction of the sexes . . . a mystical union between God and man."

The *Zohar*'s primary concern, according to Weiner, is "the tensions, antagonisms and oppositions which necessarily precede any synthesis and creative unification. Since the child and the work of art are manifestations of unification, a close connection between procreation and creativity exists in Kabbalism. The sex act, during which one "drives forward into the seat of creation," becomes allied with artistic creativity in Mailer's "kabbalistic mind" (to use his own term). Woman is desired not only in her sexual role, but because she is man's link with the cosmos. Without her, man can neither be an instrument of God's will, nor can he do the creative work God wishes of him. Thus, for Mailer, "the cunt, smelly though it may be, is one of the prime symbols for the connection of all things."

The Jewish mystics' belief in sex as a form of transcendence, or "the mirror of how we approach God," has a reverse side: sex is also perceived as a mirror of how we approach the Devil. (In Mailer's and Jewish mysticism's universe, Satan is always battling with God for Supremacy. Man's acts aid or impede God in this battle.) Promiscuity, or "ugly and vulgar" sexual acts, lend strength to the Devil, and activate evil impulses in the universe. The Kabbalists, according to Louis Epstein, believe that "a sexual connection for carnal pleasure alone opens the world to evil impulses and to that extent dethrones God. Such connections are in the service of 'Sitra Ahera,' or Universal Evil." If "good sex" always contains the possibility of conception, "bad sex" denies this possibility.

Just as he creates two kinds of women, so Mailer regards the two possible sexual orifices in a woman, the vagina and the anus, as reflections of the two aspects of femininity. In his Manichean schematization, a woman's sexuality consists of "these twin holes of life and death." The vagina is the seat of procreation, the "cave of becoming," and is, therefore, the province of the Lord. The anus is the "kitchen of the Devil," in which a man's seed "perishes" and "leaves its curse." Thus Rojack, making love to Ruta, allows "a minute for one, a minute for the other, a raid on the Devil and a trip back to the Lord."

Millett, completely missing Mailer's mystical outlook, sees only one thing in Rojack's anal sex with Ruta: latent homosexuality. But Rojack's sexual relations with Ruta are a way-station on his ascent, part of his purification rites. The whole of An American Dream can be seen as a kind of walpurgisnacht, in which the kind of sex Rojack experiences is indicative of the stage of ascent he has reached. With Ruta, he has engaged in a successful "raid on the Devil," but is not yet ready for the "grace," or reward of perfect orgasm and conception. His next step is his pure and procreative relation with Cherry, which significantly takes place toward dawn, and is strictly vaginal—in "the province of the Lord." Furthermore, it is only when he removes Cherry's diaphragm that they experience their apocalyptic orgasm, for Mailer feels that all "good sex" must contain the possibility of a child. Indeed, Cherry and Rojack are rewarded by God with the grace implicit in conception; they conceive a child that night.

Following the publication of the Masters and Johnson study, many feminists espoused the solitary joys of the clitoral orgasm. Mailer was alarmed at the implied dispensability of man, for the dialectical interplay between man and woman, and the masculine and feminine aspects of the sefiroth, was thereby threatened. The orgasm, to Mailer, must be the resolution of tensions between masculine and feminine, and should contain the possibility of conception. All this is lost if a woman can create her own orgasm. And it is therefore from a mystical perspective that he "fears in his heart the ferocity of those fifty clitoral laboratory orgasms lost by transmission into the plastic ether of some scalded libidinal psychosocial air. Where would their message go? For nothing, he believed, was ever lost, no curse, no cry of wasted come." Sexuality, robbed of its dialectics, enters the Devil's domain of "waste."

In *The Deer Park*, God tells Sergius to "think of sex as Time, and Time as the connection of new circuits." A dimension of this rather cryptic insight requires elaboration.

Jewish mystics firmly believe in *gilgul*, or the transmigration of souls; according to this creed, all souls pre-exist, and descend into mundane bodies to complete their (and God's) mission on earth, by means of pious acts, or mystical cognition of God, or working out restitution for the sins of an earlier life. Mailer similarly expresses "this belief in karmic balance—that we come into life with a soul that carries an impost of guilt and reward from the past. And at the end of each life we may be reborn, which I think is a reward in itself." At the time of conception, the soul enters into a new body; indeed, Mailer believes that "a soul must be present at a conception."

Mailer's belief in transmigration strengthens his conviction that conception must be possible in "good" sexual intercourse. If there is no possibility of conception, then there is no chance for the soul to work out its destiny in the new body, to connect with a new circuit. Sex is, to Mailer and the Kabbalists, the time when man, as the instrument of God's will, conceives a child who becomes the vehicle for a "soul" which represents some of the "more poignant notions of God." The orgasm, the earthly avenue to transcendence, is a form of grace: a reward for carrying out God's mission. Thus Mailer can say "the come was the mirror to the character of the soul as the soul went over the hill to the next becoming." It follows, then, that contraceptives obstruct God's work, and it is herein that Mailer's anachronistic even contradictory stance on contraception and abortion must be understood.

He is opposed to birth control pills, although he does not advocate legal suppression of birth control information; on the contrary, he feels that feminists who demand "legal access to contraceptive information and devices" are expressing "reasonable demands." He does not argue against women's right to control their own reproductive functions, although he does not easily accept the idea, for the reasons already given. Their right reluctantly granted, he demands that they employ removable devices, like the diaphragm Cherry uses in *An American Dream*. He "found himself in favor of abortion but opposed to contraception; even, by his logic, more opposed to the pill than . . . the diaphragm. The latter offered, at least, a chance each night . . . remove the plug and have a child."

How can one be in favor of abortion but opposed to birth control? Before probing his position further, we should understand the mystical attitude toward these questions. Orthodox Jewry is, on the whole, op-posed to birth control, and the mystical sects, like the Hassidim, are even more firmly opposed to it. On abortion, however, there are two views within orthodox Judaism. The first is that a woman, like a man, is prohibited from a "waste of nature," and therefore is allowed to practice neither abortion nor birth control. The second, which closely resembles Mailer's own, is that the woman is not included in the injunction against waste. Therefore, although she may not use any device—intercourse must be natural—anything she wishes to do *after* intercourse to destroy the seed is permissible. The Jewish prohibition, then, like Mailer's, is directed at "waste of seed" more than at any action which follows the sex act itself.

Of course, Mailer, for all his mystical preoccupations, realizes that there may be real problems in the raising of an unwanted child; it is the possibility of choice at the moment of conception that he insists upon. Accordingly, he feels that abortion may be necessary if a woman cannot properly nurture the soul which has been placed in her keeping: "If she was not ready to devote herself to such a creation, then why not assume she was in her right to deny the life? For who could ever calculate the violation left on life, or the extinction of karma, which resided in the loveless development of souls who had been conceived in love?"

Evaluation of Mailer's views on these subjects is a difficult task, for most of us are not as comfortable about living with paradoxes as Mailer and the mystics are. Can we, for instance, accept abortion as a better alternative than contraceptives, in terms of the stress on the female mind and body that abortion causes? I, for one, cannot, and Mailer himself is uncomfortable with this question, recognizing that the price a woman pays for her "apocalyptic orgasm" may be excessively high: "All right, the women will counter . . . we have to get butchered by abortionists, I've never been able to answer this. I will agree that the absence of the Pill was better for the sanity of men than women. I think women . . . since they are closer to creation . . . have to pay more for the privilege." He is aware of the paradoxes in his thinking, but is unable to resolve them.

One need not be in direct opposition to all Mailer's views on Women's Liberation, abortion and birth control, however. He does not deny woman her right to practice birth control: he merely disapproves of it; there *is* a difference. He, at no time, denies her right to abortion. He even believes that woman, as a female hipster, must be as free as man in her search for the ultimate orgasm: "Women must have their rights to a life which would allow them to look for a mate. And there would be no free search until they were liberated. . . . Finally, he would agree with everything they asked but to quit the womb." Perhaps, he feels, their liberation will lead to their ultimate transcendence, as he had hoped for the hipster.

All that he asks, with a certain pathos, is that women not close themselves irrevocably to the possibility of conceiving that "exceptional soul" which is waiting to be born of their exceptional lovemaking. Nor is his fear of women's rejection of childbearing totally gratuitous; certain more extreme segments of the Women's Liberation movement do totally disavow the child-bearing role.

Mailer's controversial disapproval of homosexuality and masturbation is triggered by the same body of concerns which we observed in his other sexual attitudes. For instance, in the manner of Jewish mystics, he condemns masturbation as a "waste of seed" which is anti-life: the *Zohar* regards the "waste of nature" in masturbation as the severest sin recorded in the scriptures.

Another reason why masturbation is condemned by Mailer as "a vice" is that it involves no testing of the self, therefore no growth. Testing involves dialectics, whereas masturbation is onanistic; "If one masturbates, all that happens is, everything that's beautiful and good in one, goes up the hand and into the air, is lost. Now what the hell is there to absorb? One hasn't tested himself. You see, in a way, the heterosexual act lays questions to rest, and makes one able to build upon a few answers." Without intercourse, there is no measuring, no traffic with eternity.

Mailer feels that even violence and rape are better than masturbation, because the latter is violence to the self, a kind of suicide, and rape is violence directed outward. His justification of such a view is that in the end, if all the violence is expressed, the ones who survive, the "hero-monsters," will be the fittest to begin a new race. This kind of irresponsible statement leaves him open to the charges of those feminist critics who claim that he expresses fascist or "Nazi" ideas, and it must be admitted that such ideas represent Mailer at his worst, on the side that allows him to feel comfortable with extreme views which he sees no necessity to modify, no matter where they lead. At the same time, however, it is important to realize that this is the obverse side of mysticism, the tendency to verge on heresy, for which other Jewish mystical groups condemned and excoriated the Sabbatians (whom Mailer closely resembles).

Many of his reasons for condemnation of masturbation carry over to his condemnation of homosexuality. He dislikes homosexuality because it, too, is a "waste of nature," involving no possibility of a child, no testing of the self, and no growth through dialectical interaction. As a corollary, he objects to the non-absorption of the feminine in the homosexual act: "Homosexuals tend to pass their qualities over to one another, for there is no womb to mirror and return what is most forceful and attractive in each of them."

In all these views, he is at one with the Jewish mystical tradition, which regards homosexuality as a non-procreative, evil perversion, totally foreign to Judaism. It is associated with "dying" heathen civilizations, like the Canaanites, and regarded as so alien to Judaism that historically, "Jews were above suspicion of committing sodomy."

Mailer's views on this subject are complex, however. Just as the Sabbatians felt that one must descend into evil in order to conquer and thus rise above it, Mailer feels that it may be necessary to descend into one's own compulsions, including homosexuality, in order to ascend to self-discovery: "Implicit in all my beliefs had been the idea that society must allow every individual his own road to discovering himself. . . . Sexual relations, above everything else, demand their liberty, even if such liberty should amount to no more than compulsion or necessity." His mystical and anarchistic views make such freedom for self-discovery essential, for the alternative is the Mailerian horror: "a deadened existence."

D.J.'s and Tex's epiphany on the mountain top in *Why Are We in Vietnam?* reflects Mailer's belief in the purgative power of descent into one's compulsions. Their failure, however, is marked by the fact that they do not descend all the way into their homosexual impulses: thus they develop into killers. Mailer feels that repressed homosexuality, like any other repressed sexual urge, must be expressed or it will turn to violence, even war: "being half excited and half frustrated leads to violence. Whenever one is aroused sexually and doesn't find a consummation [Tex's and D.J.'s condition precisely] the sex in one's veins turns literally to violence." Thus although Millett states, correctly, that D.J.'s and Tex's violence "springs directly from their stifled homosexuality," she goes astray in reaching the conclusion that "Mailer's own sanctimonious sexual dogmatism regards [homosexuality] as a greater evil than murder. . . . Cruelty and violence are inevitable and beneficial . . . defenses against homosexuality." Mailer would agree that violence does spring from repressed homosexuality, but he does not regard Tex's and D.J.'s participation in the Vietnam War, which follows their sexual repression on the mountain top, as "beneficial." Millett has not caught the distinction Mailer repeatedly makes between personal and collective violence: the former may be beneficial, but never the latter.

His belief in the need of each individual to "find his own road to self-discovery," even if it be via the hated route of homosexuality, makes him see "no reason for society to punish it." Thus we have a certain balance in Mailer which many feminists overlook; although he has a horror of certain "evil" practices, typical of the traditional views of the mystics, he also shares their respect for individuality, and their consequent antagonism toward any repressive measure inflicted by society. In the end, it is usually the respect for the individual which triumphs. He thunders his jeremiads against evil practices, to make us aware of our responsibilities for God's destiny. That awareness absorbed, however, we must still pursue our own destinies, for better or worse, in a voyage of self-discovery.

An over-all evaluation of Mailer's sexual views reveals a dichotomy which is typical of his dualistic views in general, and reflects the Manichean values of Jewish mysticism. The question to be weighed is whether or not Mailer achieves, in his insights into sexuality, the unity and wholeness which is the goal of all mystical speculation and action.

One side of Mailer, the traditionalist, regrets departures from ancient beliefs and practices. He laments that "the Jewish intellect" has "emancipated itself from its own tradition," personified by "the old Kabbalists." Thus one voice, the voice of tradition and apocalyptic prophecy, warns us of the "diabolical" dangers of our modern ways. Yet Mailer's other voice reflects the obverse side of Jewish mysticism which, as we have seen, is itself two-sided. This side of Mailer respects and sees "beauty" in the individual's right to self-determination and acknowledges the truth of women's claims that they are an exploited class: "Yes, the argument [was] that women were a social and economic class exploited by a ruling class of men . . . he was obliged to recognize [that] . . . the life of the argument was on the side of the women." Accordingly, he is "willing to agree that the economic exploitation of the female was a condition in need of amendment." He becomes uncomfortable only when masculine-feminine differences are denied, when the area of "eschatology" is invaded.

In the final analysis, Mailer is not sure of any answers. The structure of *The Prisoner of Sex*, like Mailer's mind, see-saws between traditionalism and anarchistic individualism, and the closest he can come to a resolution, or unity, is given at the end of that work. Women must "go all the way" toward self-definition, as long as they do not abandon the possibility of producing a child which, he argues, will be the most creative expression life will offer them. Whether or not we agree that this is woman's most creative act, the conclusion is flexible enough to satisfy most feminists.

Indeed, not all Women's Liberationists see Mailer as their enemy; Gloria Steinem urged him to run for Mayor of New York City, for she felt an affinity for his political views. Many of his political and personal views are similar to those of the feminist movement. His views on the hipster's individual search for apocalyptic orgasm, for example, are only at one or two removes from much feminist writing. What is Erica Jong's *Fear of Flying*, for instance, if not an assertion of just such picaresque freedom for her heroine? The difference lies mainly in the non-religious dimension of *Fear of Flying*.

Although Mailer does not always resolve his mystical conflicts between conservatism/radicalism or good/evil, and often teeters back and forth between his own dualistic bifurcations, one thing does remain constant. His concern with the "embattled universe," and our constant involvement in it, has never changed fundamentally, although some of his views have become slightly more moderate or conservative with time. His idea of sex as time, and time as the connection of circuits, has not changed since he first expressed it in *The Deer Park*. With such a viewpoint, sex can be seen only as an act of the utmost eschatological import, as "the mirror of how we approach God," so that each aspect of sexuality becomes charged with a significance of which a non-mystical mode of perception is free. For this reason, Mailer is, truly, a "prisoner of sex": he is locked into its eschatology.

Perhaps the ultimate reason for his "prisoner" role is his deep-seated conviction that the sex act, and the production of children, is our most profound form of affirmation. We carry out our responsibilities to God with our "good sex," and the children who result are God's "blessing," His ultimate grace. In an age when many young people are removed from tradition, and question the desirability of producing children, Mailer's faith in children as an affirmation of God's and our own ongoing destiny has great relevance. Similarly, at its best, his insistence on the value of tradition is useful, for we who live in an age of transition, disillusionment and malaise, can profit by being reminded of traditional values, and the ideals of which they are the expression.

One of his severest feminist critics, Mary Ellmann, grudgingly but perceptively admits that Mailer, in "attempting to reconcile an acute appreciation of the present with a passionate attachment to a masculine ideal [I would call it a mystical as well as a masculine ideal] succeeds in extracting some vitality, like clotting blood, from defunct opinions," but she feels "the difficulty, and perhaps the futility, of such a reconciliation."

In the end, one must sadly agree; the reconciliation Mailer looks for is sometimes almost impossible to achieve. Yet this does not necessarily make him an enemy of Women's Liberation, as has frequently been claimed; rather, he asks the necessary questions and should be considered "the loyal opposition." In the unscholarly, but wise words of Pogo: "We have met the enemy, and he is us."

JUDITH A. SCHEFFLER

The Prisoner as Creator in "The Executioner's Song"

*The American writer in the middle of the twentieth century has his
hands full in trying to understand, and then describe, and then make
credible much of the American reality. It stupefies, it sickens,
it infuriates, and finally it is even a kind of embarrassment to
one's own meager imagination. The actuality is continually outdoing
our talents, and the culture tosses up figures almost daily that
are the envy of any novelist.*

—PHILIP ROTH

Philip Roth's description of the
American writer's dilemma in 1961 is still accurate after twenty years.
One response to this dilemma is the blend of journalism and fiction
labeled the new journalism, "faction," or, in the case of Norman Mailer's
The Executioner's Song (1979), "a true life novel." This work has drawn
criticism on two predictable fronts: as part of the general debate over the
merits of the new journalism, the story's truth is questioned by reviewers;
as a portrait of a cold-blooded murderer, the novel creates doubt about the
value of writing 1000 pages "about unredeemed sociopathic behavior"
(*Atlantic*, Jan. 1980).

A response to these serious criticisms must confront the basic
question, what is a true life novel? Although Mailer's study of Gary

---

From *The Midwest Quarterly* 4, vol. 24 (Summer 1983). Copyright © 1983 by Pittsburgh
State University.

Gilmore does contain the prisoner's own writing and although much of that writing is surprisingly good, *The Executioner's Song* certainly cannot be classified in the increasingly popular genre "prison literature," for Gilmore never shaped his letters and poems into a coherent work. The merely factual story of a highly intelligent man, imprisoned for 18 of his 35 years, whose inability to cope with the demands of society and intimate relationships results in two senseless murders, cannot explain the book's hold over our imagination. Why, then, is this, as Joan Didion claims, "an absolutely astonishing book" (*New York Times Book Review*, 7 Oct. '79)?

Reading *The Executioner's Song* in the context of Mailer's other fiction, particularly *The Deer Park* and *An American Dream*, shows how the novelist's craft of selecting and ordering fragments into a coherent portrait operates in this true life novel and makes the characterization of Gilmore fascinating, but not necessarily authentic. Despite Mailer's unprecedented absence as a voice and controlling personality in this work, he is very much the creator, shaping his material rather than merely recording fact. *The Executioner's Song* takes its place along with other Mailer works in exploring the same dichotomies of light and darkness, reason and instinct, clarity and mystery. Whoever the real Gary Gilmore was, in this book he is the figure of the artist of the self, defining and redefining his personality, controlling events and other characters, projecting a world. The opposites of Mailer's dialectic are presented as manifestations of the protagonist's mental state or development, beginning with Gilmore's almost total immersion in instinct and impulse before his murderous rage, and moving to his weaving of reason and mystery into the fabric of his controlled world.

Gilmore's lack of self-control charges the first half of the novel with the tension of impending disaster. Gary is introduced as a mistfit, whose prolonged incarceration and dependence upon drugs and alcohol darken his prospects for adjustment to the small town lifestyle of traditionally Mormon Provo, Utah. His depressions, rages, childishness, and impulsiveness seem to be the inevitable, spontaneous expression of a personality that lacks any awareness of possibilities or alternatives in handling problems. Minor annoyances like a dead battery or a broken muffler lead to helpless brooding. Anger over conflicts with others erupts in acts of wanton destruction, like the breaking of car windshields, or in ill-matched fights where Gary cheats but always loses. His blindness to reason is total: "I'm Gary Gilmore," Gilmore said, "and they can't hurt me." An irresponsible worker, a foolish consumer with an obsessive desire to possess an over-priced white truck, an impotent and selfish lover, and a stupid thief who steals without planning and without regard for risk, Gary follows the dictates of ego and blind whim: "How come people get caught and you don't?" challenges his employer. Gary said, "I'm better than they are."

The tension rumbling beneath this portrait of Gilmore builds to a climax in the unplanned, unprovoked murders of two young Mormon strangers, Max Jensen and Ben Bushnell. For readers who seek causal relationships, the shootings are clearly seen as Gilmore's response to his breakup with Nicole Baker. He writes to Nicole, before the violence:

> I don't know why I did this to myself. You are the most beautiful thing I've ever seen and touched . . . I see it in detail like a movie. And it makes no sense. It makes me scream inside.

Afterwards, at the trial and in prison, the murderer reflects upon the involuntary nature of his crime:

> I sometimes feel I have to do things and seems like there's no other chance or choice.

> I killed Jenkins [sic] and Bushnell because I did not want to kill Nicole.

Murder for Gilmore as for Stephen Rojack in *An American Dream* is the ultimate solution to the problem of complex relationships, a cleansing of the Self and simplifying of the environment. The Other, particularly of the opposite sex, poses a threat that the Self eliminates by a murder that is essentially a victory of simplicity over complexity. In this act, the murderer stands upon the brink of solipsism, where his personal world becomes the only world. Gilmore's instinct to satisfy his compulsion, whatever the consequences, is the inevitable expression of his lack of self-control.

After presenting this violence, Mailer develops Gilmore as a character exercising considerable control, as he balances the contrary pulls of reason and instinct in his personality. Serving as a foil to this act of self-creation, however, is the obviously tawdry and plastic forming of Gilmore's image by the media. Against this background of executive deals and contracts for story rights, the reader encounters Gilmore's own efforts to control his world; the overwhelming emphasis upon the media in the novel's second half highlights rather than obscures the protagonist's act of self-creation.

Everyone—from David Susskind to Tamera Smith, a fledgling reporter for the *Deseret News;* from Geraldo Rivera to Earl Dorius, Assistant Attorney General, who sees the case as the highpoint of his career—is itching to cash in on the Gary Gilmore story. It turns out that Larry Schiller is the "media monkey" who hits the jackpot, and his miles of taped interviews are the foundation for Mailer's later work. Gilmore, however, is aware of this exploitation; despite a lifetime locked away from society, he is fully in tune with contemporary media magic. In fact, pop culture subtly punctuates the action throughout the novel: station KSOP in Salt Lake City plays the doomed lovers' song, Gilmore rides to his death to the music of "Paloma Blanca," a popular tune on the prison van radio, and he has a farewell phone conversation with his favorite singer:

> Are you the real Johnny Cash? . . .
> Well, this is the real Gary Gilmore.

Gary is not always above the temptations of the media; he is, for example, fascinated by his picture in the year end "Images of '76" issue of *Time*. Occasionally he himself assumes a false macho image, asking, "Who the hell won the World Series?" after hearing his death sentence. Other times he amuses himself, joking along with the monkeys: "Who's going to play me in the movie?" Nevertheless, Gilmore is definitely not the Western hero; we see this from the start when Gary cannot endure a bus ride home over the route his Mormon great-grandfather had traveled with a handcart. Moreover, he states quite clearly and repeatedly that he rejects the publicity and its circus atmosphere:

> I simply refuse to capitalize on this in any way . . .
> This is a personal thing, it is my life Nicole.
>   I can't help getting some publicity but I'm not looking for any.

In contrast to the media's efforts to project an image of Gary the condemned man and Gary and Nicole the star-crossed lovers, is Gilmore's own definition of himself and organization of his world after the murders. Here we see Gary as the artist figure, comparable to Sergius O'Shaugnessy in *The Deer Park* and Rojack in *An American Dream*, and here we see Mailer at work on the raw material of Schiller's tapes, transforming it into a characterization remarkably consistent with that of protagonists in his previous novels.

Gilmore's sense of identity was tinged with mystery and imagination from his youth, when he found his birth certificate naming him Fay Robert Coffman, son of Walt Coffman. The surname was one alias out of many that his often absent father, Frank Gilmore, used in his travels, but Gary's mother, Bessie, soon chose a different name for her son, honoring her favorite star, Gary Gooper. Although his ancestors were mostly English and he had been raised in Utah, Gary preferred the mystique of Ireland and the roughness of Texas and claimed them for his own. Like Sergius O'Shaugnessy, he was a seemingly self-created man without a clear heritage.

In a *Paris Review* interview in 1966, Mailer distinguished static, stereotyped "characters" from elusive, changeable "beings":

A character is someone you can grasp as a whole, you can have a clear idea of him, but a being is someone whose nature keeps shifting.

Mailer's Gilmore is a being. His moods, personality, and attitudes freely develop and change in the cramped prison environment where he seems, ironically, to function best. Describing his personality as "Slightly less than bland," Gilmore belies this statement by keeping his interviewers and the reader constantly confused and guessing about his motivation and real feelings. Barry Farrell, a writer working with Schiller, classifies 27 poses Gilmore assumes in his replies to their questions:

> racist Gary and Country-and-Western Gary, poetic Gary, artist manqué Gary, macho Gary, self-destructive Gary, Karma County Gary, Texas Gary, and Gary the killer Irishman. Awfully prevalent lately was Gilmore the movie star, awfully shit-kicking large-minded aw-shucks.

In striking contrast to his brutal crime is Gilmore's poise and dignity throughout his imprisonment; often he is clearly superior to the prison officials, relatives, and media around him. Clad in white, his legs shackled, Gary looks "like an actor playing a saint" as he makes his eloquent death plea before a morally and legally confused Pardons Board, while TV cameras record the event. Gilmore balances an innate sense of public relations with an honest fidelity to his own convictions as he moves gracefully between roles. Listening to the taped interviews,

> It looked to Farrell as if Gilmore was now setting out to present the particular view of himself he wanted people to keep. In that sense, he was being his own writer. It was fascinating to Barry. He was being given the Gilmore canon, good self-respecting convict canon.

Gilmore is, in fact, a skilled storyteller. Like O'Shaugnessy and Rojack, he freely bends the truth to present himself to advantage, making up stories to satisfy his parole officer and regaling everyone he meets with the same sordid prison tales, guaranteed to shock any law-abiding citizen. Fully conscious of this convict art, he denies any insincerity:

> I like language, but I tell the truth. In jail you rap a lot, you know, to pass the time. Damn near every convict has his little collection of reminiscenses, anecdotes, stories, and a person can get sorta practiced at recollecting . . . the fact that you tell something more than once to more than one person doesn't make that thing a lie . . . Larry, I do emphasize things . . . I've spent a lot of time in the hole, and in the hole you can't see the guy you're talking to, 'cause he's in the cell next door or down the line from you. So, it just becomes necessary to . . . make yourself clear and heard. . . .

Throughout the letters and conversations Mailer has chosen for this true life novel, the mind of an author carefully selecting his material is subtly but clearly seen in the coherent body of imagery and motifs that surface. Gary had written over a thousand pages to Nicole and obviously Mailer included only a fraction,

> to show him at a level higher than his average. One wanted to demonstrate the impact of his mind on Nicole, and that might best be achieved by allowing his brain to have its impact on us. Besides, he wrote well at times. His good letters are virtually intact.

The imagery may be classified into recurring motifs exploring the reason/mystery dichotomy. Plagued by violent images, Gary dreams of a previous life when he had been beheaded and enclosed in a box that was put into an ovenlike hole in the wall. References to demons, musty oldness, and tumbrels sprinkle both his poetry and prose. They are balanced by gentle, loving images of Nicole as an elf and a white bird. Images of fear and beauty combine in a coherent picture of transcendence that reaches beyond the dichotomies to a realm where reincarnation, dream, and a silver sword protect against all demons and the temporal pain tormenting "the cobbled streets of my ancient mind." One of the more remarkable letters to Nicole explains:

> No, I ain't drunk or loaded or nothing this is just me writing this letter that lacks beauty—just me Gary Gilmore thief and murderer. Crazy Gary. Who will one day have a dream that he was a guy named GARY in twentieth century America and that there was something very wrong . . . but what was it and is it why things are so super shitty, to the max, as they used to say in twentieth century Spanish Fork. And he'll remember that there was something very beautiful too in that long ago Mormon mountain Empire and he'll begin to dream of a dark red-haired sort of green eyed elfin fox. . . .

Gary as lover is, of course, a major role in the novel, for as it precipitates the violence and expresses his concept of his afterlife, it is a measure of his growth and development throughout the events. From the start, he insists that theirs is an ancient relationship, that their present affair is but a reunion after a separation in a previous life. Nineteen-year-old Nicole shares this sense of recognition to an extent, but her confidence and fidelity are strained by her promiscuous habits learned from years of sexual freedom, a history of mental illness, and an almost masochistic need to satisfy every man she encounters. Gary's helpless pain over their conflicts is the only chink in the armor of his machismo; even in prison he writes that "you have the power to crush me or destroy me."

The media frenzy to obtain both sets of love letters as the basis for a Romeo and Juliet story shows how vast is their misunderstanding of this unique relationship. For Nicole's part, it is a mystical experience, inspiring her to a fidelity she had never before imagined, but it is Gary who wields the awesome power. High priest of their love/death cult, he writes, "By love . . . we can become more than the situation."

Here in prison, touching Nicole mostly through his remarkable letters, Gary creates a solid relationship between two of the most unlikely candidates. It is, notably, *his* creation, and he solipsistically perceives Nicole as the passive mirror of his thoughts and desires rather than as a separate personality. The inability to recognize the separate existence of others, seen dramatically in his murders, is in fact more completely and methodically expressed in his theoretical and authoritative letters to Nicole, where a calmly reasoned suicide pact alternates with vulgar, enraged expressions of uncontrolled jealousy. The complex emotional disparity between any two people, always more emphatic between the sexes, is here transcended as priest Gary charges his disciple: "You are not to go before me, Nicole Kathryne Gilmore. Do not disobey me."

This calm resolve to die is the most noteworthy aspect of Gilmore, and is certainly the one that sparks the most media attention. Gary is the Hipster figure, theorized by Mailer in his essay, "The White Negro" (*Advertisements for Myself*, 1959): he chooses

> to accept the terms of death, to live with death as immediate danger, to divorce oneself from society, to exist without roots, to set out on that uncharted journey into the rebellious imperatives of the self.

In an age of absurdity, the Hipster survives the constant threat of death by confronting it squarely. Dynamic change and relativity of identity characterize him, and he rejoices in contradiction, since it is a fact from which no man can escape:

> the element which is exciting, disturbing, nightmarish perhaps, is that incompatibles have come to bed, and inner life and the violent life, the orgy and the dream of love, the desire to murder and the desire to create, a dialectical conception of existence with a lust for power, a dark, romantic, and yet undeniably dynamic view of existence for it sees every man and woman as moving individually through each moment of life forward into growth or backward into death.
>
> ("The White Negro")

With his Hemingway code of bravery ("I just hate fear. I think that fear is a sort of sin in a way. . . ."), Gilmore challenges the society that instituted the death penalty to have the courage of its convictions. In this sense, Mailer does see Gilmore as heroic, and admiration shines through the selected material, causing uneasiness in some readers who consider the prisoner's inexcusably barbaric crime. Mailer sees him as "a genius endowed with an exceptional imagination." He possesses

> the capacity to discover an exceptional solution to a virtually impossible situation. He understands the fundamental thing that so few people understand: that it's more important to die and save your soul than to live and feel it slowly be extinguished.
>
> (*The New York Times Magazine*, 9 Sept. '79)

Clearly he did not possess this ability to solve an "impossible situation," much less fix a dead battery, before the murders. It is as though the crime and the sensory deprivation of the prison have given him a mental freedom to be constructive in balancing reason and instinct.

The final Gary Gilmore opts for free will, as do Sergius O'Shaughnessy and Stephen Rojack, though it may be purchased at others' expense. As poet and self-taught painter, he has always shown a discipline in his work that runs counter to his impulsive crimes. Prison, it seems, offers him time for thought and solitude to reduce the complex outer world to one of timeless, restricted simplicity. Here, he finally controls both aspects of the reason/instinct dialectic, expressing them in a total world view, with love and death as the cornerstones. "Nicole, I believe we always have a choice," he writes, affirming the paradoxical free will that generations of prisoners have proclaimed in journals and stone wall etchings. This choice, according to Schiller, who strives to project a sentimental yet sensational, human image of Gilmore, threatens the public who

> could live with a killer who was crazy, mixed-up, insane. But for a murderer to start controlling the issue—that was developing a lot of hatred for Gilmore. People felt as if the world was being tipped on edge.

This contrast between the media Gary and Mailer's Gary creates a constant tension in the second half of the novel, resolved only in Gilmore's death.

The Executioner's Song is a novel that uses true life persons and events as the impetus for the author's carefully crafted characterization. This basic point answers the two questions of the book's veracity and the worth of chronicling an unredeemed criminal's acts. Both questions, to a large extent, miss the point. Whatever confusion may arise from our current fashion of blending fact and fiction, the imagination prevails in a novel and need not abide by journalistic rules. An exploration of the real

Gary Gilmore should more appropriately focus on the great loss of humanity that occurs when a prison setting proves more congenial than society to a man who has spent his life incarcerated. Not at all a final triumph of the spirit, Gilmore's story dramatically shows how imprisonment can become a habit incapacitating a man to survive decently outside, with the exercise of normal self-discipline. Prison has its own code of conduct, but it is not society's code. Mailer's implied admiration for Gilmore makes for captivating fiction, telling us once again more about the author's views than about his flesh-and-blood subject. *The Executioner's Song* is a novel and a good one, but it is not true life.

HAROLD BLOOM

Norman in Egypt: "Ancient Evenings"

"Crude thoughts and fierce forces are my state." With this artful sentence, Normal Mailer begins his Book of the Dead. Our most conspicuous literary energy has generated its weirdest text, a book that defies usual aesthetic standards, even as it is beyond any conventional idea of good and evil. Like James Merrill, with whom he has in common absolutely nothing else, Mailer finds one of his occult points of origin in the visionary Yeats, but unlike Merrill, Mailer truly shares Yeats's obsession with the world of the dead. Merrill's spirits, in *The Changing Light at Sandover*, are representations of our lives, here and now. But Mailer has gone back to the ancient evenings of the Egyptians in order to find the religious meaning of death, sex, and reincarnation, using an outrageous literalism, not metaphor. What the subscribers to the Literary Guild will find in it is more than enough bumbuggery and humbuggery to give them their money's worth.

But there is also spiritual power in Mailer's fantasy (it is not the historical novel that it masks itself as being) and there is a relevance to current reality in America that actually surpasses that of Mailer's largest previous achievement, *The Executioner's Song*. More than before, Mailer's fantasies, now brutal and unpleasant, catch the precise accents of psychic realities within and between us. *Ancient Evenings* rivals *Gravity's Rainbow* as an exercise in what has to be called a monumental sado-anarchism, and one aspect of Mailer's phantasmagoria may be its need to challenge

From *The New York Review of Books* 7, vol. 30 (April 28, 1983). Copyright © 1983 by The New York Review.

Pynchon precisely where he is strongest. Paranoia, in both these American amalgams of Prometheus and Narcissus, becomes a climate.

Ancient Evenings goes on for seven hundred large pages, yet gives every sign of truncation, as though its present form were merely its despair of finding its proper shape. The book could be half again as long, but no reader will wish it so. Thomas Mann proudly remarked of *his* Egyptian novel, *Joseph and His Brothers*, that "as the son of a tradesman I have a fundamental faith in quality. . . . The song of Joseph is good, solid work." Mann gave his life to the book for sixteen years, and its quality is durable. Mailer has given *Ancient Evenings* a decade, and it is wild, speculative work, but hard work nevertheless. Its quality is not durable, and perhaps does not attempt to be. Mailer is desperately trying to save our souls as D.H. Lawrence tried to do in *The Plumed Serpent* or even as Melville did in *Pierre*. An attentive reader ought to bring a respectful wariness to such fictions for they cannot be accepted or dismissed, even when they demand more of the reader than they can give. Mailer wishes to make his serious readers into religious vitalists, even as Lawrence sought to renew our original relationship both to the sun and to a visionary origin beyond the natural sun. Mailer's later works thus strain at the limits of art.

Mailer's readers will learn rather more ancient Egyptian mythology than they are likely to want or need, but the mythology is the book, and seems more than mythology to Mailer. Like his ancient Egyptian nobles, Mailer hunts, slays, roasts, and devours his gods, in order to increase his share in courage, sexual potency, immortality. I assume that a reading of *The Book of the Dead (The Papyrus of Ani)* first alerted Mailer to the Egyptian analogues to his own ongoing obsessions, but whether that is true or not, it is of some interest to look at the translation of the ancient text by E.A. Wallis Budge (*The Egyptian Book of the Dead: The Papyrus of Ani in the British Musuem*. Dover, 1967) alongside Mailer's nightmare of a book.

The Book of the Dead exists in many versions, some of which may go back thousands of years before the 190 covered in Mailer's book (1290–1100 BCE). But they tend to tell the same stories concerning the gods and the afterlife, stories that center upon the death, mutilation, and resurrection of the god Osiris. Even as Osiris triumphed over death, so the Egyptians hoped to emulate him, and indeed to achieve a virtual identity, with that king of eternity, who in his resurrection had taken on aspects of Ra, the sun god. And even as Osiris had risen in his reassembled corporeal body, so the ancient Egyptians conceived that they would live again in more than the spirit. As resurrected gods, they would feast and love forever.

Unfortunately, the great hazards of passing through the various stages and places that lay between the tomb and heaven made this vision of resurrection difficult even for those handfuls of monarchs and great nobles who could afford properly monumental and well-stocked tombs. The *duad* or Land of the Dead swarmed with hideous monsters, and only a proper combination of magical preparation, courage, and plain good fortune was likely to get one through. This is essentially the given materials that Mailer appropriates.

What Mailer adds are his own emphases upon scatology, buggery, and the war between women and men, but the fundamental material on the wavering border between the human and the divine, and on the world of the dead, is already there in Egyptian mythology for him to develop. His book's peculiar and disturbing sincerity is its strength. The reader is likely to be numbed by the repetition of charnel-house horrors, and even the most avid enthusiasts of buggery, whether heterosexual or homosexual, may flinch at confronting Mailer's narrative exuberance in heaping up sodomistic rapes, but the religious seriousness of all these representations is rather humorlessly unquestioned and unquestionable.

"Crude thoughts and fierce forces are my state" because Mailer's narrator is the Ka or surviving double of a dead young nobleman who had been named Menenhetet the Second. This unfortunate Ka takes us on a ghastly tour of the necropolis, where it encounters the Ka of the young man's great-grandfather, Menenhetet the First (henceforth I shall emulate Mailer in calling both these personages by their shortened name, Meni). Great-grandfather Meni is Mailer's central character, and has just died out of his fourth life, at a still monstrously vigorous sixty. We are at about 1100 BCE in an Egypt all too like the United States in the 1970s, but now we are hearing the song, not of the executioner, but of the magician.

Great-grandfather Meni, a devourer of bat dung, has mastered all the mysteries, including a rather lively one of Mailer's own invention (which rather peculiarly is attributed to Mosaic esotericism). In this occult performance, one becomes one's own father, by begetting one's own next incarnation upon a woman who thus in some sense already is one's mother. Meni the First selects his own granddaughter, Hathfertiti, for the honor, which in some other sense has to be regarded as very nearly one's dying act. But I don't intend to give an elaborate plot summary, since if you read *Ancient Evenings* for the story, you will hang yourself. There is a lot less story than any summary would indicate, because this is a book in which every conceivable outrage happens, and yet nothing happens, because at the end everything remains exactly the same.

There are only two characters who matter in the book, and they not inaccurately could be termed versions of Hemingway (I mean the novelist, not one of his characters) and of Mailer himself, the heroic precursor and his vitalistic follower and son. One is the great pharaoh Ramses the Second, victor over the Hittites at the battle of Kadesh, and the other is the three-times reincarnated magician Meni the First, who fought at Kadesh as the pharaoh's first charioteer.

Ramses the Second is a beautiful and potent male god, usually called Usermare, while the scarcely less potent Meni is condemned to be the perpetual worshipper of his pharaoh, a condemnation enacted by way of a ferociously divine bumbuggering of Meni the First by Ramses, which in true Maileresque terms sets up the dilemma that all Meni's magic will never resolve. To have been bumbuggered by one's precursor is a sublime new variant on the sorrows of literary influence, but evidently it does not inhibit the strong sons of strong fathers from bumbuggering the Muse, a delicious revenge carried out by the magician Meni upon the queen and goddess Nefertiti, prime wife of Ramses the Second.

Most of the magician's story is told by him to the reigning pharaoh, a descendant of the great Ramses, in the course of an endless night of banqueting, which together with the inserted lives of Mani the First consumes about five hundred of Mailer's seven hundred pages. There is an unsolved problem of form here, but that is minor compared to defects of texture, to hopelessly unresolved inconsistencies of tone and of badly mixed imagery. Mann found a style for Joseph in Egypt, but Mann's strength was irony and Mailer's strength is never ironic. There are some horribly grand set pieces, most notably the battle of Kadesh, but there are also immense stretches through which the poor reader must crawl with an unrewarded patience, including the entire "Book of Queens," which occupies 135 pages of harem intrigues. Nothing else Mailer has published is so hopelessly listless as the "Book of Queens," which might have been entitled "The Prisoner of Sex Revisited, or The Radical Feminists' Revenge." In fairness to Mailer, I offer a single representative passage, honestly chosen at absolute random:

> Disloyalty stirred then in Menenhetet, and his breath became hushed as the water. He was ill with desire for the little queens. It was vivid as shame to be alone among so many women with not even a boy about older than ten, but then by that age, the children born here were off to the priests for schooling. All he heard were the voices of women who had no husband nor friend nor any lover but the Good and Great God Usermare. Worse. About him were all the plump eunuchs with their black muscles enriched by the air of their easy life. Thereby they were appealing to all—the hundred women and Menenhetet—attractions powerful to his senses. His loins ached, his throat was gorged, and his mouth was so hungry he would not look through their windows at the beerhouse

these little queens were making. In the dark, like the horse that hears a murderous beast in the rustle of a leaf, he started at each breeze. At this hour, there were eunuchs everywhere in the gardens, fondling one another with their fingers and their mouths, giggling like children, and the flesh of Menenhetet was inflamed.

But poor Meni's flesh is inflamed for pretty much all of these seven hundred pages, and ultimately the inflammation is the lust to be Usermare-Ramses, pharaoh and god, and so never to die except as a rapid transition between incarnations. The actual magical and physical process by which Meni begets a fresh incarnation is rather obscure. He must be able, "during an embrace, to ride his heart right over the last ridge and breathe his last thought as he passed into the womb of the woman and thereby could begin a new life, a true continuation of himself; his body died, but not the memory of his life." Whatever that gallop over the last ridge truly is, Meni the First still comes to a very bad end. Unlike Scheherazade, Meni finally runs out of stories, and is graciously allowed to cut his own throat with the pharaoh's own knife. Where has Mailer's fantasy of his magician brought us? On the Stevensian aesthetic principle that "It Must Change," Meni, once a general, can find his epitaph in Stevens:

> Nothing had happened because
> nothing had changed.
> Yet the general was rubbish in the
> end.

Why are we in Egypt? Where else could we be? Mailer's dialectics of sex and death have found their inevitable context, though the world of Usermare and Mani may not be wholly distinct from the world of Gary Gilmore. Pynchon and his newest Mailer are what Vico called "magic primitives," giant bards who try to deify themselves by the ancient praxis of divination, but Pynchon scatters himself even as he finally scatters his hero Slothrop in *Gravity's Rainbow* quite literally, by having him undergo a parody of the fate of Osiris, or as Yahweh scattered the builders of the Tower of Babel. Mailer, like his American ancestors from Poe through Hemingway, resists the scattering of his self and name. *Ancient Evenings* thus fulfills the critical prophecy of Richard Poirier's book on Mailer (1972) which found in the emphasis upon buggery a dialectic by which meaning is both de-created and restituted. Poirier argued that it is almost as though in the Kabbalah of Norman Mailer, buggery constitutes the trope of the breaking of the vessels, as a negative creation that is a prime Gnostic image.

Mailer, as a fictive theologian, has been developing a private version of an American gnosis for some time now, in the sense that Gnosticism can be a doctrine insisting upon a divine spark in each adept that cannot die because it never was any part of the creation anyway. Such a doctrine resigns history and mere nature to the demons or bad angels, and identifies what is immortal in the self with the original abyss, from which the Yahweh of Genesis stole in order to form his bad creation. Libertine and antinomian, since it identifies the law of the Torah with a catastrophic creation, such a faith is the antithesis both of normative Judaism and of orthodox Christianity. In Jewish Gnosticism or Kabbalah, the catastrophe that ruins creation is imaged as the breaking of the vessels, the shells of the cosmos and the body that becomes riddled with divine light. Consciously or not, Mailer has substituted buggery for the breaking of the vessels.

Buggery even as a word has Gnostic origins, alluding as it does to the Bogomils or Bulgar Manichaeans. As a metaphysician of the belly (self-titled), Mailer had some earlier inclination toward regarding buggery as an antinomian act—a transgression of all the rules of a deeply false order that would reveal a higher truth (see the buggering of Ruta, the German maid, in An American Dream and "The Time of her Time"). In Ancient Evenings he has emancipated himself, and seems to be verging upon a new metaphysic, in which heterosexual buggery might be the true norm (as it may have seemed to the Lawrence of Lady Chatterley's Lover), and more conventional intercourse perhaps is to be reserved for the occult operation of reincarnating oneself in the womb of the beloved. Here we may recall an analysis of the Marquis de Sade that was carried out by Horkheimer and Adorno in their chapter on Juliette in The Dialectic of the Enlightenment, in which they observed that the harangues of the Sadean heroes marked a final perfection in the rationality of the Enlightenment. Yet this seems more appropriate to the sado-anarchism of Pynchon's paranoid rationalists than to the Egyptian mysteries of Mailer-Meni, who has striven so mightily to wrench himself away from post-Enlightenment reality.

Mailer's is too formidable a case of an authentic literary drive to be dismissed, and dismissal is certainly not my intention. Ancient Evenings is on the road of excess, and what Karl Kraus said of the theories of Freud may hold for the speculations of Mailer also—it may be that only the craziest parts are true. Mailer probably is aware that his Egyptian obsessions are in the main tradition of American literature, carrying on from much of the imagery of the major writers of the American renaissance.

The definitive study here is John Irwin's American Hieroglyphics: The Symbol of the Egyptian Hieroglyphics in the American Renaissance. Irwin centers on Poe, and in particular on *The Narrative of Arthur Gordon Pym*, but much that Irwin says about Melville's *Pierre* is as relevant to *Ancient Evenings* as is Irwin's brilliant commentary on *Pym*. Irwin argues that Emerson and those he stimulated—Thoreau and Whitman positively; Poe, Hawthorne, and Melville negatively—found in ancient Egypt a vision of resurrection through reincarnation or reappearance that they could oppose to the Hebraic vision of the resurrection of the body. Certainly the attitudes toward death of the Pharisees, and of mythological Egypt, could not be more antithetical than they were, and perhaps American writers inevitably prefer the Egyptian account of personal survival, as Yeats did also. Irwin, commenting on *Pym* and on *Pierre*, sees in the Egyptian resurrection a kind of Freudian displacement of the writer's body into the writer's book, of blood into ink. As the great Western version of the *Abendland*, nineteenth- and twentieth-century American literature perhaps takes on an almost Egyptian sublimity, an exaltation of cultural belatedness as the second chance of a literal life beyond death. Mailer's *Ancient Evenings* yet may seem a work in *Pierre*'s sad class, if not quite that of *Pym*'s, an American vision of final sunset.

I call the American literary vision of death "belated" in contrast to the ideas of death first in normative Judaism and then in early Christianity. Post-Biblical Judaism associated the salvation of each Jew with that of all Jewry, and the third century CE sage Rab said of the world to come that in it "there is no eating and drinking, no begetting of children, no bargaining, no jealousy and hatred, and no strife." This is akin to the quite Pharisaic reply of Jesus to the Sadducees that "when they rise from the dead they neither marry nor are married, but are like angels in heaven." Irwin, in his *American Hieroglyphics*, contrasts the Jewish and Christian versions of personal immortality to the Egyptian notion of personal survival:

> As the empty tomb and the vanished body evoke the Judeo-Christian concept of an immortal self that is independent enough of the body to have dispensed with even a bodily image, so the monumental pyramid and the mummified corpse express the Egyptian sense that the immortality of the personal self is constitutively linked to the preservation of such an image. . . .

Irwin reads Poe's *Pym* and to a lesser extent Melville's *Pierre* and *Mardi* as a kind of Egyptian reversal of the Jewish and Christian understanding of death as God's revenge for our original sin against the Father. Like Poe and Melville, Pynchon and the Mailer of *Ancient Evenings* participate in this reversal which, as Irwin says, "refers not to death as revenge, but to a revenge against death, the revenge that man attempts to take, through art, against time, change, and mortality, against the things that threaten to obliterate all trace of his individual existence." Thus Melville said of his Pierre's Maileresque attempt to write a book of "unfathomable cravings" that: "He is learning how to live, by rehearsing the part of death."

Mailer too wishes us to learn how to live, in an America where he sees our bodies and spirits as becoming increasingly artificial, even "plastic" as he has often remarked. If our current realities, corporeal and psychic, manifest only lost connections, then Mailer's swarming, sex-and-death-ridden ancient Egyptian evenings are intended at once to mirror our desperation, and to contrast our evasions with the Egyptian rehearsal of the part of death. Myself, I vote neither for the sage Rab nor for the vitalistic magus Mailer, but I acknowledge the strength of his crude forces and fierce thoughts.

Mailer concludes his book with an enigmatic rhapsody, in which the Ka or double of Meni the First expires, and the power of the dying heart enters the Ka of Meni the Second. That combined Ka sails toward rebirth, while Mailer-Mani declares somberly: "I do not know if I will labor in greed forever among the demonic or serve some noble purpose I cannot name." That may be a touch grandiose, but it is thoroughly American, and perfectly Gnostic also in its aspiration to join itself to an alien God. Mailer, until now, has seemed to lack invention, and so after all to resemble Dreiser more than Hemingway, a judgment that *The Executioner's Song*, an undoubted achievement, would sustain. *Ancient Evenings* is an achievement of a more mixed kind but it is also an extravagant invention, another warning that Mailer is at home on Emerson's stairway of surprise.

Chronology

1923   Norman Mailer born in Long Branch, New Jersey, to Isaac Barnett Mailer and Fanny Schneider Mailer.

1927   Family moves to Brooklyn, where he attends local public schools.

1939–43   Attends Harvard University, intending to study aeronautical engineering. Wins *Story* magazine's annual college contest and writes first novel (unpublished). Receives a B.S. in engineering sciences.

1944–46   Elopes with Beatrice Silverman in February, 1944, and remarries her in a traditional Jewish ceremony in March. Enters the Army, and serves at Leyte, Luzon, and with the occupation forces in Japan. Discharged in May, 1946.

1948   Publishes *The Naked and the Dead*. Studies at the Sorbonne on the GI Bill, writes articles for the *New York Post*.

1949   Birth of daughter Susan. Speaks at Waldorf Peace Conference. Works on (rejected) screenplay in Hollywood.

1951   Publishes *Barbary Shore*.

1952   Divorce from Beatrice Silverman.

1953   Becomes contributing editor for *Dissent*.

1954   Marries Adele Morales. Contract disputes over obscenity in *The Deer Park*; after several rejections from publishers, manuscript accepted.

1955   Publishes *The Deer Park*. Founds *The Village Voice* with Daniel Wolf and Edwin Francher.

1957   Birth of daughter Danielle. Publishes "The White Negro" in *Dissent*.

1959   Publishes *Advertisements for Myself*. Daughter Elizabeth Anne born.

1960   Runs for Mayor of New York on Existentialist ticket. Stabs wife Adele with penknife; she refuses to press charges. Under observation at Bellevue for a few weeks.

1962   Publishes *Deaths for the Ladies (and Other Disasters)*. Divorce from Adele Morales. Marries Lady Jeanne Campbell, a columnist. Their daughter Kate born in August.

1963   Publishes *The Presidential Papers*. Divorce from Lady Jeanne Campbell. Marries actress Beverly Bentley.

1964   Publishes *An American Dream* serially in *Esquire*. Birth of son Michael Burks.

1965   Publishes revised version of *An American Dream* as a book.

1966   Publishes *Cannibals and Christians*. Birth of son Stephen McLeod.

1967   Publishes *Why Are We In Vietnam?* Adapts *The Deer Park* for the theater, where the play receives a limited run. Makes two films. Takes part in anti-war demonstrations. Elected to the National Institute of Arts and Letters.

1968   Publishes *The Armies of the Night*, which receives both the Pulitzer Prize and the National Book Award. Covers both political conventions, and publishes *Miami and the Siege of Chicago*.

1969   Runs for Mayor of New York in Democratic primary, advocating New York City's secession from the state; comes in fourth in a field of five.

1970   Publishes *Of a Fire on the Moon*. Elected to the American Academy of Arts and Sciences.

1971   Publishes *The Prisoner of Sex*. Birth of daughter Maggie Alexandra to Mailer and Carol Stevens. Separation from wife Beverly Bentley.

1972   Publishes *Existential Errands*.

1973   Publishes *Marilyn: A Biography*.

1975   Publishes *The Fight*.

1976   Publishes *Genius and Lust: A Journey Through the Major Writings of Henry Miller*.

1978   Publishes *A Transit to Narcissus*. Wife Beverly Bentley sues for divorce. Birth of son John Buffalo to Mailer and Norris Church.

1979   Publishes *The Executioner's Song*, which receives a Pulitzer Prize. Divorce from Beverly Bentley.

1980   Marries and divorces Carol Stevens. Marries art teacher Norris Church. Publishes *Of Women and Their Elegance*.

1983   Publishes *Ancient Evenings*.

1985   Publishes *Tough Guys Don't Dance*.

Contributors

HAROLD BLOOM, Sterling Professor of the Humanities at Yale University, is the author of *The Anxiety of Influence, Poetry and Repression* and many other volumes of literary criticism. His forthcoming study, *Freud: Transference and Authority*, attempts a full-scale reading of all of Freud's major writings. He is the general editor of *The Chelsea House Library of Literary Criticism*.

GORE VIDAL, distinguished novelist and social critic, is best known for his major historical novels, *Julian, Burr* and *Lincoln*, and for *Myra Breckinridge*.

RICHARD FOSTER is Professor of English at Macalester College, and the author of *The New Romantics*, a study of the American New Critics.

JACK RICHARDSON is a playwright and freelance critic.

TONY TANNER is a Fellow of King's College, Cambridge. His books include critical studies of Conrad, Bellow and Pynchon.

ROBERT LANGBAUM is Cabell Professor of the Humanities at the University of Virginia. He is the author of *The Modern Spirit* and *The Poetry of Experience*.

GERMAINE GREER is best known as the author of *The Female Eunuch*.

JOYCE CAROL OATES—novelist, story-writer, poet and critic—is the author of many books, including *Them, Expensive People, Unholy Loves, A Bloodsmoor Romance* and *Wonderland*.

RICHARD POIRIER is one of the editors of *Raritan*, and of the Library of America. He is Professor of English at Rutgers University, and his books include studies of Mailer and Robert Frost, as well as *A World Elsewhere* and *The Performing Self*.

RANDALL H. WALDRON teaches at Ohio Wesleyan University.

ROBERT MERRILL is Professor of English at the University of Nevada, Reno. His essays include studies of Shakespeare, Melville and Hemingway.

JOHN GARVEY is one of the editors of *Commonweal* and the author of *The Ways We Are Together*.

ALVIN B. KERNAN, Kenan Professor of the Humanities at Princeton University, has written books on the genre of satire, Shakespeare, and on contemporary literature.

JESSICA GERSON teaches at Dutchess Community College and has published several essays on Mailer.

JUDITH A. SCHEFFLER teaches at Drexel University in Philadelphia.

Bibliography

Adams, Laura. *Existential Battles: The Growth of Norman Mailer*. Athens, Ohio: Ohio University Press, 1976.

————, ed. *Will the Real Norman Mailer Please Stand Up?* Port Washington, N.Y. and London: Kennikat Press, 1974.

Begiebing, Robert J. "Norman Mailer's *Why Are We In Vietnam?*: The Ritual of Regeneration." *American Imago* 1, vol. 37 (1980): 12–37.

Bone, Robert. "Private Mailer Re-enlists." *Dissent* (Autumn 1960).

Braudy, Leo. *Norman Mailer: A Collection of Critical Essays*. Englewood Cliffs, N.J.: Prentice-Hall, Inc., 1972.

Douglas, George H. "Norman Mailer and the Battle of the Sexes—Urban Style." *New Orleans Review* 3, vol. 3 (1973): 211–14.

Foster, Richard. *Norman Mailer*. Minneapolis: University of Minnesota Press, 1968.

Goldman, Laurence. "The Political Vision of Norman Mailer." *Studies on the Left* (Summer 1964).

Gordon, Andrew. "The Modern Dream-Vision: Freud's *The Interpretation of Dreams* and Mailer's *An American Dream*." *Literature and Psychology* 3, vol. 27 (1977): 100–05.

Gutman, Stanley T. *Mankind in Barbary: The Individual and Society in the Novels of Norman Mailer*. Hanover, N.H.: University Press of New England, 1975.

Guttmann, Allen. *The Jewish Writer in America: Assimilation and the Crisis of Identity*. New York: Oxford University Press, 1971.

Hampshire, Stuart. "Mailer United." *New Statesman* (October 13, 1961).

Hassan, Ihab. *Radical Innocence*. Princeton: Princeton University Press, 1961.

Howe, Irving. *A World More Attractive*. New York: Horizon Press, 1963.

Kaufmann, Donald L. *Norman Mailer: The Countdown (The First Twenty Years)*. Carbondale: Southern Illinois University Press, 1969.

Langbaum, Robert. *The Modern Spirit*. New York: Oxford University Press, 1970.

Lasch, Christopher. *The New Radicalism in America: 1889–1963*. New York: Alfred A. Knopf, Inc., 1965.

Leeds, Barry H. *The Structural Vision of Norman Mailer*. New York: New York University Press, 1969.

Lennon, J. Michael, and Strozier, Charles B. "Empathy and Detachment in the Narratives of Erikson and Mailer." *The Psychohistory Review* 1, vol. 10 (1981): 18–32.

Lucid, Robert F., ed. *Norman Mailer: The Man and his Work*. Boston: Little, Brown & Co., 1971.

MacDonald, Dwight. "Art, Life and Violence." *Commentary* (June 1962).

Manso, Peter. *Mailer: His Life and Times.* New York: Simon & Schuster, 1985.

Marks, Barry A. "Civil Disobedience in Retrospect: Henry Thoreau and Norman Mailer." *Soundings* 2, vol. 62 (1979): 144–65.

Merrill, Robert. *Norman Mailer.* Boston: Twayne Publishers, Inc., 1978.

Middlebrook, Jonathan. *Mailer and the Times of his Time.* San Francisco: Bay Books, 1976.

Miller, James E., Jr. "The Creation of Women: Confessions of a Shaken Liberal." *Centennial Review* 18 (Summer 1974): 231–47.

Mills, Hilary. *Mailer: A Biography.* New York: Empire Books, 1982.

Muste, John M. "Norman Mailer and John Dos Passos: The Question of Influence." *Modern Fiction Studies* 17 (Autumn 1971): 361–74.

Poirier, Richard. *Norman Mailer.* New York: The Viking Press, 1972.

Radford, Jean. *Norman Mailer: A Critical Study.* New York: Harper & Row, 1975.

Richler, Mordecai. "Norman Mailer." *Encounter* (July 1965).

Rosenbaum, Ron. "The Siege of Mailer: Hero to Historian." *The Village Voice* (January 21, 1971).

Schrader, George A. "Norman Mailer and the Despair of Defiance." *Yale Review* 51 (December 1961): 267–80.

Siegel, Paul N. "The Malign Deity of *The Naked and the Dead.*" *Twentieth Century Literature* 4, vol. 20 (1974): 291–97.

Solotaroff, Robert. *Down Mailer's Way.* Urbana: University of Illinois Press, 1974.

Tanner, Tony. *The City of Words: American Fiction, 1959–1970.* New York: Harper & Row, 1971.

Toback, James. "Norman Mailer Today." *Commentary* (October 1967).

Acknowledgments

"The Angels Are White" by Gore Vidal from *The Nation* (January 2, 1960), copyright © 1960, 1962 by Gore Vidal. Reprinted by permission.

"The Early Novels" by Richard Foster from *University of Minnesota Pamphlets on American Writers, No. 73*, copyright © 1968 by University of Minnesota. Reprinted by permission.

"The Aesthetics of Norman Mailer" by Jack Richardson from *The New York Review of Books* (May 8, 1969), copyright © 1969 by the New York Review. Reprinted by permission.

"On the Parapet" by Tony Tanner from *Critical Quarterly* 2, vol. 12 (Summer 1970), copyright © 1970 by *Critical Quarterly*. Reprinted by permission.

"Mailer's New Style" by Robert Langbaum from *The Modern Spirit: Essays on the Continuity of Nineteenth- and Twentieth-Century Literature* by Robert Langbaum, copyright © 1959, 1964, 1965, 1966, 1967, 1968, 1970 by Robert Langbaum. Reprinted by permission.

"My Mailer Problem" by Germaine Greer from *Esquire* 3, vol. 76 (September 1971), copyright © 1971 by *Esquire*. Reprinted by permission.

"Male Chauvinist?: Out of the Machine" by Joyce Carol Oates from *Will the Real Norman Mailer Please Stand Up?* edited by Laura Adams, copyright © 1971 by Joyce Carol Oates. Reprinted by permission.

"The Minority Within" by Richard Poirier from *Norman Mailer* by Richard Poirier, copyright © 1972 by Richard Poirier. Reprinted by permission.

"The Naked, the Dead, and the Machine" by Randall H. Waldron from *PMLA* 1, vol. 87 (January 1972), copyright © 1972 by The Modern Language Association of America. Reprinted by permission.

"*The Armies of the Night*" by Robert Merrill from *Illinois Quarterly* 1, vol. 37 (September 1974), copyright © 1974 by Illinois State University. Reprinted by permission.

"*The Executioner's Song*" by John Garvey from *Commonweal* 5, vol. 107 (March 14, 1980), copyright © 1980 by Commonweal Publishing Co. Reprinted by permission.

"The Taking of the Moon" by Alvin B. Kernan from *The Imaginary Library: An Essay on Literature and Society* by Alvin B. Kernan, copyright © 1982 by Princeton University Press. Reprinted by permission.

"Sex, Creativity and God" by Jessica Gerson from *Mosaic* 2, vol. 15 (June 1982), copyright © 1982 by *Mosaic*. Reprinted by permission.

"The Prisoner as Creator in *The Executioner's Song*" by Judith A. Scheffler from *The Midwest Quarterly* 4, vol. 24 (Summer 1983), copyright © 1983 by Pittsburgh State University. Reprinted by permission.

"Norman in Egypt: *Ancient Evenings*" by Harold Bloom from *The New York Review of Books* 7, vol. 30 (April 28, 1983), copyright © 1983 by The New York Review. Reprinted by permission.

Index